Industrial Poetics

Joe Amato   **Indu**

CONTEMPORARY NORTH AMERICAN POETRY SERIES

Series Editors   **Alan Golding   Lynn Keller   Adalaide Morris**

strial POETICS

Demo Tracks for a Mobile Culture

UNIVERSITY OF IOWA PRESS   IOWA CITY

Copyright © 2006 by the
University of Iowa Press
http://www.uiowa.edu/uiowapress
All rights reserved
Printed in the United States of America
Design by Richard Hendel
No part of this book may be reproduced or used
in any form or by any means without permission
in writing from the publisher. All reasonable
steps have been taken to contact copyright holders
of material used in this book. The publisher
would be pleased to make suitable arrangements
with any whom it has not been possible to reach.

The University of Iowa Press is a member
of Green Press Initiative and is committed to
preserving natural resources.

Printed on acid-free paper

Cataloging-in-Publication data
on file at the Library of Congress

06 07 08 09 10 C 5 4 3 2 1

for the have-nots
I have
and have not known
and for Kass

Some have at first for Wits, *then* Poets *past,*
Turn'd Criticks *next, and prov'd plain* Fools *at last;*
—Alexander Pope, An Essay on Criticism

I insist on the imaginative relation in the critic's life because I sense that without it, without poesis, the critical relation becomes a form of Nietzschean ressentiment, a consummation of the ironic self, a spite of mind.
— Ihab Hassan, "Parabiography:
   The Varieties of Critical Experience"

Contents

~ Construction Note xi

Acknowledgments xiii

How to Tell the Difference between Life and Art
   A Grant Proposal (Take 1) 1

TRACK 1

Industrial Poetics: A Chautauqua Multiplex in Fits and Starts 7

How to Tell the Difference between Life and Art
   A Grant Proposal (Take 2) 65

TRACK 2

Technical Ex-Communication: How a Former Professional Engineer
   Becomes a Former English Professor 73

How to Tell the Difference between Life and Art
   A Grant Proposal (Take 3) 97

TRACK 3

Labor, Manufacturing, Workplace, Community:
   Four Conclusions in Search of an Ending 105

Notes 161

Bibliography 179

Index 201

~Construction Note*

"industrial" → metaphor + ~metaphor
"A Grant Proposal" = industrial metaphor = funding request + ~funding request
"A Grant Proposal" in three takes, interspersed 1-2-3 between tracks 1, 2, 3
"track" = industrial metaphor
track 1 = industrial performance
track 2 = industrial narrative (didactic)
track 3 = industrial components (i.e., labor, manufacturing, workplace +)
"industrial discourse" → matter of vocabulary + ~matter of vocabulary
   Q: What is real?
   A: What hurts.
   Q: Is that all?
   A: No.
Hence,
   "industrial" → hurt + ~hurt → ~deferral + deferral → ~$ and $
   = follow the money to the mysteries that prevail, laughing until it hurts

HARD HATS REQUIRED BEYOND THIS POINT

* ~ = symbol for negation

Acknowledgments

As of this writing, literature would seem to persist in the public domain as a sacred cow, venerated or offered up for slaughter as the occasion warrants. Within academe and largely under the auspices of cultural studies, scholars have meanwhile sought to discern a broader social context for the reception and interpretation of literature. This latter effort, while laudable for having mitigated any number of formal and institutional insularities, has not infrequently repackaged literature into hamburger patties.

There are writers and poets and critics, employed by academe or employed elsewhere, who resist the implication that a work of literature is either a sacred cow or a hamburger patty. Some of these writers and poets and critics are vegetarians. I acknowledge first and foremost, alas, that I am not a vegetarian.

To help flesh out the terms of my casually carnivorous leanings, or yearnings, herewith is Sven Birkerts's opening paragraph in his review of Margaret Atwood's *Oryx and Crake*, which appeared in the *New York Times Book Review* on 18 May 2003:

> I am going to stick my neck out and just say it: science fiction will never be Literature with a capital "L" and this is because it inevitably proceeds from premise rather than character. It sacrifices moral and psychological nuance in favor of more conceptual matters, and elevates scenario over sensibility. Some will ask, of course, whether there still is such a thing as "Literature with a capital 'L.'" I proceed on the faith that there is. Are there exceptions to my categorical pronouncement? Probably, but I don't think enough of them to overturn it. (p. 12)

I acknowledge correspondingly, then, my dismay that "Literature with a capital L," whatever it is, might be advanced by M. Birkerts—a very nice chap, for all I know—as a means of discrediting "conceptual matters." To which conceptual matters I will return in what follows, with abandon and ever offbeat.

This book would not have been brought to the table without the help and steadfastness of multitudes, two among which I must next acknowledge: first, and first always, Kass Fleisher; second, Charles Bernstein. As such, Mme. Fleisher and M. Bernstein share considerable blame for what you hold in your hands.

Fair shares of culpability for the (literate?) anguish and (literal?) indigestion likely sparked by these proceedings must be assigned as well to my series editors, Alan Golding, Lynn Keller, and Adalaide Morris, without whose editorial patience and perseverance readers would doubtless have been spared said anguish and indigestion. I am especially grateful to these three and to Holly Carver and her staff at University of Iowa Press. I must also express my thanks to Robert Mandel and his staff at University of Wisconsin Press, who supported an earlier version of this work. And a bear hug each to Jed Rasula and Lisa Samuels, my outside readers at UWP, for their careful appraisal of the strengths and weaknesses of this project in manuscript, their help in fortifying the former and mitigating the latter.

Deeply felt thanks to Steve Tomasula, compadre and fellow enthusiast; to Laura Mullen, kindred co-conspirator; to Michael Joyce, unwavering archaeologist of the real; to Anselm Hollo, whose lead I and others can only hope to follow; to Don Byrd, Greg Hewett, Pierre Joris, and Jody Swilky, Albany pen pals and stalwart supporters; to Marjorie Perloff, long may you run; and to Charles Alexander, Doug Barbour, the late Paul Barrett, Perle Besserman, Christopher Breu, Vanessa Carroll, Brian Collier, Ricardo Cortez Cruz, Mark DuCharme, Susan Duran, Kristin Dykstra, Lucia Getsi, Gabriel Gudding, Roberto Harrison, Elizabeth Hatmaker, Gail Hawisher, Judith Johnson, Kent Johnson, Steve Katz, Julie Kizershot, Andrew Levy, Nick LoLordo, Stuart Moulthrop, Aldon Lynn Nielsen, John O'Brien, Nathalie op de Beeck, Lauren Pretnar, Patrick Pritchett, Bin Ramke, Tara Reeser, Manfred Steger, the late Ronald Sukenick, Cole Swensen, Joe Tabbi, Michael Theune, Maria Tomasula, John Tranter, Mark Weiss, Ian Randall Wilson, Amy Wright, and Laura Wright, each of whom has better sense than I. Voluminous and circulating thanks to members of the SUNY/Buffalo Poetics List, which forum has for years proved the noisily productive source of my highly unoriginal and labored efforts. Thanks to the Naropa Summer Writing Program, which kept my brain alive a mile above sea level, and to Illinois State University, which as of this writing is putting food on our table. Thanks to "my" students, and thanks beyond thanks to my family. Countless steadfast and abiding others inhabit this volume and its contents utterly—for which I thank my lucky stars.

Naturally I take full credit for any infelicities, improprieties, or indiscretions that give lasting offense, including the undiscriminating culinary sensibility with which I correspondingly summon questions of aesthetic efficacy. You can tell: the conventions of academic discourse do not come easy to me. But I've learned to be persistent in my failings, and this may have to do more than anything else with my origin, my point of departure.

One way or another, the tracks that follow lead back to Syracuse, New York—my place of birth—and to the nearby towns of North Syracuse and Liverpool, where my kin and kind once thrived, often despite difficult circumstances. So while my fabrication of the whole may most immediately bring to mind packaged aural or visual content—an aesthete's libation to aestheticism—my tentative refiguring, here in this preface, of all as foodstuff says a great deal about the domiciles I was raised in, places where, and times when, securing a livelihood generally made for animated suppertime talk—*sans* the sort of literary allusiveness to which any author must occasionally fall prey. Sometimes I wish I could be more, what, cosmopolitan?—and the distance I find myself from such ten-dollar tropes probably helps to explain my continuing pursuit, without apology, of a poetic theory that might invoke both a stylistic literariness and a practical literacy, a lived and living scrawl that would demonstrate against legalistic pros and cons, even while performing the singular and unavoidable work of *passing judgment*. If I've become something of a textual specialist in the process of searching and researching, it's been strictly by default.

I feel compelled to acknowledge, finally, that I suffer occasionally from chef envy. But I'm no chef, as I don't have the stomach for compulsive verticality, and as I tend to settle for the so-so ingredients of your local regional chain grocer, the better to keep my finances in order and my feet planted firmly on terra firma. Still, I love to cook, rustic-style, and have a knack for working with what's in the fridge. So eat, please, and should you find yourself losing your appetite, do what what my Sicilian grandmother used to tell me to do: take a breather.

Then eat some more.

Portions of this book were published earlier in the following journals and magazines, often in different form, to which grateful acknowledgment is made:
Takes 1, 2, 3: "How to Tell the Difference between Life and Art:
   A Grant Proposal." *88: A Journal of Contemporary American Poetry* 4
   (October 2004): 76–96.
Track 2: "Technical Ex-Communication: How a Former Professional
   Engineer Becomes a Former English Professor." *Postmodern Culture* 10.1
   (September 1999).
Track 3: *Conclusion the 2nd: Manufacturing*: "A Treatise of Whole Numbers."
   Notre Dame Review 19 (Winter 2005): 1–14.
   Conclusion the 3rd: Workplace: "We Interrupt Our Regularly Scheduled
   Programming." *Denver Quarterly* 33.1 (Spring 1998): 7–23.

How to Tell the Difference between Life and Art
A Grant Proposal (Take 1)

.0 This is a request for funding in order to develop a new interface for poetry and culture, tentatively entitled *Industrial Poetics*. This interface will require a no-holds-barred engagement.

.1 There are times when one must permit certain words or concepts to operate in the absence of hard-and-fast definition. This is one of those times.

.2 Art is not the guy or gal next door. The guy or gal next door may very well lead a happy and carefree life in the short term in the absence of artistic provocation. The guy or gal next door may very well lead a lonely and impoverished life in the long term in the absence of artistic provocation. (1) Will they know it? (2) And who's to say?

.3 Art is a judgment call. Today we can rely neither on connoisseurs of taste nor eternal verities to make that judgment call for us. But if you have do-it-yourself art, you must have do-it-yourself criticism. The function of do-it-yourself criticism at the present time is to foster the production of better art at the present time. By "better art" is meant art whose purpose ultimately is to transform the social domain for the better. Art may serve this purpose in perverse or contingent ways—one can never be certain. Such is the nature of social circuits.

.4 Careful readers will be sure to note that I hedge for the moment on the word *better*.

.5 Taste? OK, so here's what I have to say about taste: Winston tastes good, like a [two beats] cigarette should.

.6 At any given instant, life demonstrates art's convictions. At any given instant, art exceeds life's demonstrations.

.7 Answers: (1) Believe it or not, people are often aware that their lives are lonely and impoverished. They just don't know what to do about it. (2) Passing judgment is something most of us do most of the time, and we'd do it better if we gave some thought as to how we ourselves are implicated in our judgments and assumptions, why we think the way we do. Trying to avoid the difficult work of judgment—aesthetic, aesthetic-ideological, what have you—has become a means of avoiding responsibility for thoughtful making.

.8 We ought not in any case to place ultimate emphasis on end product *or* process.

.9 Neither life nor art is like a box of chocolates—but chocolate may be essential to the life of the artist.

.10 Art is at work in all human activities, and thus cannot be construed a luxury. Yet art is rarely an initial response to security or survival needs, and to admit as much is hardly to the detriment of art.

.11 Preheat oven to 400 degrees.

.12 It very likely requires a supportive and ambitious public, a public willing to risk emotional and cognitive complacencies and certitudes, for ambitious art—art that frowns upon training wheels—to make a real and lasting difference in the lives of nonartists. Let us not be overprotective of our arts, but let us do everything we can to create an environment congenial to the demands of ambitious art.

.13 Let the bird stand for ten minutes or so before slicing.

.14 Insert thermometer into thickest part of polemic.

.15 Ambitious art—ambitious making of any kind—is a prime reason why we have the expression *weep for joy*. You cannot be an artist if you are never humbled by art.

.16 Art changes the world not because of some intrinsic form presumed to attend to a specific transformational politics, and not because of preset social configurations, which amount in themselves only to the conditions of and for change (and which must of course be given their due). Art changes the world because people change the world, people who find themselves in countless situations, interacting with other people in countless ways, and transforming *themselves* in the process. Sometimes this can amount to a desperate or quixotic activity, sometimes a hopeful one. It is always, at some level, a pedagogical activity when understood not as a function of the artwork, but in terms of the person or people involved.

.17 But art has changed the world, sometimes for the better, sometimes for the worse. Ante up.

.18 Collaboration = a clash of convictions tempered by the prospect of love.

.19 This grant proposal is in essence an act of collaboration. Or so say all of us.

.20 The chief value of conceptual art has been that it has forced us to confront as sensation the immediacy of embodied thought. Speaking pragmatically, that is.

.21 Style as substance, substance as other, other as purpose, purpose as soul, soul as longing, longing as death. Death as reach. Reach as laughter, laughter as laughing so hard it hurts.

.22 Like life, art may be full of surprises. When it's not, we may need to get a new art. Like art, life may be predictable and boring. When it is, we may need to get a new life. Getting a new life is more difficult than getting a new art. Getting a new art is more thankless than getting a new life.

.23 We must, as artists and critics, plumb the breach between what an artwork says and the cultural work that it does. This is the breach between the perception of embodied meanings "inside" a work and the realization and manifestation of effects and affects "outside" the work, some of the latter being all but imperceptible. Plumbing the aforesaid breach applies both to the artist—who is variously aware of her own motivations, intentions, and assumptions (or should be)—and the audience, or reader, or viewer, or user, or listener, whose speculations regarding motivation, intention, etc., will remain speculative, but are no less, for that, a part of that complex whole that includes saying and doing, and the breach between.

.24 The mystery of art resides in this breach, in what keeps us coming back to art and taking it with us, but this is no reason not to explore the phenomenon with teeth intact. Theorize your practice, and try not to get hung up in your theories.

.25 A brief note on artistic community: community helps put food on the table. The meaning you assign to "helps" will dictate the kind of community for which you yearn.

.26 Being an artist does not make one a good human being, anymore than does reading a book or voting Democrat. I generally prefer the company of artists who read books and are Democrats.

.27 One must distinguish between the various modes of art and their demands on our lives, our lifeways. Architects in particular often neglect the fact that the mind to which we casually refer in such locutions as "the life of the mind" requires constant sustenance. To "inhabit" a text is a figure of speech, then, in a way that to "inhabit" a physical structure is not. I am an old-fashioned postmodernist who likes to cook; who has still lifes on his walls (painted by long-since-dead European members of his family); a large TV; a modest CD collection; a comfortable Sealy; some nice kitchen knives; and too many books I don't get a chance to read. I am not very postmodern in my lifeways, and neither is my postmodernist mate—and we have no desire to live in anything resembling Schwitters's *Merzbau*. We do, however, enjoy tinkering with words.

.28 We must ever seek out new means of making art and commerce work together—for the benefit of art, and for the benefit of commerce.

.29 Artists need to be public intellectuals. That is, they need to be intellectuals about their publics, about their art, and about intellectual work, and this may require a capacity and a willingness to talk in different languages, employ different codes, milk different theories—a capacity and a willingness to engage multiple contexts.

.30 Artists occasionally need periods of intense solitude, for reasons that remain unclear to nonartists.

.31 Artists occasionally need immersion in social discourse, for reasons that are painfully clear to artists.

.32 Art can and has saved lives—but in saying so, it must be admitted that "saved" operates most of the time in largely figurative terms. A better word might be *salvaged*. Some take the idea behind this statement too far, however, sounding much as though they'd long to experience an occasion when art is quite literally a matter of life and death.

.33 In some countries, of course, art still *is* a matter of life and death. This is a Bad Thing. Art on the North American continent today is rarely if ever a matter of life and death. This is a Good Thing. Art in the U.S. is a matter of the life and death of U.S. culture, which is both a good and a bad thing, especially as "U.S. culture" does not exist in a cultural vacuum.

.34 Ideology: there, I said it.

.35 Anything may be political, but not everything has to do with politics. Failure to distinguish the adjective from the noun will likely lead to insubstantial art.

.36 Paying your dues to the system will eat up at least one (1) decade of your life. Try to learn something useful meanwhile.

.37 Artists who do not work to shape the context for reception of their art may or may not be irresponsible. Artists who do not work to shape the context for the reception of other artists' art *are* irresponsible. We owe something, finally, to our networks.

.38 The intrinsic formal attributes of any art object, so identified, are often of less consequence than the context for the reception of said art object, but this does not mean that they are of no consequence in considering its effects. Scholars—listen up.

.39 Artists are never solely artists. Artists are thinkers, citizens, heroes, cowards, thieves, cops.

.40 You can fake it for only so long before you become genuine. This is a source of great consternation for those preoccupied with origins.

.41 Sick and blunted with community? Authenticate yourself interest free.

.42 Art has less to say about quality control than it does about quality. But quality can be manufactured, as can art, and industrial manufacturing processes produce much of the material (e.g.) out of which artists construct their art. Or so say all of us.

.43 But can art really be manufactured *in toto*? That is, can it be reduced to the very routines and automations that generally prevent art from being art? How to set the material parameters of symbolic action.

.44 Snap! Crackle! Pop! Stop bumming rides, and buckle up that repertoire.

.45 How to rethink *industrial*: it's a word that tends to come in the back door, and sometimes this back door consists of authoritative commentary—which tends to take for granted [ahem] its fully industrialized (patriarchal) power. There is no form of labor, in any case, not even network labor, that is likely to operate independently of industry, conceived broadly.

.46 Power is as power does.

.47 Upper limit craft, lower limit manufacturing = the range of ordinary constructions. Extraordinary constructions (such as ambitious art) generally require an additional integration. And please to note that the ordinary is a necessary part of the extraordinary.

.48 The elemental can be extraordinary, the complex can be ordinary.

.49 Don't sit under the apple tree with anyone else but me.

.50 Art has as much to say about value as it does about quality. Value can be manufactured, but never for once and for all.

.51 Art is a vast democracy of habit. Wait a second   I didn't say that, Twyla Tharp did.

.52 The arts comprise highly ritualized practices. Though anything can be deemed a work of art—perceptions vary—the success of artifacts so deemed will ultimately be measured by their embodiment of these practices and the meanings and actions attending thereto.

Track 1

Industrial Poetics
A Chautauqua Multiplex in Fits and Starts

pour Charles Bernstein

Calling to mind a Rube Goldberg contraption, both anchored to the real and, within this apparently stable, if adjustive, scaffold, sustaining all manner of motion and transformation. Perhaps the Earth as it tracks around the Sun, perhaps this essay as it spins around the block, tethered by touch and willingness, around *you*. In which manifold human universe, any number of figurative (combustible?) and literal (recto-verso hand-eye) displacements are not only possible, but inevitable. If "the language of poetry is the language of inquiry" (Lyn Hejinian), this writing, this system of writings would make of the language of inquiry a fraught, tensive language of *industry*. I could draw you a picture, arcing—

1   *And introducing*
2   A quarter-century ago, and faced with something of a Hejinian dilemma
3   Please ignore, or try to, that passing whiff of authenticity
4   So there I was, riding roughshod over plant purchasing procedures
5   Coasting downhill now, temp just fine
6   Uphill again, and the gauge is showing it
7   Uphill still, gauge needle nearer the red zone
8   A few words about salary issues
9   That cooled things right off

10   (My lord but this is deadly stuff
11   Let us pretend (some of us) to be scholars
12   Date: Mon, 07 Nov 1994
13   *Before I* get to the question of scholarship
14   Get a refereed article, get a few such articles
15   Oh, you say, but you forgot that little matter of "refereed"
16   [Full stop. Again.
17   Oh, you say, but this reads more like a story
18   Yes, I know—thus far, and with the exception proving the rules (of the game)
18 cont'd   She's drawing a few stares as she walks
19   In all, then, the question of the sexed body, of gender, of the more masculine

20   Just to be clear
21   Tranny downshifts into L1, vehicular hydraulics just so-so
22   This is Charles Bernstein speaking
23   This is Joe Amato speaking
24   This is Kent Johnson speaking
25   The Pass
26   —to beg a good question, the bad
27   during which activity, receptivity, nothing, there is nothing
28   thence vast, the work of work, wickedass, and the work
29   industrial poetics

INDUSTRIAL POETICS   9

Perhaps I should remark here that the execution of a poetic work—if one considers it as the engineer . . . would consider the conception and construction of his locomotive, that is, making explicit the problems to be solved—would appear impossible.
—Paul Valéry, "Poetry and Abstract Thought"

Criticism written by poets has often been misread as a deviant method of self-justification, which it then becomes the critic's job to decode and realign with the poetry.
—Jed Rasula, The American Poetry Wax Museum

As if a theory of writing poetry is useful whereas the poem is not
—Bernadette Mayer, Midwinter Day

1

And introducing, début de siècle—

A drive train for an infant poetics, as old as the ages. But the poetics of poetry, or the poetry of *poetics*? Nothing terribly new in this question, and it's a hot start off a cold line. Poetics of, poetry of, poetics of, poetry of, poetics of, they love me, they love me not.

Either way, stuck, as in stuckness, as in chapter 24 of *Zen and the Art of Motorcycle Maintenance*, and "gumption traps" abound (see Pirsig's chapter 26). Like nearly everyone else in this latter-day era of postmortem effects—post-9.11, post-Lawrence, post-Pequod—I've turned to what I know best: my trusty 3-speed Turbohydramatic (Drive, L2, L1, ca. 1969). Shifting through the shifty poetry of poetics, then, tongue occasionally in cheek, wind in my face, hoary mechanical tropes at my back, a bit gabby, but hellbent for ruins, for the love of it, for the hell of it. It's all uphill and downhill from here, not least because I'm a landlubber. The moon and New York City? No such worries. Just *go*.

Labor, manufacturing, workplace, and maybe an added surprise or two: linkages and counterweights abound, my theater of operations. No, no *Gesamtkunstwerk*, and not quite what *you* had in mind, either. Unbridled access to one's originary longings, yeah—and isn't this what you writer-readers generally look for in us reader-writers? Isn't this what gets you all goo-goo-eyed?

No apologies for that touch of prolepsis, lover. You'll just have to get used to it, along with a healthy dose of, what, Neo-Ex? And parenthesis (see Lennard), and aposiopesis, and—

Yet standing now at water's edge, the *locus classicus* of crisis-management poets, I find I've learned to forsake my algorithmic Bernoullian past for the present statistical glories of dead reckoning, and the old luxury of a Me-Generation automatic. Like so many others here in the U.S. who have learned to hit the road—the road that becomes more precarious, more mythic, and less beckoning with each passing decade—I've learned as well to

EXPECT DELAYS

(before the suspected pulling out

of all stops)

Complicating which, this conceptual motion would, even as it effects the vehicular, affect the dispersal of Energy States (~50) to jerk you through the episodic: this baby tends to overheat if pushed too hard, driveability compromised in the process. In the midst of which figurative wear and tear, you might catch a literal glimpse of how to write. Literally. Overheat, overheated: might be a bad thermostat or loose fan belt, haven't had a chance to check it out. Idling it heats up, uphill it heats up, it's tough to find the right cruising speed. What with the topography ahead, it's likely I'll have to keep my eye on the temperature gauge.

A blue-collar lament in the face of encroaching white-collar instrumentalism? Certainly. And on our shared horizons, a can-do poetics that would not stand on ceremony, that would embrace performance-enchancing subject positions even as it fuses shards of class consciousness: we use what we can.

And it's drive time too, so a lotta talk on the airwaves. Research Jane Fonda, one voice says. Research Sharon Doubiago's use of a nice Fonda snippet in *Hard Country*, says another. Research Doubiago's spiritual predecessor, Meridel Le Sueur, outstanding in a corn field, says a third. Research Barrett Watten's "The Bride of the Assembly Line: From Material Text to Cultural Poetics," I say. Says Watten, "norms are products, not deductive schema of oppressive rationality, although they can be used for oppressive ends" (p. 33). See if you can locate where Valéry says, "All theory is autobiography" (*if* he says this). See your *Owner's Manual*, and by all means, see any number of other poets, and that means prose writers too. Just watch you don't pick up a citation along the way. Like I'm always already (sorry) doing, trying so hard to measure up.

Here's another, which comes at the very end of Jean-Michel Rabaté's *The Future of Theory* and—I trust this much is obvious—at the very beginning of this, my title piece:

Theory should go back to philosophy not as a history of philosophy or a philosophy of history, but as a systematic hystericization of philosophical problems. . . . These questions, once articulated together architectonically, will then build a problematic, that is a set of problems which may or may not be traditional, and will provide a discourse allowing one to mediate between the irreducible singularity of given texts (whatever their nature may be) and the generality of repeatable principles of analysis underpinned by well-defined concepts. This is the moment that will ineluctably be present in any publishable text, not in the scholarly footnotes but in the opening pages or paragraphs where the first moves, the gambit, and the stakes appear, whether it belongs to literary studies or to cultural studies, and this is the crucial moment of justification for all these efforts, a moment that can be highlighted—and hopefully taught—by Theory. (p. 150)

Whew-ee! One helluva citation. For "irreducible singularity of given texts" read "irreducible singularity of given _____," and you have some idea of where I'm coming from, what our destination might be.

Anyway, as I was saying—I wanted *originary* (see above, someplace). And there are precedents.

2

A quarter-century ago, and faced with something of a Hejinian dilemma: I've exhibited a certain talent for overseeing large-scale construction and maintenance activities. I've got, what, four or five million annual bucks to work with, there are few spending regulations in place, and the Wild West brewery I'm working at, located ten miles south-southeast of Lake Ontario, is increasing production capacity to meet increasing demand, to meet *projections* of increasing demand, for a beer that I only occasionally drink with my friends.

Doors. Windows. Roofing. Lighting. Telephones. Paging. Lawns. Sprinklers. Asphalt. Concrete. Rail siding. Aluminum siding. Painting. Plumbing. Janitorial. Drywall. Time clocks. Striping and sweeping. Snow removal.

Snow removal, with 200" on the average per season, and forty-odd overhead doors designed (in St. Louis) to face northwest. What the hell.

But most important, it pays the bills.

3

Please ignore, or try to, that passing whiff of authenticity, the mark of a true-blue *bricoleur*. I rely on such whiffs when I sense I'm about to be brushed off, made *in*authentic—decertified—hence it's entirely provisional, this authentic, self-absorbed imagination of mine, and I tend to think of it as a defense mechanism, or survival skill. Some find me *difficult* because of this. I wonder whether, by essay's end, this difficulty (and see Steiner's *On Difficulty*) will have dissipated, or whether I'll ratchet up the stakes by virtue of further figurations of voice and voice technologies (including the ones reading this assemblage back at me). The poetics of presence(s), or the presence of poetics?

"What is in mind is a sort of Chautauqua—that's the only name I can think of for it," Pirsig writes, "like the traveling tent-show Chautauquas that used to move across America, *this* America, the one that we are now in, an old-time series of popular talks intended to edify and entertain, improve the mind and bring culture and enlightenment to the ears and thoughts of the hearer" (p. 15). Tall order for a post-haste age, an age that has little time for the sort of village life one finds in Chautauqua, New York, or for the Iroquois who named the lake there *Chautauqua*.

What say we ratchet up the stakes one click? Orientalism and anti-Modernism aside, I would mine—no, *mime*—Erich Auerbach's much-vaunted subject-positional dislocation in *Mimesis*—i.e., Istanbul ("not Constantinople")—for constant (physical) proximity to and immersion in the objects under investigation *can be* a drawback; but I don't have, as a faltering academic, this liberty of locale.

(I go where I must, as did Auerbach—but Auerbach for more pressing reasons, Edward Said rather famously unpacking and situating "the pain of his [Auerbach's] exile" as a Jewish refugee from Nazi-dominated Europe; which brings to mind, too, Bakhtin's internal exile, and brings to my mind my mother's non-Jewish [French] refugee status.

(In contradistinction to which pragmatic [metaphysical?] grasp of place, Stevens wanted us to believe that "man is the intelligence of his soil" only in "*The World without Imagination*" [Stevens, "The Comedian as the Letter C," p. 27; l. 1]). So I guess I'll take my chances in the ever-shifting earth beneath my feet, that "poverty of dirt" which grounds my relocations and "inhuman" locutions, and trust that whatever writerly horse sense I can lay claim to will ground my sporadic flights of, uhm, fancy [Stevens's, "World without Peculiarity," pp. 453–454; ll. 3, 14]).

Now comes the hard part. Or, a harder part.

Writing well about poetry is easier than writing poetry well.

This bears repeating: Writing well about poetry is easier than writing poetry well. In the long term, of course, as writing a poem is—

Well, it's *this* easy:

 ate

 rate

 lerate

 ecelerate

 decelerate

 ecelerate

 lerate

 rate

 ate

(Do the math.)

You who are still in doubt may verify this assertion by performing one of the easiest literacy (term used advisedly) tests on the planet, followed by one of the hardest literacy (term used advisedly) tests on the planet.

Easiest test first: (1) Open a new document file, and (2) type in a few thoughts—any thoughts. Or a few words—any words. Or a few letters—any letters. You get the idea. Wax poetic, as you wish. You can rhyme, or not. You can even use pen and paper, if you must.

Now, (3) call your creation a poem, and (4) offer it to a poet you know *as* a poem. Next, (5) have that poet explain to you why s/he likes said poem, or why s/he doesn't. (Give 'em a few minutes, anyway.) (6) Find a few other poets, preferably from other parts of the U.S., and do the same. (You may use e-mail.)

Be sure (7) to record these exchanges for posterity. (This latter should be especially easy, as this is what intellectuals, the best of us, generally *like* to do.)

Lather, rinse, repeat. Discuss.

Hardest test second: (1.1) Open a new document file, and (2.1) write a critical essay about a poem. You know what a critical essay is, right? At *this* point in *this* essay, we shall suppose it to be synonymous with scholarship. So wax scholarly, if you must. You can even use pen and paper, as you wish.

Next (3.1) have a group of critical essayists (i.e., scholars) read this critical essay (*as* a critical essay), and (4.1) ask them to explain to you why they like said essay, or why they don't. (You may use e-mail.)

(5.1) Record, again, for posterity. (Etc.)

Now: compare and contrast the responses to the poem (easiest to write) with the responses to the essay (hardest to write). The set of responses that exhibits the greatest apparent arbitrariness, the most tenuous assumptions regarding form-content, the greatest deviation from any mean of literary value, will likely denote the activity that is hardest to do well over the long term. *Be honest!*

QED, and so say all of us.

And please note: the activity that is hardest *to do*, in terms of literacy (term used advisedly), is *not* the activity that is hardest *to do well* (in terms of?). And the obvious reason, as captured between those parens, is that the community of poets is far less cohesive than the community of scholars. (We knowingly use the singular, "community.") Which *might* say something about the discourse of poetry, and how it intervenes, or doesn't, in the discourse of poetics.

Some say writing a great poem can take less than a minute. But again, I'm talking over the long term—and incidentally, the failure to distinguish long- from short-term objectives is one of the great shortfalls of much of what passes for intellectual [cough] culture.

Mind you—I've said nothing, *nothing at all* about great critical essays, or great poetry, or great literature. That is, there's nothing at all here about canons. Or postmodernity.

4

So there I was, riding roughshod over plant purchasing procedures, wheeling and dealing with some incredibly knowledgeable construction veterans, some of whom were downright *legendary*, and struggling with the occasional mob-based contractor, two of whom were downright *brutal*, but in any case getting all sorts of work done, and done right. I was in a very real sense a very *public* engineer—accessible, friendly, grace under pressure and all of that. Yes sir, sir. I maintained my dues in the American Society of Mechanical Engineers (ASME), and in my future self loomed the sort of engineering administrator embodied in one (of two? please check) of our twentieth-century U.S. engineer-presidents. Herbert Hoover, a mining engineer who graduated from Stanford's first class in 1895, saw the profession (his advocacy of "rugged individualism" and the like aside) in a more public, even activist, light (for helpful discussion, see Layton's *The Revolt of the Engineers*).

So like I say, there I was. And after being there for a while, I was in a bit deep. Some would say, in over my head. Some would write, "my checkered past." ChockChalkChock*Chalk* it up to the "occasional mob-based contractor," as above. After the obligatory contractor-pal-shows-up-at-my-desk-wired-for-sound-hoping-to-have-his-life-threatened-by-other-contractor-pal-and-yes-recorded-for-posterity (Jeff lifted his shirt, barrel chest covered with mikes, tape, etc.); after the obligatory FBI interview-where-I-am-instructed-to-ask-the-G-men-to-show-me-their-IDs (they were very nice about it); after the obligatory call-from-our-Purchasing Manager-in-which-yours-truly-is-advised-that-all-purchases-no-matter-how-chickenshit-must-be-preceded-by-formal-purchase-requisition-and-Plant-Manager's-approval etcetera etcetera etcetera (he was *not* very nice about it): well, I was faced with a choice, a binary, or, if you prefer, a finite reification. A dilemma.

Was I (1) to continue in the management vein, as a vestige of my former shirt-sleeved, hard-hatted self, and join the supervisory ranks, among whose similarly hard-hatted minions were a number of college-degreed engineers, a number of former Merchant Marine CPOs and Vietnam vets, and a number of—not to put too fine a point on it—asskissers; or was I (2) to plunge head-first into what many engineers, if they would but lift their heads from their *vade mecums*, might observe is the source of engineering *amour propre*, viz, design?

One trouble right off with (1), as I saw it, was that it required I become an actual, chain-of-command manager, subject to the rules and regulations and management philosophy of the brewery; which, while not exactly Disney's controversial role-playing strategy for the workplace, "pixie dust," was nonetheless onerous enough, your typical bastard version of Management by Objective (i.e., you manage by being a bastard about objectives). Other people—men—would report to me within the company's militaristic hierarchy, and I would be "tasked" with evaluating their "performance"—"on a regular basis," and "up to and including disciplinary action," and so forth.

While my construction activities also took place under the auspices of numerous chains of command, the guys who actually did the work for me, foremen to laborers, were each members of *different* chains of command. And we often worked things out on the fly—which is to say, we were equals, each in our way, despite the fact that they worked under contract for me, that I could hire or fire them, etc. Thing is, we all—or most of us—took the job before us as our first priority. At most I was a bit like an academic department head (as opposed to a chair), a *primus inter pares*. Hell, I would go so far as to say that off campus—I mean, off the job site—a couple of these guys were, well—your obligatory homosocial bonding aside, I measured my relationships with a couple of these guys in terms of friendship. There was even a little graft involved, sorry to report.

Oh, and did I say that my father used to be a shop steward? That my mother did assembly-line piecework through the fifties?

My construction pals didn't like it either way, felt I'd forsaken my calling. You're fucking up, Joe. What the fuck you wanna do *that* for, Joe? Some even offered me jobs. Some even offered me high-paying jobs.

But I'd have none of that—I'd already gotten it into my head, silly me, that I wanted to be a poet—a stubborn fact that resonates well with my stubborn disposition. Don't ask me how, or why—I still haven't entirely figured out this *poeticus mobile*, even after having written a memoir about same. (Plug: "*Up from Ellis Island*," which at this rate looks to be available at your local bookstore chain, perhaps as a nonfiction novel, sometime in the not-too-distant future. That, or posthumously.) Poet or no, though, bread and butter called, cash money to pay the bills. You do what you gotta do, and even in quarter-century retrospect, I did what I had to.

So as you might expect, and in sum, my decision as to which career path to take turned on the machismo appeal of proving myself in that highly testicular knowledge work known as *design*. If perhaps not nearly as testicular as the workaday contours of facilities management, so defined—which itself yielded testicular ground to the construction trade unions, the guys who did the actual manual work with material in accordance with my directives—*design* was tacitly understood, by engineers, as the no-nonsense side of engineering. Not supervisor (né foreman), that curious euphemism for what some understand narrowly to be company men (and now, women, Bully Broads included)—no, not for me. Instead, allegiance to the intricacies of physical laws, to the ordinary and yet so often anti-instinctual professional culture that aspires to control nothing less than the elements of nature.

Testicular, as in "testicular discourse." In the once and future hacker world, testicular discourse takes the form of who has the Biggest Balls (women included) to code in xyz. Nerdy, quirky balls, perhaps, but balls nonetheless. When I was an engineering student, it was FORTRAN; in the late eighties and nineties, it was C; a popular variant today is expertise in XML and the like. And in 1978, just pre-PC and pocket-calculator bound, the field of engineering design exhibited similar such anatomical-scatalogical-configurative proclivities. (But go read Ellen Ullman, who knows the ins and outs of the digital workplace inside out.)

Put simply: since I couldn't and wouldn't be a blue-collar man like my father, or like Ben Hamper, I wanted still to be a man, without having to report 100 percent to The Man. Design seemed a good way out, and in. And I had reason to be optimistic, knowing that my designs would take me away from my desk on occasion, out into the plant with hard hat and earplugs to check on the work, to sketch out the lay of the land.

5

Coasting downhill now, temp just fine:

As to the etymology of *industry*: the Latin root of the word, *industria*, gives us (according to John Ayto in his *Dictionary of Word Origins*), "the quality or state of being hard working, diligence," and is derivative itself of *industrius*, or "diligent," which goes back to the Old Latin *indostruus*, from the prefix *indu* (in) and the suffix *-struss* (build, from which root we get, interestingly, both *construct* and *destroy*). As to *diligence*: the "steady effort" and "painstaking attention" we associate with the word somewhat belies its roots. Ayto takes it back to a compound verb that means "single out" and shows how the word is shaped semantically over time by association with the Latin *diligere* (esteem highly, love) into our current meanings.

Industry, diligence, construction, destruction, love, steady effort: sounds like a moral universe to me. *Homo faber* is often praised as such an industrious species, if no more industrious than, say, the *Formicidae* family. Just what makes that little old ant. . . .

Here I intentionally pick up that "human quality of sustained application or effort," which Raymond Williams identified as one of the "two main senses" of *industry*, the other being "an institution or set of institutions for production or trade" (Williams, *Keywords*). Evidently, *industry* was one of Williams's five prototypical key words, along with *culture, class, art* and *democracy* (see his Introduction, p. 13).

Today *industrial* signifies an entire matrix of (usually) systematic attributes. One imagines the labor, management, and wealth associated with large-scale manufacturing, or the small-scale efforts associated with small-scale craft, or arts and crafts. *Industrial* can also be used to mean "heavy-duty," as in "industrial-strength pesticide."

(To say nothing of industrial design, regarding which I intend to say nothing, save to motion my readers toward Moholy-Nagy's *Vision in Motion* and Loewy's *Never Leave Well Enough Alone*.)

(To say nothing of industrial arts, regarding which I intend to say nothing, save passing mention of my one lackluster high-school course in Shop. See Bill Cosby.)

The word has also been applied since the mid-eighties to popular (and underground) culture and music. Industrial music (like its related offspring, Gothic) is generally thought to be comprised of hard-hitting, aggressively delivered compositions that are presumed to subvert, often self-reflexively, our technologically and media-saturated post-Fordist environs. Such music may be understood, then, to go beyond the rebellious pose of rock, to challenge those various and sundry authenticities emerging from rock's cult of personality—

But I digress. And the definition of any pop-cultural form is a habitually contested site, in any case.

As I use the word, *testicular* means something akin to heavy-duty. Industrial and testicular can be synonyms, very hard, very Goth (albeit no playing in the dark implied in my use of the term). Oddly enough, *industrial engineering* is believed by many engineers to be somewhat soft, since its focus on (human and machine) efficiencies sometimes results in little actual material (re)design.

Hard and soft, chocolate and vanilla, left and right, black and white, 0 and 1, yes and *no*.

In any case, design is commonly understood as heavy-duty engineering—hence, interestingly, design is what the lay public *thinks* engineering is, however little they (they, not us) might understand of the devil, or the god, in the details. What the general public doesn't get about engineering is how closely it's tied to business interests, and how conflicted engineers can be about same (in which regard, see Layton).

6

Uphill again, and the gauge is showing it. I'm turning on the cabin heat to provide some additional cooling, and cracking my windows so it doesn't get too warm in here:

Steam, compressed air, CO_2, water, ammonia refrigeration, HVAC, chlorine: optimizing the nuts and bolts of such systems, improving quality, efficiency, safety, ease of use, and in some cases, installing brand-spanking new such systems of pipes and pumps and valves and—and this was to be my bailiwick under my new and improved project engineering title, "Utilities Engineer." And I migrated rather quickly in fact to instrument and control system design, not least because (1) my background in mathematics turned out to be congenial to the logic underwriting this somewhat arcane, if positively mundane, field of engineering and design practice; and (2) I shared an office with one of the region's downright *legendary* instrument and control systems engineers, John Mishko (a WWII vet who's getting on these days, and who, with his wife Bernice, are my only remaining friends from my seven years in industry).

Think for a moment about the thermostat in your home—how it maintains room temperature—and you'll have an inkling of what I was into. Most of my work in fact entailed *re*design of existing systems—I would optimize performance, ultimately to save bucks, sometimes to improve quality, infrequently to enhance safety. I even joined the Instrument Society of America (ISA), in which John served as the secretary for the local chapter. Had I stayed in that field through 2006, I'd doubtless still be learning something new every other day, earning a much better wage than I am presently, and likely weighing in at thirty or forty pounds heavier.

Now, one of the more interesting textual aspects of design has to do with blueprints—not the figurative blueprints you hear about when screenwriters discuss their scripts, but actual blueprints—which, when copied from the original brown-yellow sepia prints are . . . *blue!* or a shade of blue, and come in various sizes, E being the most common I worked with at the time.

Blueprints in the instrument and control world are often diagrams of processes, what are called P&IDs—process and instrumentation drawings—drawings that map the phases of a process and the sorts of controls (and control variables) that are requisite to controlling said process.

One of the more interesting hermeneutic issues—which is to say, issues that can be stated hermeneutically—that arises from reading (and drawing) such blueprints may be stated as follows (and I forget where I read this): "A design, like a bridge, can fail in many ways. And it can fail in communicating proper content improperly as much as it can fail in communicating improper content properly."[1] Setting aside the apparent emphasis on communication, propriety, and the like (and the fact that the sentence itself seems to point up its own failure to communicate proper content properly), the gist here would seem to be that drawings and blueprints, the material evidence and means of design, are symbol-ridden artifacts; hence that the process by which we render such material artifacts into things—a different kind of matter, or a matter we perceive differently—is fully susceptible to those difficulties attendant to all textual artifacts.

By analogy, then: I can fail in this Chautauqua in communicating what I would like to communicate, whether message or affect, because (1) I don't say what I want to say as efficaciously as I might; or (2) I say the wrong thing. Not that Chautauquas need be eminently, immediately useful—all acts of communication invoke some measure of redundancy (if merely by virtue of how language works), and anyway, only by situating reception *in context* can one begin to appreciate how contingent the question of symbolic use value really is. There are occasions, as this utilitarian discussion will labor to show, when uselessness itself is useful.

Once an engineer, always an engineer.

So: a quarter-century ago, I found myself earning my keep based in part on my facility with *symbols*. When you toss in my more bureaucratic-organizational writing duties—writing and rewriting capital appropriation requests, memos, and so forth—the scene at the brewery becomes that much more literary, which doubtless means, for some readers, that much more exotic.

But this is to take design as a process in and of itself—fine as far as it goes. In fact, the paperwork labor that comprised my design activities pointed, strictly speaking, to an *outside*, a set of boundaries, marking out rather precisely planned changes in nonpulp products (stainless steel pipe, propylene glycol) as well as different stratifications of workers (hourly, salary), with respective duties corresponding to the nature of the work sites (having all converged together on said work sites, for instance, there were times we worked at odds with one another). Once my designs were tested against other material forms—i.e., once construction began—they were often found wanting (sometimes severely so). This learning process—learning from various modes of failure—provided feedback into the design process, yielding only at its end point what might be fairly called a final design, a shooting script.

And now I find I need to work out a few things for myself, which all interested parties are invited to peruse. I prefer to lay bare this meandering bit of thought *as* a meandering bit of thought in order to elicit something along the lines of what Ronald Sukenick has described, in *Mosaic Man*, in the following terms:

> Besides, he has the intimation that though there's something doing here, for him, other than the pleasure of mere doing, it will emerge only if he lets his normal analytic habits of mind become undone, giving himself up to the apparently aimless drift and eddy of incident, the profane course of event which, faithful to nothing, comprises nonetheless a kind of fateful language if you know how to read it. (p. 174)

If you find yourself growing impatient with *my* mosaic, please skip ahead to part 7.

Henry Petroski has written engagingly about failure in *To Err Is Human: The Role of Failure in Successful Design*, but for those of you holding a PhD in English, his discussion of literary masterpieces—which for Petroski, like masterpieces of structural design, issue forth from failure—may be found wanting.[2] I am provoked here, however, to consider whether we humanists have been far too easy on ourselves and on our discourses regarding failure in general.

For starters, and in terms of pedagogy: shouldn't writing classrooms provide room for failure (without, that is, failing grades)? In terms of career orbit, and obit.: if the *theoria* of failure attendant to my second [gulp] tenure denial (and will this play in *Peoria*? it's a half hour drive from where I've subsequently landed) constitutes something like the theory-death half of some constitutive postsecondary dialectic—to pursue a figurative, if not fanciful, rendering of Paul Mann's work on the avant-garde—how, exactly, is my tenure-track "death" to be recuperated by the circulation system, aka job market, as a symptomatic "effect" of academic culture? (Word is out, but I'd love myself to know what the word is. It's clear that, professionally speaking, the final resting [work]place for so many who have faltered so is adjunct life, which is in fact the life I presently inhabit.) And in terms of textual practices: isn't it abundantly clear that the very item you hold in your hands, to whatever degree one may conclude that it "succeeds," was successively, if not successfully, modified because some cadre of thinkers, some with a little say and some with quite a lot, found prior iterations wanting? (It's clear to *this* bloke, on that you may hang your hat.)

To speak of this Chautauqua "by analogy," as (far) above, does seem at any rate to obscure a profound working difference between engineering design and Chautauqua design, because even granting that this talk-essay is the result of applying careful design parameters (conventions) to the writing process within the limits of an intended material substrate (paper, say), this implied design schematic will, like the thing designed, concern itself primarily with the selection and placement of (at the moment I am revising this work, pixelated) words, to create such and so semantic/syntactic effects. Texts may be things, then, but to speak of them in terms, for instance, of their inertial (material) attributes is to understate that aspect of their heft that makes text, and not concrete, conceptually formidable (apologies to St. Augustine and I. A. Richards).

One can speak of design, no doubt, without implying an actual conversion of word-things into thing-things, for symbols slip and slide from one medium to the next. One does, indeed, use HTML to *design* a web page, creating specific effects via a "code" that instructs a "program" how to "read" it. (Scare quotes are meant to indicate the high degree of control entailed in this "interpretive" loop.) And in truth, even writers who use outlines (you will guess correctly that I do not) might balk at the idea that their work is a matter of design, for most writers would like to imagine their work as unencumbered by any but their imaginative aplomb, entirely open to the spontaneous combustion of ideas, the intuitive leap, etc. Design for these writers would constitute malice of forethought. And the less *willful* the end product—those presumed flights of fancy that characterize poetry (for some) as opposed, say, to poetics—the more malice in speaking of the corresponding writing process in such programmatic, ego-saturated terms. (Interestingly, a John Cage or a Jackson Mac Low would often undercut ego-driven aims precisely *through* premeditative ["chance"] measures and structural patterning. Ditto for OULIPO.)

Even writing that would seem (to writers) to embody a design only in retrospect is therefore informed by any number of provisional decisions (by writers) as to which parts (words, sentences, paragraphs, lines, stanzas, fields) will go where to make up what sort of whole. These decisions are hardly a matter of revision alone—they're a matter of consciously working through cognitive-affective moments, a process that is less than methodical sometimes, at times adamantly so, and a process that, while we may be aware of it while we're *at it*, is thereby no less subject to forces beyond our control, to contingencies of context. (And again, chance methods, like procedural or automatic writing, imply a willful decision, *prior to* the hermeneutic circle taking shape, as to the sort of method to be employed to generate product.)

To some extent the, or my, difficulty in even writing about this question of writing matter versus other kinds of matter turns on the twin . . . matters of *intention* and *purpose*—on who's doing the intending, and what is intended, and why, and how purpose is conceived (if indeed a purpose *is* conceived beyond merely satisfying the immediate desire to write—which possibility I will explore in some detail in Track 3, *Conclusion the 1st*). I have glossed right along the etymology of "design," which according to Ayto "is a little complicated," his exposition of associated roots and branches yielding many of the words I've used above: "mark out"; "point out, denote"; "plan"; "purpose, intention"; and "pattern, drawing." Yes, I've used—or if you will, employed—these words *by design*.

In point of fact, a good engineering designer—a good engineer, "good" boasting not merely QCEL-style functionalism (see Track 2), but having also aesthetic and ethical import—owing to the pragmatic circumstances that underwrite the demand for design work, generally thinks along more determinate lines than might a fiction writer or poet. But in point of fact, a good engineer knows too that there are forces at play that exceed her grasp. The real is often a real freakin' mess, and basic physical variables—temperature, level, flow—don't always behave as you might expect them to. But if writing, as Cixous has it, may be understood as "applied to" thought to yield *"applied thought"* (*Hélène Cixous,* p. 42; emphasis in original), then engineering design ought to be viewed not as the direct application of a rigorous set of parameters to this messy reality, but to our apprehenson *of* this reality. Thus, engineers might be well served by imagining their more and less thoughtful interventions into everyday life as an application of symbolic parameters "to something that presents itself . . . as unknown and as mysterious"—on a par, say, with examining an ostensibly ordinary bodily response such as "the phenomenon of tears" (ibid., p. 42).

Structurally and in philosophical terms, then, we might (purposefully) explore the form—in particular, the "final form"—of this essay by considering the purposive matter in terms of Aristotelian "form-in-motion." This would take us to Books VIII and IX of the *Metaphysics* and the *Physics*—where I most decidedly do not wish to go. Alternately, and with due regard for those many factors (that is, in addition to authorial intention and motivation) that have a role in bringing thought to life in words, we might consider the new sciences of complexity and self-organization, and the extent to which what you hold in your hands sits at the crosshairs of cognitive, phenotypical, and cultural vectors. Margaret A. Syverson's *The Wealth of Reality: An Ecology of Composition* would be the likely place to start.

Still, since I am busy marshaling my metaphors toward the grander contours of the industrial, I can ill afford another meta-concept.

7

Uphill still, gauge needle nearer the red zone. Not much I can do but push ahead (and there's a McDonald's not far down the road . . .):

The move into supervision, as one might expect, alters one's sense of loyalty and obligation. Historically, in the U.S. technical professions, this management path was devised by the business world to redirect engineers' loyalties away from their profession and to their employers. Sadly, engineers are generally the *last* to learn that the engineering profession was making some serious noise about collective bargaining early last century (again, see Layton). Hence we get that well-wrought move into a more lucrative management position, we get the "engineering manager," we get the MBA with an engineering undergrad degree.

That's some Big Balls, yeah—but Big Corporate Balls (BCBs).

I didn't want BCBs. From where I sat, BCBs were an illusion. It was clear to me that, once in, I'd never get out, that I'd have to keep up appearances of which I wanted no part. Hell, I didn't even want to be an engineer, remember?—I wanted to be a poet. So the absolute last item on my punch list of last items was to move into quasi-bossman status, corporate logo on my ass.

No. If I was to be an engineer, goddammitall, I wanted Big Engineering Balls (BEBs). With BEBs, I could remain aloof from the nastier, more Orwellian aspects of Fortune 500 bureaucracy. I could revel in my elite (if oh-so-white and Western middle-class) knowledge base without ever having to discipline anyone for not meeting "objectives"—save for the plant hourly personnel, unionized I(nternational) A(ssociation) M(achinists) A(erospace) W(orkers), who would ultimately serve as my in-house contractors. But I knew, or thought I knew, how to handle mechanics and technicians, because I knew, or thought I knew, that we plain got along, push come to shove. Besides, as a design engineer, I could actually (over)see things, material things, taking shape (as Hoover said—I forget when). And whatever I decided, I could still buy a motorcycle—or two. No Organizational Man for me, nosireeBob. Eros and civilization (that other Herbert) would become my personal projects, never mind Carter's 68-degree thermostats and double-nickel speed limits, never mind the incumbent eighties, the onset of AIDS, the overblown rhetoric of dialectical materialism, and materialistic overconsumption.

Never mind the history of ideas, and the idea of history. I hungered for the derring-do of design.

Still, there were hoop-jumps, there were do's- and dues-paying. If you want a state license as an engineer, you become formally, via eight-hour exam, an Engineer-In-Training (EIT). Four on-the-job years later, another eight-hour exam later, you become a Licensed Professional Engineer, or PE. Provided you pass your exams.

Some don't. And some engineers I've known put PE on their license plates, it means that much to them.

In the trades you become a journeyman. More hoop-jumps.

8

A few words about salary issues while I fuel up on drive-thru fries, fretting over carbs and carburetor jets as those distant higher elevations seem suddenly less distant. (Carbs can be tricky things.)

When you work in a factory as an hourly worker, or in a business as an office worker, you retire at night to a home suited to factory work or office work—a house of relatively modest proportions. Some factory workers and some office workers make a very good wage and live in exceptionally beautiful houses, but in general, factory workers and office workers live relatively modest financial lives, in relatively modest houses, regardless of the retirement monies they may have in the Dow.

When you work as a faculty member in an academic department, you may retire at night to a veritable mansion. Or you may retire at night to a home more modest than that of factory workers or office workers.

When I worked as a salary (not hourly) engineer, in a factory, I retired at night much as a middling academic might retire at night. For four years of my life as an engineer, my father, brother, and I paid less than $125 per month rent for a two-bedroom upper flat. For three years of my life as an engineer, I rented an apartment with full appliances and a gas fireplace—while I supported my dad. In 1999, my wife and partner, Kass Fleisher, and I paid $1,000 per month rent for a new-ish two-bedroom (two-bath) townhouse in Boulder County, Colorado. Among other things, we greatly enjoyed the obligatory cathedral ceiling which is now a regular feature of all such townhomes. Some of our (former) colleagues lived (and still live) in Boulder proper, in houses worth more than a half a million. (Median housing cost there topped the four-hundred-thousand dollar mark in 2003.)

9

That cooled things right off. Moving along and the road leveling off some, gauge in the normal range:

On the surface of it, for me to move into design—to do the testicular work I'd imagined myself to be doing as an engineer—would be not unlike my decision to write this would-be Chautauqua. To write this talk-essay—to write it well—would be to take command of my wits, to undertake the steely work of creating a prose machine dedicated to plumbing a diverse array of discursive conventions. Prosaic prose, prose with a purpose.

None of that hallucinatory funnystuff you call poetry. Not here, no way, and not on an academic press.

Collapsing all distinctions, and still on the surface of it: this essay would be testicular, would be heavy-duty, would be designed with due respect for conventions, certainly. This essay would be, then, *industrial*—in the pre–Henry Rollins, pre-cyborg, post–Industrial Revolution (ante-Newtonian?) sense of the word.

But if so: what would an industrial poetics be?

And why not a *professional* poetics?

Why not indeed. I am a professor, after all; I profess (a lot of things); I belong so obviously to a profession. (Some very smart latter-day Marxists would observe that I'm nothing but a glorified professional-managerial worker—*like them*, I would respond.) And in fact "professional" has actually replaced "industrial" in the past decade or two as the heavy-duty ad copy of choice. Our current chaos-bound, quantum universe boasts "Professional Strength LIQUID PLUMR" (see gray bottle under our sink).

That's right—I'm a pro of sorts, there's no doubt about it, if being a pro means that I get paid (not too awful much) to profess. And I was an engineering pro, too, was paid (quite a bit) to engineer—up to and including myself, or so it seemed at times. Nothing against amateurs, nothing at all. And I mean, poets don't generally get paid as such.

But.

But have a look at that poor word, *professional,* the work it's being asked to do these days, and the current hyper-turbo-quantum-professional privatization trauma experienced by any number of postsecondary faculty and grad students throughout the U.S. "Specifically, at many of the nation's four-year institutions," concludes Ernest L. Boyer in his Carnegie Foundation study of higher ed, *Scholarship Reconsidered,* "the focus had moved from the student to the professoriate, from general to specialized education, and from loyalty to the campus to loyalty to the profession" (p. 13). Boyer's point is that professional mandates have overriden campus-*qua*-social mandates, hence that the mission(s) of higher education "must be carefully redefined and the meaning of scholarship creatively reconsidered" (p. 13).

I can dig it, if perhaps not the way Boyer would have me dig it.

So no, not professional. I needed something more archaic, more out of fashion—i.e., black tint and black leather fashion. I needed something a little dingier, a little rougher, something I could dress up rhetorically and use to drag you kicking and screaming, backward, toward my epiphanic, virtual conclusion. And I needed a word, too, that would bring to middle-aged minds, at least, the only real liberal-left-leaning infrastructure the postwar U.S. has ever had—that of industrial (traditionally, blue-collar) labor.

(And woe betide you blue-collar Republicans.)

(OK: my old man—he was IUE, a shop steward, as I say, the neighborhood I was raised in was predominantly postwar working class. No, we don't want to go back there, or back to Emerson's American scholarship—but yes, something salvageable may endure in the ruins of modernity, which are the ruins of our time.[3] Paul Krugman and Kevin Phillips may not be on the same political-economic page, but they both have some helpful things to say about this, too. Don't believe that brand strategy stuff.)

I need, *we* need, in a word, in three words: industrial-strength poetics, heavy-duty poetics. And if this dictatorial moment invokes an occulted dogma (see next page), its tenets are avowedly jocular—and noncomedogenic, to boot.[4] Doomed to mechanical wear and tear and, ultimately, to failure, certainly. Planned obsolescence.

I don't have the bucks to be a *real* pro anyway. Just ask any dot.com entrepreneur.

I know this: poetry tools thought, and an industrial poetics demonstrates the contrasting properties of machine-tooled cognition correlative to individual and collective action. If along the way I give the impression that, like the Cyd Charisse–Ninotchka character of Rouben Mamoulian's *Silk Stockings*, I'd rather be exploring (not working at!) a foundry than enjoying a *pas de deux*, this is probably because my materialist passions are quite literally that.

And sure—I'm smitten by the architects of industrial-age triumphs, from Georges Eugène Haussmann's mythic (re)design of Paris, to the Brooklyn Bridge, to the muscle cars that caught my adolescent eye. Conscious of the misuse of metaphor, myth, and matériel, I venture forth with profound ambivalence, then, skeptical of the armchair ease with which I wield my rusty hammer; alerted by thinkers like Derek Owens to my professional responsibilities as a teacher of writing in providing for a sustainable society; aware of Hart Crane's eventual disillusionment with The Bridge; ever fearful of crematoria technology; wary of assembly-line monotony; attentive to Rachel Carson's and Sandra Steingraber's and Marc Lappé's and Barbara Freese's and Bill McKibben's eco-concerns; distraught in the face of Bhopal, Chernobyl, and similarly lethal industrial terrain; on edge, with Richard Manning, at the detrimental long-term effects of a thoroughly industrialized agriculture; like Manfred Steger, dismayed at the global prevalence of urban slums (having spent enough time on public assistance to know what this means for us all); forever in awe of Kong's stop-motion fall from the spired grace of the Empire State; and *goddamn pissed-off* to see war continue to be hawked by military-industrialists as the instantiation of "progress."

Venture forth we must, though, (New York) Yankee ingenuity intact, with a deep regard for the lived environment, creek to factory lot—an industrial ethic that, push come to shove, ought never to be trumped by our geopolitical wanderlust, with its associated yearnings and earnings and appeals to empire. What was it Marjorie Perloff said about the avant-garde, the Eiffel Tower and the *tour d'ivoire*?

Pity me all day. And I like what Smithson says about rust. Onward, onward, oy and ahoy!

:=:=:=:=:=:=:=:=:=:=:=:=:=:=:=:=:turnbuckle:=:=:=:=:=:=:=:=:=:=:=:=:=:=:=:=:=:

Michael Heller has published a useful, searching précis on poetics and its possibilities in *Samizdat*, a small, newspaper-like poetry mag published by Robert Archambeau, an English prof at Lake Forest College in Illinois. In "Aspects of Poetics," Heller does a nice job of sketching the history of this "beclouded field" (p. 3). After dispensing with poet Devin Johnston's concerns regarding the "slippage" between poetics as generative principle and poetics as ideology—Heller comes down on the side of ideology if only as a function of those "traditions and psychologies" that guide poetic work (p. 3)—Heller neatly and with enviable erudition unpacks how the mechanisms of a "dictatorial" poetics can create a "hidden opposition" between an "occulted dogma" and the poet's "craft" (p. 3). He describes the movement of poetics as a "future-looking dynamic" (p. 3), and borrows from the late philosopher Gillian Rose to advance an "anachronstic" and defamiliarized future (p. 4) that evinces neither the more optimistic proportions attending to Shelley's seer-(legislator)-poet nor the more foreboding aspects of a Benjaminian "dark muse" (p. 3).

For Heller, a constructively alternative poetic platform would owe not a little to Ernst Bloch's twin notions of an "authentic end" and "the *unfated*" (quoted in Heller, p. 4), an end absent "preconceptions" and needless "psychologizing" (p. 4; Heller cites Bloch's *The Spirit of Utopia*). An "'unfated' poetics" would initiate the "open-ended architecture" requisite to a fuller grasp of Otherness, and would precipitate a "form of humility" in the face of that profound emptiness which the future in fact augurs (p. 5; this notion is not unlike Buddhism's supreme mantra/paradox, "form is emptiness, emptiness is form," and indeed Heller glosses Buddhist *shunyata* and Hindu *Maya*).

The method Heller proposes to reach this unfettered, unfated state is what he calls "phantomology," which will presumably present us with "a new poetic real, perhaps closer to the essayistic assay or try-out than putative distance or objectivity or reading the *zeitgeist*" (p. 4). This is to be a poetics both of "precision" and "uncertainty": precision as a means of "uncovering the seed-syllable of poetry in thing and event"; uncertainty as "the registration ... of one's phantom-like existence" (and of existence itself), "a condition induced by knowledge of our unreliability, our deference if you will, before the limitations and understanding of language and of otherness" (p. 4).

Very well then. For the sake of a poetics, as opposed to, say, a pedagogy—and Heller discusses Poundian vorticism as having a "pedagogic relation to the future" (p. 3)—I would forgo the fatalistic, obtaining my sense of beginning, for instance, only at the end of the line. Still, Heller's "phantomology" smacks a bit of the old UnCola ad campaign—not a cola perhaps, but still just soda pop (I hear Harry Potter won't be drinking it)—which method, or antimethod, or unmethod, brings to my regrettably associative mind that "spectral evidence" marshaled during the Salem witch trials.

And apropos of my beef with poetics as discursive SOP, I simply must interject here: did I really need those little parenthetical numbers, (3), (4), (5), to reference a 1-2-3-page essay? And aren't BCBs (Big Citation Balls) in fact a variant of BEBs? (I'll be trying my hand at same most vigorously in Track 3, *Conclusion the 4th.*)

But OK: even with the critical advantage of Heller's helpful clarifications and unavoidable adumbrations, why succumb in the first place to the fastidious binary of poetry (the application, let's say, of a method or methods, as above, to produce something called "poems") and poetics (a generalizable statement of methodology presumably owing something to the methods of poetry)? To hazard a(nother) tautology (this time of the A = A variety): what if one were to propose, instead, poetics as a creative discourse in and of itself—i.e., as its own example, and *as* its own example, one that amounts neither to a statement of generative principle, strictly speaking, *nor* to an ideological program, speaking broadly. Moreover, what if we posited such a poetics as a function of generative-ideological *demonstration?*

One problem with such self-reflexive variations on singularity—that which exemplifies or proposes itself, an attribute customarily assigned to works of poetry and art in general (whether or not we imagine the work of art as a proposition *about* art)—is that most of what we writers dash off fits the bill, if trivially so (take, for example, this paragraph). Another problem would seem to center around what one might *do* with an example of such degree-zero proportions—i.e., aside from reading same. Of course one might ask what to do with a poem, for that matter—albeit poets might observe that the primary doing of the poem has been done once a poem has become a poem—but as we slip into a discourse presumed to have specifically informational-descriptive-polemical aspects, this issue becomes somewhat more pressing. How do we follow the singular example, how do we remain singularly true to its precepts? At the same time, if poetry is (as I interjected parenthetically, last para) but the application of a method or methods, it runs the risk of being merely methodical.

When we talk of poetic method and poetic methodology, we are generally referring to discursive activities that work along critical and theoretical coordinates, respectively (a generalizable theoretic being the equivalent of what we might call normative poetics, which in its simplest manifestation may amount to a how-to). These latter exercises in symbol-strewing frequently comprise *post facto* approaches to generative concerns, the poem itself, discourse itself viewed as an aftereffect, always already (sorry) adduced as primary evidence of (at most) a backgrounded originary effort. If the poem has a perceivable design, then, it "makes sense" critically or theoretically to the extent that it embodies certain effects, which we (often tacitly) attribute to authorial motivations, on the one hand (down to and including intention, if there is such a thing), or which we can regard as symptomatic of "larger" sociocultural trends (in which latter case, the originary effort of the poem is social in character). In both cases the poem has been understood through its effects, again, or as a bundle of effects, and its generative (or as Olson might aver, proprioceptive) moment is obscured (*this* moment, the moment I first wrote "this"—and even "moment" is technically and temporally imprecise). These critical-theoretical methods tend to beget more methods (let's set the etymology of "method" aside), and anything deemed inexplicable via the methodological becomes ever more mysterious.

Still, there are advantages to maintaining that poetry stubbornly persists at the crosshairs of trivial singularity *and* precariously programmatic method. If trivial and self-exemplifying, we can set aside, for one, those nagging questions of uniqueness, of the "unparalleled" nature of the poetic act (in which regard singularity, to be candid, has often struck this reader-poet as something of a dodge). If methodical, the poem may be understood in the abstract as a continuance of something prior, as "original" (hereafter, unoriginal) in the sense that this term might have been used during the Middle Ages. Ergo poetry as a trivial, unoriginal activity and—through my promptings here—ditto for poetics (and it is not without some irony that I refer you here to the work of Rosalind Krauss); on which basis, *here*, we may begin, have begun already to demonstrate corresponding (literary and other) value.

Yet if poetry is presumed to be a trivial and unoriginal affair, as ordinary as a heartbeat, why do we bother with it as writers or readers? The answers are to be found at the varied thresholds of our reading and writing experiences— and maybe this is as much as can be said of such events in the abstract. A poetics fashioned after such poetry might demonstrate and exemplify, among other things, its own trivial and unoriginal character, revaluing its associated discourse (of poetics) even while proposing how poetry ought to work. Why be conceptual purists about it? Whether a poem-event has moment, and what type of moment (cultural, aesthetic) it has, will be no less vital concerns.[5]

Readers will observe that I've borrowed the unoriginal, in any case, *from* poetry, and applied it *to* poetics—I've assumed, that is, that there are origins at work in poetry, hence in poetics, and I've intimated too that poetry might be better understood in terms of poem-events, timepieces, mechanical contrivances even, with a foregrounded temporal dimension. If poems have more than a trivial, methodical value, yet are trivial and methodical by their very circumstance, this says something about language perhaps, and ultimately, about what sorts of beings we are, and hope to be (anthropologically, culturally, collectively, etc.). It also suggests that what we "do" with poems, or with a poetics, turns chiefly on the value we assign to such demonstrations, which demonstrations themselves embody value. There can be but further demonstrations, all very touch and go, trial and error (and as visionary as you like).

Admittedly, I'm splitting railroad ties here, but I offer this schema *mezza voce*. We can, alternately, emphasize the way methodology informs/begets method, which in turn informs/begets poetry; or we can, if we prefer, see poetry as the initiating event that gives us (some would argue, necessarily reductive) statements of method, hence ever more remote, and removed, methodologies; or we can regard method (pick one) as the initiating activity in this array. But by suggesting that this fine madness we call poetry is both trivial and unoriginal, as above; and by dispensing with more customary assumptions regarding conventional poetic *and* essayistic (Chautauqua-istic) form: might this bring us in fact closer to Heller's "essayistic assay or try-out"? Rhetorical question. What seems key here, too, is the matter of *agency*—how best to estimate (or guesstimate) and display the various control networks undergirding authorship functions of any sort.

According (again) to Ayto, *demonstrate* is from *monstrum*, originally a "warning of misfortune, evil omen" (e.g., monster), only later "show, inform." Am I demonstrating then, for and against, in order simply to (fore)warn? Of what?

:=:=:=:=:=:=:=:=:=:=:=:=:=:=:=:turnbuckle:=:=:=:=:=:=:=:=:=:=:=:=:=:=:=:

10

(My lord but this is deadly stuff, no?)

More along the line of perceptions steeped in realities, as we grind away on yet another uphill grade, exhaust catching up with us, needle once again nearing the red zone:

That bit about this essay being a matter of design—that was all on the surface of it, all very formalist in temper, finally.

First, note that scholars who write critical essays about literature probably *wouldn't* write critical essays about literature were they not scholars.

(And here I continue to interject, clunkily, that seemingly innocent adjective, "critical," in order to blur the distinction between essay and scholarship.)

Academic poets who write poetry, academic fiction writers who write fiction, academic writers who write writing (so defined) probably *would* continue to write poetry, fiction, writing (so defined), even were they *not* academics.

Ditto nonacademic writers. Even were they not textile workers, computer workers, service workers, factory workers.

But scholars *are* academics. Unless, that is, you happen to be an "independent scholar," as I read occasionally below defiant faces at the annual MLA convention. Adjunct faculty, like unemployed faculty, are often "independent scholars." On my last campus, such faculty were paid—not wages, but—"honoraria." Kass was paid honoraria ($4,000/course, which is far above the national average). We needed her "honoraria" to make ends meet.

Well it's an honor to teach, you know. Really.

Below the surface, then: though the imperatives of the design world would seem in many ways (and as I've offered it) to correspond to the imperatives of working the talk-essay genre (as I've offered it), the essay as a scholarly form (*before I, before I*—see below) demands a certain allegiance to academic discourse. Demands allegiance, that is (along, usually, with a certain pedigree), to a preset sphere of possibilities, as to what can possibly be said, which is to say, what can possibly be published, and more, what can possibly be accepted as legitimate publication—not simply by a publisher, but by, for instance, a hiring committee, or a tenure committee.

And how. *And how.*

You see what I mean?

So: Demands an allegiance to academic discourse, *which could be an allegiance to academic life* (and culture) that you generally won't find among poets and writers. I won't go into the historical reasons why this is so—Kass and I have written at length about the writers-as-teachers complex, from a teaching perspective, and it's fair to say that writers who shirk their teacherly duties really burn our ass(es).[6] My reason for bringing this up here and now is because I wish to align scholarship—scholarship as a lived experience, as a lived process, as a set of allegiances—not with design, but with *supervision*.

Design moved me toward the nuances of engineering thought, yes, but I was still an employee of the brewery (owned by a transnational corporation that, as reported, has recently sold off the brewing company). Had I entered the supervisory ranks, though, I would have found myself that much more fettered to the demands of management—*as* a manager. Crudely (because the mechanism is a crude one): I would have been viewed *by* middle and upper management as participating in a smaller-scale version of their own duties. As an engineer, I could always shrug my shoulders and blather on about the technical intricacies of a specific job.

So yes, design did, in effect, enhance my professional allegiance to the engineering profession, thus deflecting my Miller Brewing orbit (and, thank the lord, my Philip Morris orbit). Likewise, one might surmise that scholarship would enhance a scholar's professional allegiance to (in this case) the profession of English studies, thus deflecting ideological-payday orbits accordingly.

One would surmise so, and such a surmise would not be entirely wrongheaded. But my aim is to show how and why it just ain't *entirely* so in practice. Thus my next task, simply put: scholarship = supervision.

But *before I*—*before I* do so: I want now to unhinge *this* Chautauqua and say what should be so painfully obvious by now (not least because I've been at such pains): who am I bullshitting, this is no academic essay! After all, I've called it a Chautauqua (first clue). The labor that I commit to this labored piece of writing is of a much different mindset, of a much different set of loyalties, of a much different approach to discursive practices and conventions, of a much different understanding of intellectual-historical-artistic context, of a much different *literary register* (KA-CHING) than scholarly, run-of-the-mill, and often quite valuable exercises in seemingly more "objective," literary-theoretical explication. (I can see now that I must regrettably cite, and soon, Charles Bernstein's writings, *pour* whom, titularly, *this*. Hold your horses. First—)

11

Let us pretend (some of us) to be scholars (you scholars can just go on being scholars), and let us have a quick look at one such valuable scholarly exercise by (my former colleague, the scholar and poet) Jeffrey C. Robinson, his *Romantic Presences: Living Images from the Age of Wordsworth and Shelley* (1995). And I quote:

> But maybe "poetry"—that is, its essence, if it has an essence, a root drive (Schiller's *trieb*) that the poet and the reader can acknowledge, deny, or cynically distort—*is* excess, particularly if you locate its opposite in

"work," which is required to keep the human social system going. Poetry breaks the plane of ordinary work; being work of its own kind, it also—in the Romantic tradition—signals its opposite, leisure. Wordsworth and Coleridge (e.g. "the Eolian Harp") are poets of leisure as excess. The reclining Romantic poet, to whom I am walking [sic] in this book, is the figure of excessive leisure. He does not merely lie down but, in poems, becomes or implies a rootedness, earthward in the timelessness of that supine position, driving down among chthonic forces. As my language here reveals, behind "leisure" lies a more vital apparent opposition to work, eros. Eros, as Bataille says, is silence and solitude, violence and entropy (even as it anticipates reproduction). Work—either in its quotidian form of keeping stable, as in Hannah Arendt's term *labor*, or in the form of making or having made permanent, *opus*—should therefore strenuously resist eros. Yet the poetry most useful to the spirit from Romanticism onward risks extending the capacities and hopefulness of the self by insisting upon the place of eros in work. The poem is a metonymy for the fullness of creative experience insofar as it takes this risk. (p. 6)

The leisure-ly work of the lyrical poem (and poet), in Robinson's intriguing peripatetics, opens to a renewed understanding of work itself. If ours is a savagely industrial, post-Romantic era, we might nonetheless regard the inexorable call to labor as an occasion, too, for permitting the workaday self its fair share of (lifeway, roadway) autonomy, of erotic self-definition—that is, *if* we "listen" to poetry, as against Spicer's lament (or rebuke) that "no one" does. Such is the concealed surplus (if not synergy) of all systems that attempt to organize the human, and the risk is nothing more, and nothing less, than one's livelihood.[7] Most workers come face-to-face with this kind of risk when reprimanded by the boss for spending too much time over coffee and donuts, shooting the breeze with coworkers. (It's happened to me. You too?) Most teachers come face-to-face with this kind of risk when they disregard grading policies predicated on unchallenged, and unchallengeable, assumptions about quality work, which policies arise from the edicts of learning institutions dedicated to the proliferation of expertise-based models of knowledge production and consumption. (It's happened to me. You too?)

The workplace for teacher-employees, then—the workplace that, let us be clear, students inhabit—is often modeled on the retrofitted corporate workplace (as I will attempt to demonstrate in Track 2). In the corporation, individual (employee) growth, to the extent that it occurs on-the-job, is put in the service of continued production of quality manufacturing products, further facilitated through inculcation (training) of professional-managerial workers in the gummy metaphysic of pragmatic, follow-the-leader, "team-based" cooperation and the like. Perhaps, then, we might align learning (not training) with precisely that transformative eros that repudiates undue risk to selfhood, *risk* here understood as a stratification of self, and selves, in compliance with externally fixed patterns of identity. Thus the downside of socialization is, if you'll pardon the pun, self-evident—viz, obedient human widgets.

And how will students learn to "[insist] upon the place of eros" in their work (Robinson) if they are always already (sorry) at the mercy of those very institutional forces that permit for socialization in the first place? Good question, and something of a hermeneutic conundrum, as posed. I offer here but a lyrical injunction to whet your appetite: *Don't let the past remind us of what we are not now.*

There's an industry for just about everything, phatic statements included. Design is an industry, scholarship is an industry, poetry is an industry, supervision has become something of a meta-industry (more below). This is hardly an academic concern: to varying degrees, most in this country are involved in any number of industries, from the airline industry to the computer industry to the textile industry. My emphases here are meant to foreground this fact and see where it takes us. My polemic is geared, admittedly, toward the more positive aspects of a poetic industrial—an industrial poetics. To see where this takes us.

12

```
Date: Mon, 07 Nov 1994 11:17:55 -0800
From: XXX@XXX.ORG
Subject: Re: Submission to XXX
To: HUMAMATO@minna.acc.iit.edu
Message-id: <199411071917.LAA17488@weber.ucsd.edu>
Content-transfer-encoding: 7BIT
Dear Joe,
What timing . . . a decision was made on your paper
just last Friday.

We gave your paper careful consideration but have
decided that we cannot publish it. A copy of one
reviewer's comments are included here; we trust you
will find them useful.
```

Thank you for submitting your paper. We hope that you will continue to find the Journal of interest in your work.

   Sincerely,

   XXXX

****

I really think you should NOT publish this. You have a theoretical and empirical agenda for the journal, and your tone should be serious and rigorous as well as exploratory. This probably means that your poetry section should be small, to the point, and not too experimental; that is, it should speak directly, albeit through a different genre, to the issues that the rest of the papers in the journal speak to in a more mundane way. This poem is too long, too out of control, and too demanding for most readers.

One version of poetry is that it should be more difficult to write than prose. Attention to structure and rhythm should result in more than prose as usual, albeit with a lot of font variation and clever work at the space bar. By no one's definition should poetry be disorganized prose arranged in unusual patterns on the page.

I would not be surprised if there were a set of contexts which, if well articulated, would allow us to see this poem event as a work of great genius. The author does not deliver these contexts, and hard work by this reader could not turn up enough of them. Frankly, it made me dizzy. I am sure that this harsh review is unfair to someone else's incredible cleverness, but the early issues of your journal should not commit this kind of risk. A person doesn't have to be as conversational as Robert Frost or as quick as Langston Hughes, but if it is going to be 30 pages, it should be precise and available.

```
28 May 2002
Dear Colleague:
I am writing to you on behalf of the MLA Executive
Council about a serious problem in the publishing of
scholarly books. We seek your assistance. . . . Some
junior faculty members who will be reviewed for tenure
in this academic year are anxiously waiting to hear
from various university presses. These faculty members
find themselves in a maddening double bind. They face a
challenge—under inflexible time constraints and with
very high stakes—that many of them may be unable to
meet successfully, no matter how strong or serious
their scholarly achievement, because academic presses
simply cannot afford to publish their books. . . .
Above all, at this moment I urge an intensified
awareness of the problem: departments can no longer
routinely expect that the task of scholarly evaluation
will be undertaken by the readers for university
presses and that a published book will be the
essential stamp of a young scholar's authenticity and
purpose.
   Sincerely Yours,
   Stephen Greenblatt, President
```

13

Before I get to the question of scholarship as a form of supervision, though: it might help if I modify my prior claims and observe that design, whatever else I've said it was, wasn't *quite* what I've said it was. I didn't quite get those BEBs I initially spied, fuck me.

The plain and simple and sad fact of the matter is that—once I started working as the Utilities Engineer; once ten hours of each waking day (and considerable dreamtime) were saturated with the arcana of my various design projects, a few of which I inherited half-finished from my predecessor; once I began to appreciate, yes, the very real beauty of control (temperature, level, flow, phase, etc.), but as well began to appreciate how difficult it can be to work with a relatively fixed group of hourly and salary plant personnel, some of whom were quite brilliant, some downright *asskissers*—well, I began to overload a bit. And then a bit more. And toward the end, more than a bit more.

I kept getting handed more and more projects. And I kept getting ordered, in so many words and gestures and by any number of managers, not to spend so much damn time on my designs. To do it right, yes, but to do it quickly, and most importantly, to do it *inexpensively*.

John—remember my friend, John Mishko?—he would laugh at this bottom-line rationalizing, and sigh. *Used to be,* he would say, *I had no more than a half-dozen projects at a time* (this is the early, cold-war fifties). Not today.

Had I just a little foresight, I would have foreseen that I'd end up working for someone (such as the guy I was working for at the time) who had little working knowledge of the technical as a daily design challenge, and whose youthful organizational exhuberance would no doubt grate on my wisdom-laden twilight years. So whether I liked it or no, I was headed either for a management slot, or for the elephant's graveyard—like John, who'd been canned after more than a quarter-century of chemical plant design, and who had stubbornly refused to take up supervisory responsibilities even when the boss left town for a few days.

In fact, that dumbfounded look my engineering manager occasionally gave me in the face of my desire to persist with the design track approximates the look I've gotten from the occasional educational administrator, who can't seem to fathom my obstinate commitment not to the business of books, but to the books themselves. One thing was certain, then as now: I didn't want to see the vestiges of that look staring back at me each morning over donuts and coffee.

I learned this lesson the hard way (see Sally Hacker). I learned this lesson at the brewery, and I learned this lesson, with even harsher repercussions, at Bristol-Myers Company. And as they say in westerns, it weren't pretty.

14

Get a refereed article, get a few such articles, get a book on a good academic press, get tenure. *Then* do the writing you really *want* to do. The writing that really *needs* doing.

Sound like a game plan? And if it's *not* a game plan, or not *exactly* what you find in the *Chicago Guide to Your Academic Career*, then what have I been listening to all of these years? And why have I been greeted with so many game faces?

What *about* those refereed articles?

(Remember now: I've said nothing, *nothing at all* about great essays, great scholarship, great poetry, or great literature. That is, there's nothing at all here about canons. Or postmodernity.)

Well, we all know what a refereed article is *not*. It's not, among other things, a poem.

Then again, why isn't it a poem? If I can call anything I want a poem, why can't I call anything I want an essay, or a Chautauqua, or a talk-essay? What *is* a talk-essay, anyhow?

And in particular, why can't I call a poem an essay?

I've got news for you, by the way: *this* is a poem—this talk-essay, this Chautauqua.

That's right—you've been reading a poem. I've been fibbing all along, beginning with my title.

(And since this Chautauqua *is* a poem, all by my say so and all issues of fair use to the wind, industry practice will have copyright reverting to *me*, yes? Perhaps this latter is too important to be left in parentheses, so:

15

Oh, you say, but you forgot that little matter of "refereed."

Well you ought to know, you scholars among you, that most creative publications (term used advisedly) are *not* refereed, technically speaking. We creative writers, in writing up our tenure portfolios, often fudge that one. I mean, why sell ourselves short?

As to referees: even setting aside what we all know to be the commonplace, practical lapses in the ostensibly hermetic system known as "('blind') peer review"—which at times I feel we in the poetry world could stand more of, and at other times, no more of—the fact is that *what is being refereed is the game* (see game plan and faces, above). The refereed journal is thus a simple feedback mechanism designed to regulate "quality," yes, but "quality" of the game itself, delimited as that which does not make one (e.g.) *dizzy*.

Here's how it works:

- The proper and appropriate (smooth and efficient) advance of knowledge requires for its operation that The Man have Knowledge-In-Advance (KIA). Not everything can pass for knowledge, for one; for two, only that which *is* knowledge can be deemed knowledge. This foreknowledge constitutes KIA.
- The Man (i.e., men and women) therefore asks each of us to submit our individualized knowledge-bodies to thermo-regulating subcommittees, which employ (usually gratis) peer review mechanisms nearly as cooperative as our submissive selves (and which mechanisms must, among other things, peer at our work).

- Each thermo-regulating subcommittee accepts and rejects submitted knowledge-bodies to maintain professional, *sangfroid* environs, setpoint 68 deg. F., with ±2 deg. F. permissible variation.
- If the knowledge-body is found to contribute to environmental conditions that fall outside *sangfroid* tolerances—if it's running too hot, or too cold, excessively emotional, or insufficiently analytical—it is generally not tolerated, and is vetted (i.e., vented) *outside* the system. (—And into the mails via SASE, with wording to this effect. Once in a great while an inordinately hot knowledge-body is accepted to offset an inordinately cold-knowledge body.)
- Thus does The Man regulate, via KIA, the "advance" of knowledge, the controlled flow of vaporous knowledge-bodies. What is not tolerated, then, is deemed unadvanced knowledge, among which forms of knowledge one finds, for example, *dizzy knowledge*.[8]

(Pardon my rather foreboding industrial control analog here [and my continuing fascination with boardroom formatting, the language of protocol, and acronyms], but what with student bodies and bodies of knowledge and teacher bodies and my forty-nine-year-old aging body and the like, and as I've experienced all of these, I find this trope ineluctably sensitive to your aesthetic needs, Dear Reader-Peer. And of course the review process I describe is mirrored, in part and in whole, by any number of publishing venues, but often without such dire consequences for creative approaches to what is, in essence, or should be, creative work.)

Does this constitute supervision?

Hell YES. (—Though this quick outburst, sans citation, minus plodding analytical exposition, and displaying insufficient modulation or excessive dishabille, might strike the thermo-regulating subcommittee as mere exhortation, deriving from mere anecdote.)

To supervise means, quite literally, to oversee. "Peer" overseeing of this sort (panoptical or no, and including teaching observations and the like) is hardly an institutional oversight—such crypto-management practices are encoded into the bits and parcels of academic discourse, and managing such communicative proprieties (theoretical, critical, creative, discursive, take your pick) will comprise but a rudimentary aspect of our very own rules of the game.

That's showbiz. And if this be professional autonomy, sayeth the industrial gadfly, there be corporate complacency in 't.

And sliced one way, that's pretty much what I was doing in industry, *all* of my time there. Which isn't to say that all overseeing is a bad thing, hell no. The difficulty that arises here is less a matter of supervision in the abstract—which suggests, to my way of thinking, a potentially elevated form of (potentially untelevisual) *vision*—than of laying bare the machinery of supervision, supervision that oversees, yes, and that calculates while thus "checking up on." Which calculations, sliced another way, may be put to distinctively unbecoming purposes.

But I would not make of all professional activities a variation on management practice, for there remains in all human activities a residue of social knowledge (and then some) that cannot be controlled, and that we would-be social engineers would do well not to attempt to control. Would-be anthropologist Charles Olson (whose formidably phallic example as an essayist so obviously haunts this poem-that-is-a-BBE-Chautauqua-talk-essay) has it right when he writes, of his mail-carrier father:

> Today [ca. 1948] he'd be fired. Or not hired in the first place. Or, if a company had to show a payroll for a contract, be the first laid off. Ground has been lost. But a good worker still knows, and can tell you, what my father knew. He just happened to be one of the first, and it was clearer earlier in the postal service than in heavy industry. He was at the switch point when the turn came. He was no enemy. He was opposition. He was fighting for pride in work which is personality. It is that simple. We have forgotten what men crave. We think that all workers want is pay. But that's all they are left with, where production, and that rot of modern work, efficiency, rule. (Olson, *The Post Office*, p. 46)

It *is* that simple, that elementary, although "personality" can be so very complex when linked to "pride in work," whether mason, engineer, teacher, or poet. And here's a little nugget that I offer entirely without substantiation: what distinguishes the public intellectual from the man or women of letters or numbers is the capacity to wrench open her or his respective discourse, to spell out for all to see the calculus of knowledge as such, and with the risks attendant to simplification, to illustrate how and why such interworkings play a vital role in everybody's autobiography.[9]

In any case Dewey disputes succinctly the instrumentalist approach to the arts and sciences by showing how, under the creative gaze, external and internal become one, thus offering the proper measure of *humilitas* for a world measured with increasing accuracy and precision by instrument men and women (and my leap from Olson to Dewey is hardly an accident—see

Magee): "In creative production, the external and physical world is more than a mere means or external condition of perceptions, ideas and emotions; it is subject matter and sustainer of conscious activity; and thereby exhibits, so that he who runs may read, the fact that consciousness is not a separate realm of being, but is the manifest quality of existence when nature is most free and most active" (Dewey, *Experience and Nature*, p. 318).

Mass cultural effects of the last century, though—the social pressure cooker that frequently forces insides out, and outsides in—would imperil such holistic capabilities. Perhaps the issues are best summarized encyclopedically (and this particular conceptual leap *is* a happy accident, as I just happened to be thumbing through my *Britannica* while revising):

> Ultimately, the ideology of mass society emphasizes the negative effects of the rise of industrial society; and, since only a part of the answers to the questions raised by the theory of mass society can be answered by empirical research, part of the issue will always remain in the form of stubborn ideological differences concerning the good, the true, and the beautiful, and the most desirable way of life. . . .
>
> Finally, it should be said that precisely because of its ideological elements, the idea of mass society will continue to have appeal for social scientists interested in specific problems associated with modernization, urbanization, and industrialism. The best one may hope for is a productive tension between these ideological elements on the one hand and an empirical concern for what is really happening, what is actually the case, on the other—in the best tradition of modern social science. (Bramson and Schudson, "Mass Society," p. 604)

16

(Full stop. Again. I needed a few parts to fix my kitchen sink, spotted a Home Depot just off the exit. Some guy nearly clipped me in the parking lot, old man with a hat in a Buick.)

Oh, you say, but who says just *anything* can pass as a poem?

Well, Duchamp and Warhol as much as said it—while demonstrating it, and Arthur Danto and like-minded souls stand ready, willing, and able, honed literary-critical-philosophical tools at their fingertips, to ply every genre-mixing, artifactual, ready-made layer. But there's another tack to take here, too, having more to do with poetry vis-à-vis prose—*this* poem, that is, which some will find poetic and some will find, again, prosaic.

(If the sign says, *No Parking or Standing*, I may be back in New York.)

To test the prose-poetry waters, I quote at length from the following exchange in which the editors of *Occident* are responding to an essay by David Antin in *Boundary 2* (see Antin, "Some Questions"). This exchange took place some *three decades* ago:

> Editors: "Modernism and Postmodernism" is partly concerned with distinguishing modernisms which are usually thought of as cognate—for example, Eliot's from Pound's. Since Eliot and Pound are usually associated with Joyce and the modernist prose movement your argument clearly would have consequences there too. Briefly what account would you make of the moderns in prose as related to the poets?
>
> David Antin: Why do you ask about "prose"? It's like saying to me "You've been discussing modernist developments in mathematics and have developed a notion of modernist mathematical styles, how would you apply these notions of modernism to accounting?" The only way that I can even approach the question is by supposing that you don't really mean "prose" writers; and I'm sure you don't. Because if I said that the only modernist prose writer is Wittgenstein, you'd say "That's not what I mean." And of course, it isn't what you mean. Which is a relief for me, because I don't really think that the notion of prose exists on the same plane as the notion of poetry. As far as I'm concerned there is the language art. That's poetry. All of it. There are then genres within it. Like narration. And there's a subform of narration. Called fiction. And a subform of that called "the novel," a narrational form with an enveloping commitment to a certain notion of "reality," constructed out of commonsense intuitions about character and objects, and social and psychological events and probability. That's not "prose." The idea of "prose" is only an additional prop for the novel. "Prose" is the name of a kind of notational style. It's a way of making language look responsible. You've got justified margins, capital letters to begin graphemic strings which, when they are concluded by periods, are called sentences, indented sentences that mark off blocks of sentences that you call paragraphs. This notational apparatus is intended to add probity to the wildly irresponsible, occasionally illuminating and usually playful system called language. Novels may be written in "prose"; but in the beginning no books were written in prose, they were printed in prose, because "prose" conveys an illusion of a commonsensical logical order. It's as

appropriate to the novel as ketchup to a hamburger, which is to say that it's not very good but the hamburger wouldn't go far without it. This is not to say that once you start to notate talk into "prose" that it doesn't exert a coercive force upon what you say and how you say it. As with all notations it has conventions, writing rules and the like, that will prevent you from saying a lot of things, or at least make it difficult to get those things notated clearly, or in their full energy and perspicuity. It will also encourage you to talk in such a way as to make it easier for you to use the notation. So the conventions of printing and the "prose" notation that developed out of it encouraged the use of certain kinds of language and discouraged other kinds in the books that were printed in "prose."

As a friendly amendment to Antin, I would argue (with Antin) that you needn't identify prose *or* poetry as the larger, more encompassing language category—you need simply be aware of your emphases as such, which could include, for instance, the overarching category of "rhetoric." (You get the idea.)

(And you had better check my citation, as I pulled all of Antin verbatim from a post by John Lowther to the SUNY/Buffalo Poetics list, what, nearly four years ago. See the archive at epc.buffalo.edu. Tracking down these small press journals has been a nightmare from which I'm trying to awake.)

An issue that arises here (and has arisen right along): poets might not write *about* poetry so much as inquire into, and bicker about, its cultural or textual status, and that of the language arts in general. Ergo, poetics. Fiction writers? As a modern commodity, conventional fiction is the more popular and more profitable upstart, though the jury will ever be out as to whether narrative or poetic utterance distinguishes humankind's first speech acts. Is it the pulpish lure of story or the desire to have one's novel optioned (or both) that dulls the wits of so many "successful" novelists, and a sizable number of laureate or laureate-bound poets, as they drag into the limelight, along with their carefully manicured personae, all manner of universalist and essentialist and often anti-intellectual platitudes regarding the hearts and bowels of artistic practice? This is not to suggest that poets are the more inquistive tribes because they have smaller savings accounts and accordingly more modest Dickensian expectations; or because their art is more difficult than the prose arts; or because they're born that way. But *writers*—of poetry, fiction, nonfiction, hyperfiction, scripts, what have you—who entertain rejection and (academic) indifference on a regular basis probably *do* enjoy some additional incentive to ask *why* this might be so.

17

Oh, you say, but this reads more like a story, and as Gertrude Stein might say ca. 1935, it has a certain narrative thing happening, as "[n]arrative is what anybody has to say in any way about anything that can happen has happened will happen in any way." (Oh lord. Where did she say this?) Thus it's clearly more like fiction than poetry.

It's a *poem*, Stein or no Stein or some Stein is a Stein is a Stein. With handholds fore and aft for internal combustion experts and external combustion beginners. Poets have been known to sub/title their poems *An essay on* such and such with a sly wink at prose, yes—but rest assured, no sly wink implied or intended here. It's a *poem*, Kilroy, and what this implies is that no theory of poetic affect and effect can anticipate the sphere of possible utterances some *we* might eventually associate with poetry.

Sincerely yours, Joe Amato.

(And it's OK with us if you insist on trying to articulate an anticipatory theory, based on past—verse?)

Yea, verily, the word *industrial* shall continue to slip and slide, for any attempt to align one lifeway (engineering) with another (poetry writing, or writing poetry) is bound to produce, along with conceptual-practical correspondences, at least a few gaping inconsistencies. I wrote *align*. I don't imagine for a second any one-to-one correspondences (anymore than might Jack Spicer). Experience, whether white or blue or baby blue collar, does not convert automatically into poetry (see Track 3, *Conclusion the 1st*); one's workaday persona may be helpful as a means of accessing material issues, but one ought not to put too much faith in one's unadulterated sensations, either. Gimmicky soul thus elevated to Poe-like heights, I fudge in particular on the v——.

I would not, should not wish them away, Paul and Ringo, Ringo and Paul.

18

Yes, I know—thus far, and with the exceptions proving the rules (of the game), this has been something of an advanced exercise in white boys advancing white boy-ishness, in male-sexed bodies getting their rocks off (as we poor boys used to say) by checking flows, making diagrams, and drawing analogies.

OK: so she, the sexed body, steps up onto the trolley. I'd estimate she's around, oh, sixty or so. Glasses, gray-blonde trim-cut hair, longish skirt, clothing all very muted. White like me.

(Well. In my one and only conversation with the late great poet Ed Dorn [*North Atlantic Turbine, Gunslinger*, etc.], Ed explained to me, somewhat to my surprise and with a wink in his eye, that I wasn't quite white. Essential, that wink, at that moment. Ed was of course self-consciously overstating my Sicilian and welfare-class heritage, which for the obvious reasons made the white boy feel kinda, well, *special*.)

Where was I? Oh—the sexed body is with briefcase.

I figure her right off for a middle-level exec of some sort. Or maybe just A High-Toned Old Christian Woman.

So the sexed body starts talking with the bus driver, whom she evidently knows. Small-talk at first, about the weather in the Bay area. I lean in to eavesdrop. I like to eavesdrop.

Next thing I know I hear the word "structural." Then I hear the sexed body utter "loads." Then "cost estimates." She's talking *design*, what the hell. I lean in closer, obvious by now, but I can't resist. She's talking about a project she's working on—and not from an architectural perspective either.

(Don't ask me how I know, I just know. Like you know when the letters on a blueprint are made by an architectural draftsman [illegible] or a mechanical draftsman [legible].) Another half-minute or so

and it's clear she's a, a—

an engineer, for chrissakes. In an instant the sexed body becomes a woman, a woman engineer, a rare bird for her age, and most assuredly a *gendered* body.

Man, does *that* do a (salutary) number on my interpersonal skills when I arrive minutes later at the MLA convention.

18 cont'd

She's drawing a few stares as she walks into the office area on her first day on the job. Len, another WWII vet who owes his baccalaureate in engineering to the G. I. Bill, corners me in the hallway.

Hey Joe.
Yeah Len?
Do you know if what's-her-name's got a license?
You mean a PE license?
Yuh.
Don't know. She's got a Master's, I know that.
Huh.
Yeah.

19

In all, then, the question of the sexed body, of gender, of the more masculine, heterosexual (and homosocial) aspects of the scientific and technological professions (and communities); the epistemological controversies surrounding the applicability of gender to the disciplinary knowledges associated with such fields as engineering; the sociological and practical concerns relating to the influx of women into these historically male and "manly" fields—including the North American (pardon the expression) avant-garde, in all of its particulars (to stick with the European reference point for just a moment)—

These are beyond the scope of this poem-that-is-a-Chautauqua.

:=:=:=:=:=:=:=:=:=:=:=:=:=:=:=:turnbuckle:=:=:=:=:=:=:=:=:=:=:=:=:=:=:=:=:

The young mechanic is closest to me, he knows me well,
—*"Song of Myself," section 47, l. 1257*[10]

In order to know what literature is, I would not want to study its internal structures. I would rather grasp the movement, the little process, by which a type of nonliterary discourse, neglected, forgotten as soon as it was made, enters the literary field. What happens? What is triggered off? How is this discourse modified in its efforts by the fact that it is recognized as literary?
—*Michel Foucault, "The Functions of Literature"*

If Greek philosophy was correct in thinking of knowledge as contemplation rather than as a productive art, and if modern philosophy accepts this conclusion, then the only logical course is relative disparagement of all forms of production, since they are modes of practice which is by conception inferior to contemplation. . . . But if modern tendencies are justified in putting art and creation first, then the implications of this position should be avowed and carried through. It would then be seen that science is an art, that art is practice, and that the only distinction worth drawing is not between practice and theory, but between those modes of practice that are not intelligent, not inherently and immediately enjoyable, and those which are full of enjoyed meanings.
—*John Dewey, Experience and Nature*

:=:=:=:=:=:=:=:=:=:=:=:=:=:=:=:turnbuckle:=:=:=:=:=:=:=:=:=:=:=:=:=:=:=:=:

20

Revenons à nos moutons, and just to be clear—

—as we head out of these sprawling boomburbs for good, and within sight now of that clear blue mountain pass, traffic thinning with the oxygen—

—this is Colorado, folks, the originary place of this writing, where the malls butt up against the mountains, and where these winding, steady ups and downs are bound to cause some overheating, regardless of how diligently you mix your coolants or torque your harmonics—

—Calling or no, poetry hardly operates absent career concerns. Here I am, a poet, catering or playing to the critical tribes, dropping every name I can think of (Bourdieu, Rifkin), imagining a community of readers (Anderson) for whom my name has brand-name recognition (Hoover—not Herbert, or Paul, but the one that actually sucks).

Celui qui veut, peut. But as I'm not much of a translator (see, uhm, Dictionary.com?), my options are limited to (not relatives, but) relations (dearly departed Blanchot).

Or is it that I don't care enough about poetry to translate it (Joris, say), to anthologize or edit or recuperate it (Rothenberg, Gizzi, Nelson, say), to pen biographies of poets (Clark, Ellingham, and Killian, say)? That I don't care enough about poetry to write brilliantly about it (Perloff, Nielsen, Damon, Fredman, Rasula, Golding, say)? Is it that I've just gotta be *me*?

Then me it is: teaching pays (most of Kass's and) my bills—my poetry motives thereby entirely compromised, as some would have it—hence I'm left as a poet with the mere poetry that I write, that I aspire to write, my correspondence about same (primarily online), and my occasional Chautauqua-that-is-a-poem. Oh and talktalktalk, provided I can find someone with whom to talk. Does this constitute a right and proper *ethos*, this assemblage of authorial mechanisms? Or has authorship by design thus subverted the whole, *bildungsroman* run amok?

Language is a wrap, its grammar permeating even the most solitary mind, and writing the self proceeds not as a batch process, but as a perpetual purge of incremental selves from a continuous process system (Broderick, *Practical Brewer*).

21

Tranny downshifts into L1, vehicular hydraulics just so-so, temperature gauge climbing as we climb our steepest grade yet. (How's my driving? Call 1-800-2-INFORM.)

In "Artifice of Absorption," Charles Bernstein makes what is now a somewhat famous (some poets would say, infamous) phenomenological case against one kind of poetry and for another. And because what you're reading is a poem, I thought it wise to include more than a few line breaks from another (poet), so thought it wise to excerpt a wee portion of Bernstein's poem—or is it essay? Will the real Alexander Pope please do stand-up? Anyway:

Still, the image of spellbinding fictions
that hype the most mundane of
literary deteriorata, & the nexus of
suspicions that has arisen in reaction
to this type of work, has
usefully led some writers to try to create
nonabsorbable or antiabsorptive works.
For these writers,
there has been a useful
questioning of what we are normally
asked to be absorbed into &
an outright rejection of any accommodation
with or assimilation into this "bourgeois"
space. Moreover, spellbinding doesn't have a
monopoly on creating meaning or pleasure
& may (I like Dashiell Hammett too)
inhibit both. The use of nontransparent
& nonunified modalities may produce far
more resonant music & content than
otherwise possible, just as it may produce works that are boring
& didactic. For many readers
& writers, the limits on what
can be conveyed absorptively are too
great, & the products of such
approaches are too misleading. For such
writers, the project is to wake
us from the hypnosis of absorption. (p. 54)

(Correct, reprinting these lines meant requesting permission, in writing, from Charles himself. Sometimes I wonder, with John Perry Barlow, why we do this to ourselves.)

Ahem. I can understand that my quoting Bernstein may make some of you feel better, more at ease, more securely moored to the foundations of poetry knowledge and its steadily personified advance toward the comedic-enlightenment light. But trust me—it won't last.

You will note Bernstein's emphasis not simply on the formal properties of text ("absorptive" or otherwise), but on readers and writers. A close reading of the salient lines will reveal that he is denoting flesh and blood (living) primates of the *Hominidae* family, primates that laugh on hearing themselves referred to as "archbishops."

What draws me to this excerpt is Bernstein's concluding reference to "the hypnosis of absorption," the notion that some writers wish to "wake" their readers from this "spellbinding" state. The language here suggests that Bernstein imagines mainstream literary culture-*qua*-entertainment—and both André Schiffrin and Jason Epstein have drawn out this connection too—as mesmerizing its readership, sucking its readers into the impeccably vacuumed (see Hoover, above, but not too far above) and intellectually torpid (if highly profitable) parlor of the "bourgeois" (check out those scare quotes) subject, with all of its associated, well-documented ills, its false ideology currently prone (ca. 2005) masquerading as—false ideology. Publishers *and* writers (*and* distributors) would be complicit in this enterprise, which enterprise is Williams's target in "Asphodel, That Greeny Flower" (published the year I was born), that bit about how difficult it is to "get the news from poems" (etc.). Not to be too awful clever about things, but if, as Pound put it, poetry is "news that stays news," then getting the news from news that stays news shouldn't be all that hard to manage. One might ask, *Whence the interference?*

Anyway. As Bernstein has elsewhere written, in homage to poet Jorge Santiago Perednik's remarks as to the "impossible" and "for that reason" necessary struggle against political terror in Argentina (quoted in "Poetics," p. 113), "the task of creating this poetry is impossible and for that reason takes place" (p. 137). (Regarding which, did you happen to catch Neil Young's positively defiant 9.11 benefit performance of "Imagine"?) So, to paraphrase Adorno (see *Aesthetic*, somewhere): does art that renounces the industrial do so for the sake of the industrial?

22

This is Charles Bernstein speaking. Joe Amato gave me permission to use his name when submitting this poem for publication—a portion of which was composed by Joe Amato, with my editorial input (the majority of the engineering parts), a portion of which was composed by me; but the whole of which, we both agreed, would properly and officially be understood (for the sake of *vitae*, future ISBN, etc.) as the work of one Charles Bernstein.

Why I participated in this ruse is quite simple, really: I hoped to deflect, *by design*, tried-and-true fictions of authorship. What you've been reading is in fact an amalgam of authors, authorities. Unlike the Yasusada hoax, however, in which the question of motivation inevitably falls, to a substantive degree, on the ethnicity of the perpetrator ("white") vs. the ethnicity of the pseudonym ("Japanese"), the perps here are arguably of a similar ethnic valence: Italian American, Russian-Jewish American, first and second generation, French-German American, etc. (This is to assume, of course, that we ascribe authorial agency in generative terms to the author(s) of *Doubled Flowering;* also that Kent Johnson *stands in for* "Araki Yasusada," however he does so.) Hence my motivation cannot be, strictly speaking, to reveal how the marketplace privileges specific ethnicities, in the pursuit of which agenda—which, again, Amato and I do not pursue here—it would seem reasonable to articulate a generative positionality that registers at least some awareness of "white"-guy backlash. Nor did we, Amato and I, hope to pass as each other.

No, this is the work of two authors, one of whom claims authorial primacy, and is hereby to be understood as The Author: Charles Bernstein.

23

This is Joe Amato speaking. Part 22 may be thought a (relentlessly linear, if you've dipped in only *here*) thought experiment. Its purpose is quite simple: if you talk with Charles Bernstein, you'll learn that his work has been rejected, via blind review, with readers' reports to the effect that *this would be OK were it written by Charles Bernstein*. I was hoping to point this up by exploring how "Charles Bernstein" might serve, momentarily, to amplify (by adsorption?) my own subject position. "Charles Bernstein" has a certain cachet to it, let's face it. So accuse me, if you must, of DUI (Driving Under the Influence of Bernstein anxiety), but drive on I will through this troubled intersection, risking a wrong turn down a one-way street.

It may be, too, that part 22 is *not* a thought experiment. And does this gratuitous feint at the propositional which could make of this paragraph, and of part 23, something of a thought experiment—amount to more horsing around on my part, or does it begin to surface a broadband of authorship functions against which the authorial servomechanisms of my archaic industrial calculus seem by contrast not a little quaint?

And please note: reference to the "Yasusada hoax" must be attributed in part to a face-to-face discussion between Amato and Bernstein on Thursday evening, 11 October 2001, in the Hotel Boulderado Corner Bar, Boulder, Colorado. No photographs were taken, but receipts were retained to corroborate the occasion (and secure reimbursement), which occasion was duly witnessed. In a world of nonstate actors who employ team-based management practices, a world in which organizational hierarchies, however necessary to village life, have learned to cloak their motives in more fluid, more horizontal rhetorics, a literary practice that seeks to disperse identity ought to be considered as to some degree circumscribed by such macrocosmic ploys. Does anyone really believe that in our efforts to admit, finally, to another, or to the other, yet *another* mask is necessary? And even if we posit a revitalized, less-entrenched copyright system, how are heteronauts to collect royalties, exactly? Or are we to forgo a discussion of personal, and impersonal, finances? Are we really "above" talking cold hard cash?

All of this notwithstanding: specifically with regard to the Yasusada affair and whatever my reservations—harumph!—I would concede that it *has* had value as a means of provoking public discourse regarding the messy, often fetishized convolutions of authorship and race.

Perhaps the drift of a question posted by listowner Patrick Herron to the (now defunct) Imitation Poetics online discussion list, and reiterated by Cris Cheek, highlights a key issue, especially in light of the existing and venerable body of anonymous, pseudonymous, and anonymously published literature. In Cheek's formulation: "Why can't the writing make its way in the world without any mode of authorial mediation?" Cybernauts dreamed of transcending the meat; in an uncanny parallel, heteronauts dream of transcending, by way of subverting, the author-function. That (even gift-economic, avatar-bound) utopias tend to be dangerously "perfect," or perfection-driven, cognitive habitats prompts me to ask, *Might we do well to distinguish, ethically, between the author-function and the Author-function?*

24

This is Kent Johnson speaking, channeled through Joe Amato. Joe Amato (and the benighted Charles Bernstein? one ought always to be on one's guard) is clearly toying with heteronymic ideas of which he has little real working knowledge, finally, and with regard to which, I myself hardly qualify as (North American) contemporary poetry's chief proponent. For one, I am but the caretaker of Yasusada's *Doubled Flowering*. But permit me to borrow from the interview Bill Freind conducted with me for *VeRT*: "Who is more authentic, who is less a reproduction: the poet who markets his person and career, proudly hoarding his cultural capital into the mutual fund of résumé and copyright, or the poet who creates another poet or more and refuses, to his dying day, to claim this writing under his own name?" (Johnson, "Interview").

In particular, with regard to this question of "White Male Rage"—at which Amato-*qua*-Bernstein hints at rather slyly in part 22—and as I answered, again, Mr. Freind:

> I've been told by people who were there [the 1999 MLA convention] that Mr. Bernstein read the paper [on Yasusada] with quite a bit of venom in his vowels. And of course, for some of the reasons I touch on above, Yasusada can't help but turn a radical avant-gardist Charles Gray Professor of Poetry [sic] into an angry white male who gets so hopping mad that he can't see how poignant and funny the situation really is. And it's a very interesting situation, that of the politically proper postmodernists: When it comes to multi-culturalism they want to have their cooked non-white poet and eat her too. And, of course, they want to do it with everyone's name cards on the banquet table in the English Department dining hall. No heteronyms allowed! (ibid.)

And "as to politics in the stricter sense of it," perhaps the core of my response to Mr. Freind:

> Insofar as US poetry is a miniature and marginal but complete economy, dependent, like all economies of private gain, on a certain fictive correspondence between values of worth and exchange, and insofar as the legal Name in commodity-driven culture assumes the status of "brand" that is carefully and zealously superimposed on its product in preparation for circulation in the market, I suppose that heteronymic writing—in addition to the above-mentioned creative and critical take-off a shadow economy of heteronymy would provide—could well represent a symbolic and principled resistance to the appropriative functions of the Institution of Art—a kind of civil disobedience, so to speak, against the IMF of the word: "Oh, so in your generous openness you'll include us in your End of History if we privatize? Well, Fuck You, you haven't seen anything yet." As we saw recently in Seattle, civil disobedience can sometimes have a salutary impact. And as I was suggesting earlier, there are manifold versions of such "civil disobedience" waiting to be brought, through poetry, into the world.
>
> But poetry's role in any real-time undermining of global capital will be quite minor, I'm sure. (ibid.)

Then again and in fact, this isn't even *me* speaking, so what in hell am I doing here?

25
The Pass
[in precise and available and newly postindustrial picket l.i.n.e.s., w/mascara and work ethic]

begins to resemble
Hoo-ray for and so forth
and in such effects so
specializing, courtesy now of
Industrial Light and Magic
[see Revenge of the Frodofuturists bent on detourning that coup de dés
or your local
["The mechanic, the engineer, even the user, 'speak the object'; but the mythologist is
operating system, i.e., homespun digital [condemned to metalanguage."—
R.B., ca. 1957
son et lumière, whistles and bells, bells
and whistles, the work whereof
[crossing?
avails itself of smash hits too
(this being a future such hit—included, bada bing
in a book of sp-sputtering essays the author has/had in mind, *Industrial Poetics*
to be edited, bada boom
[Feyerabend would prove useful here, esp. his remarks on "argument"
by Bernstein?
["Over the top," he sd. "Please excise."
and including a poem by that name or
[ideology:politics::theology:religion::poetics:batting practice
nature, a project owing more than a little to a demography
of reading, which means, or should
[cf. K. Burke, "There is pamphleteering; there is inquiry."
for (all) those who write, a demography of
[ID theft?
writing, occluding but not limited to
exploring ruins, i.e., 'collapse,' and smack

[See Duncan's
and mash? (wanting to type *and a young man,* says Mose, bleeds Roger, *ain't
got nothin' in the world these days*
"ways," but resisting presently
[*la danse à-gogo*
then, the impulse to simulate, simulations
"which have the power to reproduce themselves
in the exact likeness of any form of life"
(*Invasion of the Body Snatchers* [1956])
hoping thereby
["Jolson, Hope & Benny all for free
to resolve, or communicate
resolve, a lifeway, Der Weg)
["there is steam coming now from under the hood
at the risk of home-fried provincialism
["engineers of the soul," Stalin to Gorki you missed the pun on "unreconstr
a way of asking,   again and   again, skin off
our asses, But what are   *you   doing*
with *your* technology, *your* [hyperactive] machines
made of words
[i.e., no *perpetuum mobile,* entropy increasing w/mileage, run out of gas,
post-
made by machines? human metaphors, die, etc.; cf. "The connectionism is
a Surprise Machine" (Bruce Andrews 9.25.01 (my brother's 45th bday)

26

—to beg a good question, the bad
vs. good bomb (*Bomb*) is a flower? an immersion? (*Take me—*) a virus?
(*I love you*) an alias? ("Smith & Jones")? a *flâneur?* (No)
    The literary become tired with
    itself, become tired of the textual
    itinerary, itinerant, the approach [*rapprochement?*] of   Kultur
    Literature *and* literature. The literati turn to
    gaming, literalizing the turn to Douglas
    & Penn in *The Game,* Mamet's House of
    Games?   culture
    Chicken-egg-chicken-egg-duck-duck
        But why the bother with little letters, why
    bother with payloads anyway, what a bother [origin unknown]

   when monopolies abound? What
   would Olson, Jimmy? say? Shall we refuse all
   judgment?"[11] O to liberate
our mis-fit lingo? (& for some real words, see that little kid's book by Zim &
Shaffer.
I just loved it.)

[" Il y va de bonne fois." & *bringing you real solutions to imaginary problems.*™]

Even, then, a, what, heavy-duty, heavy extra de-
onto—or *heavy*
must make makeshift do
gizmo [origin unknown]
with cranks too, &
cranking, there persists a poetic
of terror, as well, the devil
his & her due, passing
wind, the scatalogical, that being

& becoming, *if you wanna*

get to heaven, or no, stars in your
crown, or no, revanchist
or no, would
imagine

.

.
>   Axiom iii: this is literature, you
>   & I are not
.

.

.

not to give a reading ever again
not to write a page ever again
not to com{pose} a screen ever again

& skip to m'loo my
darrrr-lin'

58 TRACK 1

.
\>   CLIQUE submission policy: 50% over the
.   transom, 50% solicited (by volume)
.
\>   I am looking to hire an experienced epic writer
.   who is familiar with Greek & Japanese history.
.
\>   \\first conjecture\\   Beneath the grime, we will want
.   to detect, as reported by Tom Clark
.   "Down with materials, and moving parts!"

.   a hankering to parse the didactic
.   the "fakelore," all the way back
.   to peanuts.

27
during which activity, receptivity, nothing, there is nothing
whatever of just urgency ('push, press, compel'), the absolute ur-urgency
of things that are just
happening
to industrious people doing things industriously
to industrious life & industrious circumstances
formally, contentiously, of substance &
with will, what does not change
to be changed, action or
reaction, for which we would predicate besides
countless industrial predicates, go so far as to say planetary
provocations, but absolutely nothing, *nothing*
that, laughing, would take us away from our self-critical & civic
designations, the ideological breaking the line/breaks through the
   sentence/takes a different/trajectory

the work, laughing, that labors forth
the work, laughing, of readers & writers
the work, laughing, of publishers
the work, laughing, of the marketplace[12]
the work, laughing, of the construction site, hammering or
   yammering
the work, laughing, of the office

the work, laughing, of the home
    of domesticity
the work, laughing, of the farm
    of farming
the work, laughing, of the citizen
    of the city
the work, laughing, of the suburbs

the work, laughing, of the exile
the work, laughing, of the immigrant
the work, laughing, of the children of exiles & immigrants

the work, laughing, of the factory
the work, laughing, of the engineer
the work, laughing, of words
the work, laughing, of engineering with words[13]
the work, laughing, clicking,
        chattering, of controllers

the work, laughing, of the artist
the work, laughing, of the virtuoso
the work, laughing, of the classroom
    of the scholar, of the teacher
the work, laughing, of prayer
    of prophecy, of profiteering, of professionals, of free agents, of loyal
        subjects
the work, laughing, of acting
the work, laughing, of passing
    false & true
the work, laughing, of the sea,   you there   you
the work, laughing, of the dreamer
the terrible work, laughing, of the soldier
the ritual work, laughing, extolling   the joyful work   laughing of the
    friend, friendship, over easy, plus the revolutionary potential of eating
    your spinach dotdotdot[14]
    (we grow alienated from those who would profess
        alienation) & observe how the present

unfolds itself, presently, where w   ite
                                could just as well have been, b
                                                                ack

28
thence vast, the work of work, wickedass, & the work
[Did someone say *sequel*?
of laughter, laughing harmlessly
[e.g., "creative opacity more suspect than theoretical opacity my
& stainlessly at our industry of earthly progress
[Man, this is one longass *feuilleton*   man   *ifesto*?
& heavenly regress? final design
["ph for phony, phake, carriage, phlogiston, phraud, philan
looming ahead, or someplace, or *here*, yes, more telos
[*hemp? metrosexual? antepoetic?*
telegraphed, the work of love
[Mike Davis recalls Ernst Bloch's "The Anxiety of the Engineer"
& love of work, which to love
["miles & miles of limes. Em il? Smile, bub—it's a strange theory
would bring meaning, meaning =
[an example of itself, its intentional, international vector? the argument
from, by, reverse engine
fullness, with & without
["pocketful of posies, poesies, posing, poise, *avoirdupois*,
poet, is this one of Rosenberg's
fervor (±), laughing still, laughing harder, laughing
[My job as a poet, Libbie   @ 1:53 PM   "anxious objects"
like hell a baker's dozen times, would be all, *all*
[EST. Buckle up? fuck that noi
one could ask, say, shopping, say, ask, say
[Harvey: But flexibly accumulated?   neocon (1952), neolib (1945),
      neoteric, neotype
of a Robin William
["& if you think that wine's got legs, you should see this sham
Carlos Williams, of flesh & blood (living) readers, or is poetics a subset of
scifi or [see Abrams
what architects call "security creep"?
[expressive>mimetic>pragmatic>objective to au[to?]ratic]
& writers, viewers & listeners, performers & audiences, shamans

["poetry to protect
& shareholders of the *Hominidae* family
["F=votiveMA, pa, but 2009 is three years from now
archbishops one & all
["Radical Empiricists Need Not Comply"—ersatz Marcel   Broodthaers
laughing mercilessly at our industrious, industrial SELF
["textual conditions = ma
decontaminating mail, degaussing ship
[cf. Virilio's "industrialization of vision" & *industria militaris* & Toffler's
"prosumer"
& screen, failing to extrude
["& that are prohibited by governments worldwide, in particular ma
the masculine, to ak-centuate
["If the job of poetics is the productive destabilization of the poetic act
the positive & negative, deviations from that
["Ladies, start your   cottage industries? & would you still say that if you
       knew how the in
lethal mean, one & all, real [intelligent *designer*, perforce *intelligent* design?"
[dustry worked, that "Bolero" is a factory song?
characters
["& open, secret & classified documents—but not limited   to
       electromechanical   *advantage*
is incessant   entrainment
[Chesterton: "The world will never starve for wonders, but only for
want of wonder."
Inscription, General Motors Building
Century of Progress Exposition, Chicago
1933/34 Chicago World's Fair
"The popularity of a book varies inversely as the square of its originality."
Carl H. Grabo, *The Creative Critic*, 1948
& the means by which we've arrived, together @

29

INDUSTRIAL POETICS

you opened- &
closed-captioned
capstans of the A≠B≠S-e-a-s
over-seers of the cosmic ins & outs
whose scattered forms, googled

& rustic frames
would mock the drifting
logos of the tides, sustainable
undertow of inter- & trans-
missions, recalibrating all
>   \\last conjecture\\   We will forgo for a change the compost
.   bin, with its stubborn anarchy
.   of the soil, to troop henceforth
.   to the junkyard, with its bits
>of refuse, virtuous, consanguine   (try to keep   up?
.   a half-mile down on the right, its own
.   anarchy of remanufacture summoning
.   us steel-eyed—neither terrorists, nor
.   tourists, but
>folksy, foxy folk to
.   "hard work, long hours, low pay
.   & must have own tools"
.

>Bummer
.   If You Want It
.   You Must Need It
.   Minimum Charge $1
:   & note that I've said nothing
nothing at all about great
essays, great scholarship, great
poetry, or great literature; that is
there's nothing
nothing at all here
about canons or postmodernity, its radical initiative
of radical modernism, its partial assemblies, disassemblies
& dissemblers
notwithst&ing—
                    \I'd rather drive a Chevy
                        than a go-kart.\
               [If you're not Joe Amato, click here.]
               ADRESSE DU TITULAIRE A L'ETRANGER:

INDUSTRIAL POETICS   63

To: undisclosed-recipients
Are objectivity and transparency the only conceptual antidotes to subjectivity and opacity?
And must metaphoricity always outstrip an understanding of mechanism?

 An older item named CONTEMPORARY POETRY already exists in this location. Do you want to replace it with the one you're moving? Cancel | OK

:=:=:=:=:=:=:=:=:=:=:=:=:=:=:turnbuckle:=:=:=:=:=:=:=:=:=:=:=:=:=:=:

The Works, Slighted

Baumeister, Theodore, Eugene A. Avallone, and Theodore Baumeister III, eds. *Marks' Standard Handbook for Mechanical Engineers*. 8th ed. New York: McGraw-Hill, 1978.

Dodsworth. Dir. William Wyler. Screenplay by Sidney Howard (based on Sinclair Lewis's novel). Perf. Walter Huston, Ruth Chatterton, Paul Lukas, Mary Astor, David Niven, Gregory Gaye, Maria Ouspenskaya, John Howard Payne, Spring Byington. Samuel Goldwyn Company, 1936.

Hardy, Phil, ed. *The Encyclopedia of Horror Movies*. By Tom Milne and Paul Willemen. New York: Harper and Row, 1986.

Jay, Ricky. *Jay's Journal of Anomalies: Conjurers, Cheats, Hustlers, Hoaxsters, Pranksters, Jokesters, Impostors, Pretenders, Sideshow Showmen, Armless Calligraphers, Mechanical Marvels, Popular Entertainments*. New York: Farrar, Straus and Giroux, 2001.

Sinclair, Upton. *The Jungle*. 1906. New York: Penguin, 1986.

Thomas, W. A., H. A. Spalding, and Zarko Pavlovich. *The Engineer's Vest Pocket Book*. Dennison compact series. Baltimore, MD: Ottenheimer, 1960.

Weschler, Lawrence. *Mr. Wilson's Cabinet of Wonders: Pronged Ants, Horned Humans, Mice on Toast, and Other Marvels of Jurassic Technology*. New York: Pantheon, 1995.

:=:=:=:=:=:=:=:=:=:=:=:=:=:=:turnbuckle:=:=:=:=:=:=:=:=:=:=:=:=:=:=:

How to Tell the Difference between Life and Art
A Grant Proposal (Take 2)

.1   Poetry is an art.

.2   Art is labor.

.3   I prefer difficult intellectual labor, intellectually speaking, even when I'm on the skids.

.4   Most readers don't get paid to read. In fact readers often pay *to* read. Work out the implications for yourself.

.5   Labor occurs in a place, usually a place of work, or workplace. As labor can be a joy, workplaces can be joyful places. Most of us agree: workplaces should be more joyful than they generally are.

.6   But work is also, you know, *work*. Even if it's not all pick and shovel work, it's *work*.

.7   Poetry is a form of labor, then, some would say pleasurable labor, or beautiful labor, or erotic labor, or talented labor. But poetry is a form of labor.

.8   Poetry can be joyful labor, but is sometimes not as joyful as it should be. We all know when we're working, but we don't always know when we're playing, or making poetry happen, or making love. For this reason we need to learn how to dress for the occasion.

.9   Poetry is poetics on-the-job. When it's not, it usually bears a striking resemblance to greeting card verse. And there could be something wrong with greeting card verse, yesindeedy.

.10   Claims made for a work are not to be confused with the claims a work actually makes. Claims a work actually makes are not to be confused with a work's demonstration *of* those claims. When any discourse begins to demonstrate its claims, it becomes subject to the caprices of literary value. You break the expository/explanatory codes, you pay the piper.

.11   In theory, all theory is just that—theory. Theory often becomes, in practice, that old time religion. Give me that old time religion, at least once in a while, if only to remind me that some ideas have a shelf life longer than the life expectancy of a fruit fly.

.12   That said, too many people who should know better do not take the time to listen to what theory is actually *saying*.

.13   A good critic keeps you honest. A good theorist keeps you on your toes.

.14 Literary discourse abhors a vacuum. Still, we can't help but operate within (legible, tacit or unwritten) parameters (note the page margins of this book, for example), hence we would do well to proceed with an awareness that there are always limits at work in what we do and say, and that transgression for transgression's sake is apt to have mixed results.

.15 Steal this book.

.16 Let's stop kidding ourselves: it is impossible to distinguish today, in formal terms, between contemporary poetry and contemporary prose (in English especially). This has, or should have had, vast consequences for English studies at all levels. Most major publishers will doubtless resist this inference for as long as it's profitable to do so.

.17 But there are times too when one would do well to define one's terms: a poet is someone who writes poetry. Whatever one means by poetry.

.18 Research the various meanings of "demo," and be sure to do a Google search for "demo failure." Next, interpolate. The hits will date quickly, as will the tracks.

.19 Let's stop kidding ourselves: there is nothing inherently good or bad about teaching in order to support one's artistic pursuits, any more than there is something inherently bad or good about selling popsicles in order to support one's artistic pursuits. (Both teaching and selling popsicles can be rewarding activities, but I'll settle for teaching.)

.20 Teaching is a job, and we should think of jobs in terms of loyalties, and obligations, and sure, paychecks. It must be granted, however, that academic employment does at times make one's ass twitch.

.21 There's a story in here someplace, if you cared to write it.

.22 The narrative trajectory will be punctuated throughout by a compulsion to say something important.

.23 Those writers for whom I have the most respect, as writers, are keenly aware of the ritualized nature of art, its deference to past forms and contents as well as its requisite nod toward future possibility. The written work of these writers exhibits equal measures of care and wild abandon. In the twentieth century, on the North American continent, most of these writers, but not all, have been poets. These poets have given equal attention to form and content, but for most, form and content are indistinguishable, finally.

.24 Our close readings may be equally close and yet oceans apart. Don't sweat it.

.25 Some of the writers for whom I have the most respect were (and are) miserable human beings. Period. Whether this miserableness is evident in their actual writing is a matter of careful interpretation by human beings who know horseshit when they see it.

.26 Poets do a great disservice to themselves and to their publics when they pretend to have no obligation to one another and to their publics.

.27 Popular culture is not the problem. The problem is the public's inability to grasp the limits of popular culture. This is fundamentally an educational problem, which is to say, a problem that has everything to do with class realities (among other things). A related problem is the general inability of academic culture to recognize that the wholesale consumption of pop-cultural artifacts is not in itself a measure of value, but a statement about *demo*graphics. Producing and marketing desire is a tricky business, but crap is crap. You can say a lot of smart things about something that didn't take much effort to produce, something that says very little, something that so many seem drawn to. Why produce such a thing in the first place? And why have a hand in promoting the proliferation of piss-poor work? I think we know in general why crap sells, and if we don't know, I'm pretty certain that advertising and PR firms *do* know. This constitutes the chief lesson of Marketing 101.

.28 "Serious" or "literary" fiction is hardly immune to such charges, to an extent even greater than the Dale Pecks of the critical establishment are willing to allow. Even scholars of pop culture, inured to the mega-incomes of the celebrity cultures they circumnavigate, might be more than a little bemused to learn that many subpar trade authors are regularly landing six-figure deals, and then some, for their latest hack jobs. This might (might) persuade such scholars to reconsider their role in the moneymaking orgy. Again—this is not directed at ghostwritten celeb bios, or the gods and goddesses of pulp, or the better known pseudoliterary scribes. This is directed at authors in the gray zones of trade publishing, whose doctored books (and doctored *sub rosa* for a steep price, mind you) nonetheless sell in the tens of thousands.

.29 A distressing situation to those of us who understand how much labor goes into the often-lovely productions one finds in the small press world—which produces its share of clunkers, to be sure, off of which *nobody* is getting rich.

.30 Item 29 applies as well to the academic presses, which are themselves struggling to stay alive—and often ending up leaner, and meaner, in the process. Of course the academic presses are the chief outlet for the scholarly discourse that interrogates, and in some sense recycles—i.e., pays homage to—pop culture.

.31 But if one is going to suffer the slings and arrows of literary fortune *anyway*, one might as well resolve to do so in style, I agree. Enter the writer-for-hire.

.32 Like all writers, writers-for-hire ought to work out a writing ethic for themselves.

.33 There is good pop culture and bad pop culture. Some people like to distinguish between pop culture and mass culture, but I find that distinction, while accurate, a bit ponderous.

.34 Please don't misunderstand me—there is room for endless analysis of all manner of cultural production. But, but: attention span may be a nonrenewable resource. We're only *mortal*.

.35 So analysis of consumption trends and of the artifacts, textual or otherwise, that participate in these trends renders a judgment call in the simple act of selecting a given trend/set of artifacts, and thus ought not to be shy of making other sorts of judgment calls.

.36 If you don't believe me, write a poem.

.37 Making money remains a vital concern. No money, no eat. Me like eat.

.38 If you don't believe me, write poetry.

.39 And sometimes I do like crap. But *good* crap.

.40 Producing, or packaging for consumption, or whatever, is something that those of us in the avant-garde, or post-avant, or whatever, probably ought to spend more time thinking about. To want one's voice heard is not careerism.

.41 To want one's voice heard can lead to careerism.

.42 Careerism can be defined, roughly, as stepping on someone else's head in order to get where you're going.

.43 Do I need to cite someone?

.44 Violence and sex, while motifs, ought to be treated, by artists, as *devices* that can be used to access more urgent cultural logics, more pressing social issues. Especially here in the U.S., violence and sex, like technology, tend to become ends in themselves. But pulp, even carefully manufactured pulp, can usually take you only so far. Hear that, Quentin?

.45 Censorship is not, is never the answer. The answer, unsurprisingly, is responsible thinking and making. The complication, of course, hinges on the word *responsible*. We artists might begin to address this complication by recognizing that the word *didactic* need not necessarily mean *preachy*. Responsible agency, whether kinetic or relatively inert, is to some degree unavoidably autodidactic. Or so I keep telling myself.

.46 Word violence is often a precondition for extraverbal violence, but they are not the same things. Just ask Quentin: the narration of violence can be redemptive in a way that actual violence rarely or never is. Depends upon the narration, and the narrator. Words words words and deeds. Floss, *then* brush your teeth.

.47 One can find constructive lessons for thought and experience in belief systems predicating groundedness *and* groundlessness, outwardness *and* inwardness.

.48 Intellectual thought still requires for its public dissemination access to constructs like "the spirit of the age" and "the history of ideas" and "root beer float."

.49 I still like those little Peter Paul Almond Joy bars, especially around Halloween—a sign, no doubt, of my stubborn insistence on clinging to bygone patterns of behavior. Of my refusal to grow up. Of my fear of death. Of my inability to overcome the nostalgic impulse. Of my habitually bourgeois sensibility. Of my poor taste, my lack of self-control, my complacency in the face of newly discovered Belgian chocolates. Of my class anxieties, my sugar habit, my sweet tooth, my unwitting complicity in commodity culture. Of my entirely willful pursuit of that leisure-class affectation implicit in the purchase of retro goods. Of my resistance to the tacit dictates of academic orthodoxies. Of my flamboyantly reactionary rejection of academic orthodoxies. Of my seduction by the indescribably delicious. Of my desire to be simple in a complicated world. Of my secret longing to be one of the huddled masses. Of my attraction to a name, to the colors white, blue, red, and brown. Of my loyalty to Hershey Foods. Of my denial in the face of change. Of my occasional yen for milk chocolate and almonds and coconut. Of my frugality. Of my being haunted by my past.

.50 Writing poetry is fundamentally not the same activity as reading poetry. Giving is not the same as taking, making is not the same as making meaning, generating is not the same as receiving, producing is not the same as consuming—and talking is not the same as listening. Sometimes more credit ought to be given to the reception side of the equation, sometimes to the generative side. One thing: when producers seek to bring consumers into the production network as would-be co-creators, they often forget that they have to produce something that is worth the consumers' effort. There's no business like show business.

.51 And there's room in this business for more than one comedian. Think mogul, act loco?

.52 You're entitled to say anything you want about everything and anything. Doing so has very little to do with rendering a critical judgment.

.53 There are two major problems facing writers today: (1) blind adherence to convention; and (2) aesthetic preciosity, whether among more conventional or more unconventional writers. With the possible additional complication that relatively few people are willing or able to entertain the questions posed by difficult literature.

.54 There's no law against asking questions, difficult or otherwise. And no, I'm not an elitist. You are not an elitist to believe that something better is possible, that it's up to each of us to make our contributions accordingly.

.55 Careful readers will be sure to note that I hedge for the moment on the word *better*.

.56 Change from below *and* from above. With a little help from our friends, yes, always with a little help from our friends.

.57 Not think outside the box, but think outside the head. Do your homework.

.58 As an artist, I am aiming for an effect just a wee bit shy of elevating your soul. *I'm joking!*

.59 Elsewhere in your literary travels you will likely find much attention paid to translation. If we're honest about art and intellectual work, those of us without a second language must deem ourselves as working at something of a cultural deficit. We ought to do something about this, much as we ought to do something about our tendency to take our highly specialized knowledges too seriously. Too, serious intellectuals often neglect, for instance, to question the widespread desire among the intellectual classes to own a Volvo, or to shop at Whole Foods, or to hire a housekeeper. This is well documented, and goes for translators as well, and would-be translators, and translator-poets, who sometimes offer up shoddy work in order to build cultural and symbolic capital. And maybe one day own a Volvo, and shop at Whole Foods, and hire a housekeeper.

.60 I do not have a second language, and possibly not even a first. I shop at Whole Foods when I can afford it, generally for specialty items. I do not own a Volvo. Maybe someday.

.61 Oh, and I'll never hire a housekeeper. Never's a long time, I know.

.62 Being a bard in the twenty-first century ought to presuppose a lay knowledge of evolutionary theory or, say, John Lee Hooker. Just for example.

.63 Where one lives and works always has something to say about how one lives and works, about how one perceives one's life and work, and others' lives and works. Whether as construct, commodity, natural resource, or earthly provenance, place is inescapable.

Track 2

Technical Ex-Communication
How a Former Professional Engineer Becomes a Former English Professor

I

1. Imagine: Once upon a time (1984), I left the corporate world to join the academic world, thinking the lofty latter would tower above the corruption of corporate complicity.

2. Yup. I really thought that. Imagine.

3. Picture this: you're seated at a table (1992) with nine other faculty, all strangers. Five such clusters of ten fill the carpeted room—off-white walls, acoustical ceiling tiles, fluorescent lighting—and everyone boasts a terminal degree in science, engineering, architecture, law, psychology, or design. Everyone except you, that is—you hold a doctorate in English.

4. Before you, on the table, glares a ream of white, 20-lb., 8.5″ x 11″ paper. A beaming but otherwise nondescript man looming at the front of the room announces, "You have one half-hour in which to devise a high-quality paper airplane. The team whose airplane hangs aloft for the longest stretch of time will be judged a true success—a leader in quality." Everyone in the room chuckles. "Let's see who the winner will be," the nondescript man teases. And with that he props a large digital timer on the table before him and slaps the start button.

5. All but five of the fifty strangers in the room are men. Most are white, eight speak an inflected English that indicates an Asian upbringing. Most of the men are middle-aged, some are older, nearing retirement. Most of the middle-aged men wear trousers, oxfords, ties, rolled shirtsleeves. Most of the older men relax in three-piece suits. Most of the men sport beards. Four of the five women in the room are all business—navy or black suits, skirts just above the knee, heels, lipstick, eye liner, nail polish. The four younger men and one younger woman are, like others of your generation, dressed casually—new jeans, polo shirts, sweaters.

6. As the timer begins its countdown, most people begin chatting, noisily, to others in their group. About their families, about the weather. One of the engineers seated at your table immediately takes command. He urges that the team proceed, first, by taking note of specific aerodynamic principles—lift, for example. He lectures the team on such principles. A few of the engineers in the group get antsy, grab a few sheets of paper from the ream, experiment by folding their sheets this way and that. The self-elected leader seems annoyed, barks a few orders. A few people in the group, intent on making progress, are willing to cooperate.

7. But you, you're someplace else, because you've been here before.

II

8. You may have heard of the Illinois Institute of Technology (IIT) in Chicago. The school has been splashed across the Windy City news in recent years. IIT's College of Architecture has a worldwide reputation for housing the program that Ludwig Mies van der Rohe directed during his post-Bauhaus years. IIT: the campus Mies built, the campus that boasts Crown Hall, the campus whose buildings announce in bold the Miesian orthogonal imprint, the less-is-more flatland structures of steel and glass and high HVAC bills.

9. Thanks to one of the largest (matching) gifts ever made to a postsecondary educational institution—120 million dollars, courtesy of two wealthy members of IIT's Board of Trustees—plans for a new student center were hoisted onto the drawing board, with leftover dollars to fund much-needed building and equipment upgrades and to endow engineering-only full-tuition scholarships (at the time of the gift, in 1998, IIT's tuition was roughly $17,000 a year). The international design competition for the student center attracted all sorts of media attention, with the commission awarded finally to the renowned Dutch architect and architectural theorist Rem Koolhaas. After several delays, the structure was finally completed in 2003, a convenient cornerstone in IIT's ongoing effort to reset its collegial clock.

10. I wasn't around to see the center open. I was happy for the students, though it remains unclear to me whether the surrounding community has reaped any actual material benefits from the hoopla. For decades IIT has been situated on the northernmost edge of the largest public housing project in the U.S.—the Robert Taylor Homes-Stateway Gardens complex, which at one point housed nearly 40,000 African-American residents, most of whom

receive public assistance, as I once did. (The project's aging high-rise structures are today, mercifully, being torn down.) Directly to the north of IIT are more projects, beyond which is the frenzy of development and gentrification that marks Mayor Daley's and the city's continuing efforts to move the South Loop frontier further south. As you might imagine, IIT has had a tough time responding to its location over the years. So perhaps the attention given to the new student center, and to a revitalization effort currently underway along Thirty-fifth Street—the historic Bronzeville area, part of which has been tagged a federal "empowerment zone"—*will* help to invigorate neighborhoods suffering from decades of neglect, of racial and economic segregation. Hence perhaps I should be spending my time, and yours, talking about the sorts of social, political, and cultural conditions that have permitted the situation on Chicago's South Side to decline to such a degree. But I'm not a sociologist—I'm an English prof who happens to be a poet. And to paraphrase Wallace Stevens, part of my work *as* a poet is to help people live their lives—an ambitious agenda, to be sure, whether one is (to borrow Richard Nixon's quip) to campaign in poetry or to govern in prose.

11. My tenure with the Department of Humanities at IIT began in August 1992. Like my former employer, the University of Illinois at Urbana-Champaign (UIUC), IIT hired me primarily because my undergrad math scholarship and seven years of plant engineering experience, followed by a doctorate in English, seemed automatically to qualify me to teach technical and professional writing. As an aspiring poet and a single white heterosexual male of thirty-seven, I was happy to be afforded the opportunity to live in a more "happening" environs—and in any case, I had no choice. My two-year "visiting" stint at UIUC had expired, and IIT was offering me a tenure-track position with a "3/3" teaching load—three courses per semester. Not something one in my notoriously job-depleted profession, with my credit card debt, turns down.

12. When I arrived at my new school, demolition of the old Comiskey Park, just the other side of the Dan Ryan expressway from IIT, was nearly complete. The new Sox stadium (renamed U.S. Cellular Field in 2003), standing alongside the old, gleamed across the Ryan at the projects, daring South-Side African Americans to make the trek into Bridgeport, where racial tensions have always run high and would explode most notably in 1997, upon the person of young Lenard Clark. On campus, things weren't quite what I'd expected. There were rumors that budget deficits were reaching a crisis

state. And IIT exuded a certain corporate ambience—reflected both in the language of my senior colleague in English (a person prone to going on about how her technical communication program is "technology-driven") and in the market "savvy" of our upper-level administrators (who were just then learning to mouth the now-ubiquitous student-as-consumer rhetoric). The corporate lip service disturbed me, not least because I thought I had left behind such thinking eight years prior, when I left my second Fortune 500 job as an engineer.

III

13. Picture this: you're seated at a table (1979) with five other people, all strangers. Five such clusters of five fill the carpeted room—off-white walls, acoustical ceiling tiles, fluorescent lighting—and everyone holds an undergraduate degree in engineering or business. All but two of the twenty-five strangers in the room are men. Most are younger, a few are middle-aged, two are black. Most wear shirts and ties, a few lounge in their sports jackets. The two women in the room have opted for solid-color blouses, and skirts well below the knee.

14. You're handed a three-ring binder, inside of which are sequenced instructions that describe a series of role-playing exercises (red, orange, yellow, green, blue tabs). Each exercise will require a high level of cooperation among members of your group. "I think we should start out by trying to—." "Wait a minute," the only woman in the group interrupts you, smiling but firm, "who put *you* in charge?" "Well, *nobody*," you respond, "but *someone* has to be in charge, no?" You look around at the other faces in your group. Two look vaguely uncomfortable, one seems to want to follow your lead.

15. By the end of that first day, the group has—simply by doing what you suggest—informally chosen you as its leader. At least one person in the group is not a happy camper. And after four days of working together, arguing together, and sweating together, everyone is asked to evaluate—not, as expected, the work accomplished—but *one another.*

16. A four-quadrant blackboard grid is used to map personal qualities, warm/cold on the abscissa, dominant/submissive on the ordinate. Everyone has his or her day in the Cartesian sun—or, as the case may be, gloom. Participants take turns shouting out adjectives that describe each monkey-in-the-middle, with a time clock to make it seem either a pressing exercise or a game

show. Each adjective is chalked into a given quadrant. If you're lucky, you might learn that you're primarily a dominant/warm personality—excellent leadership material. If not, you might leave that intense final session, as some have been known to, in tears.

IV

17. "Dimensional Management Training" is what they called it—part of the corporate training package I'd received while employed at Miller Brewing Company in Fulton, New York. My job with the Philip Morris–owned brewing giant was my first after graduation, and Miller would send me to corporate headquarters in Milwaukee for a week at a crack. Days were spent in seminar rooms; evenings, gulping down mugs of beer. Most of this training was geared ultimately toward helping trainees account for theirs and others' motivations, with the mutual goals of enhancing organizational cooperation and enlightening employees as to their latent or manifest leadership qualities. I often returned from the training seminars eager to test on-the-job my newly acquired *interpersonal skills*, as they called them. In this sense, such training cultivated in me the desire to *lead*. I guess I was lucky. In some it may well have cultivated the resignation to *follow*.

18. But leadership training or no, there seemed to be little I could do to shake my new-guy status at Miller. At twenty-six, I'd found myself stuck after four years, unable to advance beyond my entry-level engineering position with the nation's second-largest brewer. So I'd gone on the market intent, as only a former welfare recipient can be, on landing a job with Aramco. By my calculations, a mere two years in Saudi Arabia and I'd have enough cash saved to handle my father's expenses until long after he was eligible to receive his whopping $500-per-month social security check, and his $80-per-month pension check from General Electric—the latter so absurdly low because of his decision to withdraw his severance pay after the company had laid him off, with hundreds like him, in 1969. That was the year after my folks' divorce, the year after my old man started hitting the bottle. The way I'd figured it, me and my adolescent dreams of fortune and power, I'd have enough cash saved to live like a working-class hero.

19. But after six months of applying, and waiting, and inquiring, the previously optimistic job placement agent wound up with a frown on his face. "They want only seasoned veterans now," the headhunter informed me, "guys with ten or more years experience."

20. And so, with failed postcolonial aspirations, I applied for a senior project engineering position with the local pharmaceutical plant, Bristol-Myers Co. (now Bristol-Myers Squibb). This plant's claim to industrial fame was that it had at one time manufactured half of all the penicillin produced in the U.S. The interview went well. The person I'd be working for directly was a former West Point cadet who had that ingratiating habit, or tactic, of inserting "sir" into every other sentence. The cadet's boss, the plant engineering manager, was a strictly-by-the-book, suit-and-tie man, very old school, with a master's in engineering-based, Taylorized management—the type who doubtless tends to be receptive to "Yes sirs."

21. After exchanging industrial horror stories with the cadet—bonding—I was ushered into the engineering manager's office by the office manager. (They still used a secretarial pool there.) "Please take a seat," she instructed, nodding vigorously at the chairs across the desk from the engineering manager, who was momentarily preoccupied perusing what looked to be a budget report of some sort, all rows and columns. "Just a moment, Joe," he said, without looking up through his bifocals. Just then I noticed that my chair sank low, so low in fact that this older man, perhaps an inch shorter than me standing, loomed several inches above me. An old trick, I thought, and gazing around the office I spotted a portrait depicting a Canadian Mountie against an alpine backdrop above the caption, "One Canadian Stands Alone."

22. My interview with the engineering manager was a tight-lipped affair, and I'd learned by then when to be tight-lipped myself. I even started mouthing a few "Yes sirs" myself, which were snapped up approvingly. But there was one final hoop-jump to go—an interview with the plant manager. The cadet was commanded to hand-deliver me.

23. He marched me through what seemed an ancient maze of seeping and odoriferous production areas, laced with piping and crowded with chemical processing equipment, in the midst of which were constructed makeshift white-collar habitats. It was nearing lunch, and I caught a glimpse of several salaried employees seated at their desks, chomping down their brown-bag goodies. When we reached the plant manager's office, he greeted us at his office door. My escort abruptly relinquished his duties with an enthusiastic "Thank you *sir*," and the plant manager whisked me past his high-heeled young secretary. I did my best not to stare at her black fishnet stockings.

24. At first this manager seemed less officious than my prior interviewers. A well-groomed, not-unhandsome man of perhaps fifty, his clothes were elegantly, if conservatively, tailored: navy double-pleated trousers, white-on-white oxford, red-and-blue-checkered silk tie, silk navy jacket. He seated himself behind a large wooden desk in a lush, paneled office that, in my view, reflected his rank without pretension. I sat in a leather-cushioned chair, almost at ease. The blinds were shut, the desk lamp lighting the room with a warm, subdued glow. The plant manager was clearly taking his time. "Would you like a cup of coffee?" he asked. "No thank you, sir," I replied. He cupped his impeccably manicured hands and finally began, casually.

25. "What do you think of change?" he asked, smiling.

26. Bastard. He was toying with me, and he knew I knew it. I bit my tongue, hard, struggled for composure. "Depends what kind of change you mean," I replied, surprising even myself with my reciprocally casual tone, "organizational change, or evolutionary change, or social change, or—"

27. He cut me off, impatient but still smiling. "Well, let me put it differently. Suppose," he began, "—suppose you were asked by one of the production managers to retrofit a production process in such and such a way in order to increase output." "Uh-huh," I nodded, all bright-eyed and bushy-tailed. "Now suppose," he continued, "—suppose this manager, a man with some twenty-five years of experience, feels that the modifications required are thus and so. As the senior engineer, what do you feel your response should be? Do you think you should yourself investigate the process to determine the nature of the modifications, or do you think you should instead follow the production manager's lead?"

28. Trick question, of course. Why *of course* no self-respecting engineer simply does what someone else tells him to do when it comes to design. And of course this asshole wouldn't even be *asking* me this question unless he wanted to test my compliance.

29. I thought about my situation at the brewery. I thought about how the Return On Investment for capital upgrades had dropped from five years to two years in the course of my short industrial life—this was change, to be sure, but it didn't bode well for the U.S. worker, blue *or* white collar. I thought

about my father's eligibility for social security, still three years off. More change, a life change that in some sense I couldn't help but look forward to. I thought about telling this plant manager fucker to go take a good shit for himself, him and that $500 jacket and that shit-eating grin of his.

30. "Well," I said, "I figure that if the production manager has twenty-five years of experience, he knows what's going on. So I'd be inclined to do things his way." The plant manager nodded. I nodded. Everybody nodded. The job placement agent was elated. The offer came in at $34,500 per year.

31. And when I left that job in 1984—or it left me—I was making nearly $40,000 a year. This was in Syracuse, New York. To help put this in perspective: in 1998, in Chicago, as a full-time, tenure-track assistant professor of English with the Department of Humanities at IIT—and with bachelor of science degrees in mathematics and mechanical engineering, my Professional Engineer's license, and a master's and doctorate in English—my annual salary was $36,800. And as of this writing, working now (2005) as a non-tenure-track instructor at Illinois State University in Normal, my salary is—well, that might not be a fair comparison. But it's $27,000.

v

32. It didn't take a clairvoyant to see that, from the start, my days with Bristol-Myers Co. were numbered. For one, ever since my first day on the job with Miller Brewing Co. (and as I indicated in Track 1), I'd somehow gotten it into my head that I wanted to be a poet. I still don't know where this impulse came from, but in my second year with Bristol-Myers I started looking into graduate schools. I figured that I'd get a doctorate, teach college students as a means of supporting my writing. I didn't know then what I know now about the teaching profession: it's not only a job-and-a-half in itself, it's also vital social work.

33. At any rate, I'd found myself, after nearly three years at the pharmaceutical factory, wanting out of the engineering profession. I'd grown plain sick and tired of the industrial-organizational life-support system. The brown-nosing chain-of-command, along with the daily shit-shower-shave routine, conspired to create a chain of veritable *being*, my one-and-only life strapped to the capricious imperatives of plant production and the global marketplace. True, a few of my bosses saw me—despite or perhaps *because of* my outspoken nature—as management stock, attempting to lure me into the supervisory world with more money and power. But once I'd made it clear to them

that I wanted to hone my *technical* talents only, they behaved as though I'd turned my back on the company. I found it increasingly difficult to keep my mouth shut, and they found it increasingly difficult to tolerate my open mouth. The warning memo—red-stamped "confidential"— threatened me with "termination" if I didn't *just do it*.

34. But my mouth just would not close, and I was called into the engineering conference room on a bright Monday morning in April. I seated myself across the table from the engineering manager. Next to him was my new supervisor, Stan, put in charge after the cadet was canned—for incompetence brought about, in the final analysis, by excessive asskissing (so asskissing doesn't *really* work after all). "Stan has something to tell you," the engineering manager commanded. And he turned to Stan, who choked out, nervously, "We've decided that . . . we have to . . . let you go." I was immediately escorted out of the plant and told to return at four o'clock for my exit interview.

35. Later that day, I walked through the factory distributing copies of my four-page-long exit statement to anybody and everybody. Therein I explained, with quotes from Montaigne and Emerson, how I thought the company could be more fairly managed. You see, I'd seen my termination coming, and I'd planned accordingly. And like they say on the job: you plan the work, and you work the plan.

VI

36. In 1998, the second most powerful member of IIT's Board of Trustees is the former Motorola CEO, Bob Galvin. Galvin's father, Paul Galvin, founded Motorola, the company that produces, among so many other communications-based products, the 68030 microprocessor chip that powered (as they say) the aging (now kaput) Macintosh IIci on which I originally composed this essay. IIT's Board of Trustees is in fact run by two Bobs, Galvin and his (even richer) billionaire buddy, Bob Pritzker, who together are responsible for that 120-million-dollar gift. For years these two have reached deep into their endless wool-blend pockets to bail IIT's ailing, tuition-driven campus out of the red and into the black—to the tune, I believe it is, of something like ten million a year. Only thing is, in accordance with the First Law of Thermodynamics, you don't get something for nothing. (Thanks to an anonymous reader for pointing out that a variation on the Second Law—you can't even break even—appeared in the Rolling Stones sound track heard in Motorola's 1999 mobile pager commercials: "You can't always get what you want.")

37. Sending IIT faculty to QCEL training at Motorola on a Saturday was part of the payback. At the time, IIT administrators were hoping Galvin might kick some additional millions their way. So they'd agreed to bus all IIT faculty out to what is known casually as Motorola's Schaumburg "campus"—the Galvin Center of Motorola University (no shit), the company's corporate training ground. And on a bright fall Saturday there we all were, sipping coffee, bitching under our collective breath, and ready to be indoctrinated in the company's much-vaunted QCEL managerial philosophy—*Quality, Creativity, Ethics,* and *Leadership.*

38. It was quite an event. Several hundred phuds, most in the engineering and science fields and some with international reputations, marched through "creativity" sessions in which a trainer with a master's degree in creativity (no shit) inculcated them in the beauty of "convergent and divergent thinking." Or in which they were asked to work in teams to create that "best" paper airplane (i.e., Quality through teamwork, teamwork through Leadership). Or in which they were instructed in the importance of sound (business) ethics—without being asked to consider (e.g.) the ethical impact of divorcing ethics from more bracing issues of morality or politics.

39. But the IIT-Motorola *coup de grâce* was the wrap-up session, in which the powers-that-be hit upon the tactic, or strategy, of using outstanding *student* leaders at IIT to impress upon faculty the inevitable necessity of QCEL training. "We students sincerely hope you faculty take QCEL seriously," advised one especially emphatic, rosy-faced, head-shaved, undergrad ROTC engineer, "because we believe that IIT needs this sort of thinking in order to become a technical leader in the twenty-first century." The ensuing faculty response was punctuated by several outbursts from senior faculty members who, understandably, found the entire enterprise an insult to their professional integrity and expertise. "I have an international reputation in my field," one distinguished research engineer rose to exclaim during the wrap-up session, "and I find it utterly humiliating that you have brought me to this place, to be lectured at by those who could very well be my students. I regard this as a distressing, if not ludicrous, development."

40. And if I couldn't help but sympathize with the gent, I thought at the same time that he probably *could* stand to learn a thing or two about political action. I understood at that QCEL session what I'd learned the hard way years prior: to get through to the corporate mind-set requires something a bit more vul-

gar, or of the "common people," than solitary expressions of distress—something a bit more *collective*. As in *collective bargaining*, for one, anathema to so many academics because they think of themselves, with some (historical) justification, as necessarily autonomous thinkers and researchers, as free-agent intellectuals—as anything but common-cause *workers*. IIT is a private postsecondary institution, and only in the late nineties did the National Labor Relations Board give some indication that it might eventually permit faculty at private institutions to unionize (faculty are still awaiting word ca. 2005, but it don't look good). Of course, union or no, it's unlikely that intellectual freedom—and an institutional commitment to do some good in the world—will emerge from top-down enforcement of an ever-more-severe bottom line.

41. Needless to say, QCEL fever hit IIT hard, and lickety-split we were all being asked to devise a QCEL component for each of our courses and to attend mandatory brown-bag lunches with the purpose of brainstorming innovative applications of QCEL thinking. Some faculty took up the QCEL banner, but many of us just plain refused, calling the administration's bluff. Most of us readily understood that QCEL, though perhaps appropriate to a workplace bound by short-term constraints of efficiency and end product, hardly suited the long-term goals of informed personal awareness, discovery, and self-critique that true education demands.

42. And I mean, what were they going to do, *fire us*?

43. It was especially difficult for those of us in the Department of Humanities, which at IIT is comprised of history, philosophy, and English. In the minds of corporate-leaning administrators, the humanities are understood as revolving around *communication*, and this narrow conception of what we do empowers those of us in English studies only to the extent that we're willing to teach students how to structure effective memos, accurate lab reports, and so forth. Further, according to Motorola's QCFL logic, communication practices—most conspicuously *writing*—fall under the L category, L for *Leadership*. Where else? We all know that the primary purpose of words is to help you gain control over others, right? Literacy *is* power, yes?

44. In any case, IIT's ongoing public relations effort seems to suggest that, in order to produce the finest technical leaders for the next millennium, faculty must maintain close ties with the corporation. As stated in IIT's (1998) *Undergraduate Bulletin*, one of the things that distinguishes IIT is its "unique Intro-

duction to the Professions program": "Throughout the curricula, the IIT interprofessional projects provide a learning environment in which interdisciplinary teams of students apply theoretical knowledge gained in the classroom and laboratory to real-world projects sponsored by industry and government" (p. 7). Interprofessional projects, or IPROs, now displaced QCEL as the newest curricular fad at IIT. The clause "sponsored by industry and government" had given many of us conniptions, and had been met with substantial faculty resistance. Some tried to redefine the IPRO initiative to better align it with more liberal-educational impulses. For years now, engineering education has been the subject of modest reform efforts—from expanding the curriculum to require a full five years of study, to removing undergraduate area designations (mechanical, electrical, civil, chemical, etc.) in favor of a general engineering degree. From my point of view, none of these reforms satisfactorily addresses the dearth of historical, social, and cultural thinking that characterizes most engineering curricula, curricula that have begun to bear an uncomfortable resemblance to vocational ed. But the IPROs represented a truly pernicious kind of "reform." To insist that industry and government sponsor IPROs, to permit these latter consolidations to drive an educational mission "focused," as it says elsewhere in IIT promotional literature, "by the rigor of the real world": was this the best way to usher in the new millennium?

VII

45. Picture this: it's the spring of 1995, and Galvin and Pritzker have threatened to shut down undergraduate education at IIT unless the IIT administration and faculty manage to produce a convincing plan to increase undergrad enrollment. Thus, endless talk of IPROs. And to cut costs: buyouts of tenured faculty; appointment of a new VP without faculty input; and removal of the provost position. Of course the provost, as the chief academic (faculty) officer, is a key player in granting faculty tenure and promotion; any problems with tenure are typically addressed to this office. When the president, with the backing of the wool-blend trustees, removes the provost position from the organizational flow chart, he delegates tenure and promotion duties to himself—a nonfaculty administrator. Meantime, key faculty cooperate with the development of a professional, pre-professional, and interprofessional educational package. You know—professional master's degree programs (with, for instance, reduced math requirements), three-course certificate programs, and the like, programs designed primarily to *credential employees* while attracting tuition dollars from their *employers*, and marketed accordingly.

46. It's important to understand these institutional changes from the point of view of the bottom feeders. At IIT, as at many universities, "bottom feeders" equals "humanities profs." Consider: the highest paid, nonadministrative faculty line in my (former) department—which now reports to the Armour College of Engineering as a result of the 1995 disbanding of the Lewis College of Liberal Arts—was approximately $45,000 per year. Which is to say, a full (tenured) professor of history, philosophy, or English, with twenty years or more experience, earned approximately $5,000 less than the average starting *assistant* professor at IIT. Chalk up these salary disparities to those large government contracts and grants that form the staple of scientific and technological research in today's major and minor research institutions. Wagewise, IIT was in 1998 ranked near the bottom of the nation's twenty or so tech campuses—it ranks today in the bottom quarter of *U.S. News*'s best doctoral engineering programs nationwide (see *America's Best*, p. 115)—so even engineering faculty weren't exactly brimming with joy. Still, a thirty-ish engineering prof drove home in his new Chevy sedan, while I drove home in my 1986 Escort (kaput as of 2001).

47. This is IIT, folks—a school that had its beginnings in the Armour Institute of Technology, established in 1890. Yes, that's Armour of meatpacking fame—think hog butcher for the world, everything but the squeal. But it's also the IIT where Marvin Camras, the "Father of Magnetic Recording," conducted the research that led to his more than 500 patents. It's the IIT that once boasted a linguistics program with the likes of S. I. Hayakawa on its faculty. And it's the IIT where László Moholy-Nagy, another of Bauhaus fame and author of one of my favorite design books, *Vision in Motion*, founded the Institute of Design. So whatever you make of it, it's a school with a legacy, with a place in the postsecondary sun.

48. Picture this: the week after our trip to Motorola U, a book appears in all faculty mailboxes. It's entitled *The Idea of Ideas*, by one Robert W. Galvin, "Special Limited Edition" published in April 1991 by Motorola University Press.

VIII

49. *Motorola University Press?* All right, Bob & Co.—hereafter simply Bob—I get your point. You're a do-it-yourselfer, and your book is for the billionaire or would-be billionaire who has (of course), or wants to have (of course), *everything*. Like any good communications engineer, Bob begins at his beginning:

he engineers communication of his ideas by fabricating a pseudo-academic press to poke fun at (academic) book-learnin' even as it affords its wannabe author the privilege to spin his worldview in certified academic trappings.

50. It's a beautifully crafted book, believe me, at least insofar as its *design* goes. Let's start with a few design notes, as provided by the publisher on the copyright page:

> Typeset in Perpetua
> by Paul Baker Typography Inc., Evanston, Illinois.
> Five thousand copies printed
> by Congress Printing Company, Chicago, Illinois.
>
> Soft cover is Mohawk Artemis, Navy Blue; cloth cover
> is Arrestox B, B48650. End sheets are French Speckletone,
> Briquette; text stock is Mohawk Superfine, Soft White.
> Binding by Zonne Book Binders, Inc., Chicago, Illinois.
>
> Design by Hayward Blake & Company, Evanston, Illinois.
> Illustration [of Paul V. and Robert W. Galvin] on page 6 by Noli Novak.
> Quotation on cover by Robert W. Galvin.

Bob, like any civic leader who thinks global and acts local, chose wisely to patronize Chicagoland firms. Most small-press poets would be thrilled to publish a book with a spine, or a book with a print run of even a thousand copies, let alone a book of such silky smooth, hefty pages (214 of them). And the book comes with its own bookmark, folded Hallmark-card-like.

51. That "quotation on cover" by Bob: "*We can and should apply consciously, confidently, purposely and frequently, the simpler, satisfying, appropriate steps to create more and then better ideas.*" Four adverbs followed by three adjectives—Bob lays it on thick. Key words for the discussion that follows (please allow for cognates): *apply, confidently, purposely, frequently, simpler, appropriate*, and of course, *ideas*.

52. Reading over that cover sentence in fact brings to mind the old white-collar acronym, KISS—"Keep It *Simple*, Stupid." Bob wants you to know that he's a down-to-earth, WYSIWYG kinda guy. On the bookmark we find a checklist of his handy ideas, such gems as "*Set the idea target,*" "*Go for quantity,*" "*Question. Question!*" and "*Ignore quality. Don't judge 'til last.*" But bro-

mides aside, and to riff on Adrienne Rich, Bob has access to machinery that could cost you your job.

53. Bob's book has eight chapters: an Introduction followed by "The Idea Process: Its Role," "Leadership," "*Purposeful* Differences," "The Customer Idea," "Global Strategies," "Some Outside Ideas," and "Special Ideas." As I've indicated, English studies has been understood increasingly by university administrators as writing, with writing at IIT itself subsumed under the QCEL rubric, Leadership. Hence I've chosen to restrict my remarks to Bob's "Leadership" chapter—to its first subsection, entitled "The Paradox of Leadership."

54. "Leadership" begins with two quotes, one from Bob himself: "At times we must engage an act [sic] of faith that key things are doable that are not provable" (p. 24). Spoken, I might say, like a true engineer. And I should know. Engineering is not about theory *per se*, but about how to *apply* theoretical principles to produce results. And this does in fact constitute, as Bob indicates, an act of faith—a faith in *doing* in the absence of explanation. But this emphasis on doing somewhat sidesteps the sticky matter of what "key things" get done, and who is to decide what "key things" get done, and why such "key things" need getting done—why in fact they are deemed "key."

55. "The Paradox of Leadership" strikes this reader at first glance as oddly literary, which is another reason why I've chosen to respond to it. Paradox is, after all, a staple of poetry and of literary writing. Paradox is generally understood as an assertion in which apparently contradictory words, or *ideas*, reveal upon close examination a truth of sorts.

56. So what exactly *is* the paradox of leadership? Well, Bob begins by saying that this *idea* "finds its expression in a series of paradoxes" (p. 25). To put it another way, the "*idea* of leadership" (p. 25) as a paradox is realized in actuality as a series of paradoxes. Here as elsewhere, the "*idea* of" is Bob's modest way of formulating the *idea* not as abstract, but as evidenced in the particular, "real-world" example. But this constant harping on the *idea of* what is ultimately the whole wide real world—presumably including *the idea of ideas* in such a world—reveals that Bob's commonsensical, pragmatic appeal is predicated on an *idea of order*.

57. "It is neither necessary to impress on you an elaborate definition of leadership," Bob asserts, "nor is this an *appropriate* time to characterize its many styles" (p. 25). Suffice to say that leaders must have "creative and judgmental intelligence, courage, heart, spirit, integrity and vision *applied* to the accomplishment of a *purposeful* result." "When one is vested with the role of leader," Bob grudgingly concedes, "he inherits more freedom" (p. 26). Yet the leader is at the same time subject to "responsibilities that impose upon" this freedom (p. 26). Hence the first paradox of leadership: that the apparent "independence" of leaders may in fact be offset, if not checked and balanced, by the "dependence of others" *on* the leader (p. 26). Powerful leaders like Bob are evidently accountable to their followers.

58. "For one to lead implies that others follow" (p. 26). Uh-huh. "But is the leader a breed apart," Bob asks, rhetorically, "or is she rather the better follower?" The answer is as expected—the latter—which yields our second paradox: "to lead well presumes the ability to follow smartly" (p. 27). So smart leaders are not entirely free, because they are responsible to others and must, as leaders, learn how to follow wisely. By this odd if obvious bit of logic, the workplace is divided into leaders and followers, but everyone is in essence a *follower*. Hence, paradoxically, leaders are in fact merely *better* followers. And thus leaders have attained their role as leaders not through politicking, or manipulation, or (gosh!) inheritance—like Bob, who "inherits" only "more freedom" (as above). Nope. Instead, a leader becomes a leader because she "learns more quickly and surely from the past, selects the correct advice and trends, chooses the *simpler* work patterns, and combines the best of other leaders."

59. "Because a leader is human and fallible," Bob overtheorizes, "his and her leadership is in one sense finite—constrained by mortality and human imperfection" (p. 27). Yet "in another sense, the leader's influence is almost limitless," for the leader "can spread hope, lend courage, kindle confidence, impart knowledge," etcetera etcetera etcetera (p. 27). In fact, the "*frequency* with which one can perform these leadership functions seems without measure" (p. 27). "Again we see the paradox of the leader," Bob concludes, "a finite person with an apparent infinite influence" (p. 28).

60. This third paradox reveals Bob at his most—elegiac? Leaders labor under an Olympian strain, forced to *apply* such infinite "influence" (= power?) so *frequently*, and to such magnanimous ends, capable of doing so much good

for others, yet ultimately frustrated by their inevitable, all-too-human demise. One wonders whether Bob—the physical Bob—harbors notions of biostasis, cloning, perhaps even network consciousness à la Max Headroom, in order to provide a personalized hereafter for his elderly, leaderly, upgradeable self. (*Max Headroom?* I'm dating myself.)

61. "A leader is decisive, is called on to make many critical choices," and may therefore "thrive on the power and the attention" (p. 28). And yet—here emerges our fourth and final paradox—"the leader of leaders moves progressively away from that role" (p. 28). In fact, according to Bob, a chief responsibility of leaders is to delegate to others the "privilege" of "decision making" (p. 28), of *leading*, within an institution that, through such leadership, "generates . . . an ever-increasing number of critical choices" (p. 29).

62. A key to leadership, then, is the ability gradually to convert followers into would-be leaders, spreading the upwardly mobile aspiration throughout the management and worker-bee ranks. (Think, for instance, of those hourly workers who make the often difficult move into supervisory positions.) And this conversion process is necessary in order to cope with the decision-making demands of a larger and larger institution. So though we were given to understand in a prior paradox that all leaders are in essence followers, we are now given likewise to understand that followers are themselves potential *leaders*, and that cultivating these acorns of leadership, paradoxically, is one of the chief responsibilities of true leaders. With U.S. universities graduating 90,000 or so MBAs every year, we're talking a whole lotta acorns, folks.

63. For both followers and leaders, this game of follow-the-leader, like all games, requires a willingness to play by the rules—requires *cooperation*. And cooperation might not be the benign process entities like Bob make it out to be. Much has been written about the emergence of cooperation as a chief organizational variable, from Chester I. Barnard's classic business treatise, *The Functions of the Executive* (1938), in which authority becomes "another name for the willingness and capacity of individuals to submit to the necessities of cooperative systems" (p. 184), to Robert Axelrod's *The Evolution of Cooperation* (1984), in which cooperation evolves strategically and in accordance with game-theory logic, making it applicable even to trench warfare. But I've never found discussions of cooperation as such to square with my experience in the trenches: information-age push-pull come to shove, your boss is likely to demand of you that you *just do it*.

64. Bob wraps up his thoughts on the paradox of leadership with vague mention of "others which, if not paradoxes, at least are incongruities" (p. 29). He states that "each one of us is at once part leader and part follower as we play our roles in life" (p. 29). Bob concludes with the following tidbit from Walter Lippman: "The final test of a leader is that he leaves behind in other men the conviction and will to carry on" (p. 29).

65. I couldn't help but think here of Bob's desire for a legacy—of Bob's son Chris, in fact, himself a CEO of Motorola, whose compensation in 1997, while a sizable two million dollars, was itself small potatoes on the *national* CEO scale. Paul, Bob, Chris: that's three generations, dear readers—I guess it's in the blood.

66. In the face of which we have four paradoxes that, contrary to—conventional wisdom? popular opinion?—work successively to reinforce the logic of benign corporate leadership: (1) leaders are dependent on followers; (2) leaders *are* followers; (3) leaders are all-powerful but "human and fallible"; and (4) leaders convert their followers *into* leaders.

67. In 1970 it was, for some very good reasons, Everybody is a Star. Today—1990, 2001, and as this book goes to print—for some not-so-good reasons, it's Everybody is a CEO.

68. That so?

IX

69. Bob—the corporate entity Bob—is much like his book: judged by his career, his *cover* as multizillion-dollar corporate concern, he seems to reek of good intentions combined with cutting-edge quality objectives—good things brought to life. But when you get *into* his book, into his narrative of corporate expansion, you find a life-form that insists on being judged by its own criteria. As the aspiring global leader of communication leaders, Bob would be the measure of all company men and women. To lift from Eliot: in (the aging) Bob's corporeal end is his and your beginning. Or, Be Like Bob. Yet Bob, dear readers, amounts only to the *message* of his *medium*.

70. Now medium may itself be understood as material form, so a few words about form here: people who spend an inordinate amount of time studying

texts are used to distinguishing between content and form. It's a nice shorthand, but then too there is what Hayden White famously referred to as *the content of the form*, which should give some *idea* of the vexed nature of any form/content dichotomy. Even poets and those who study poetry often come to believe that a specific form—whether deemed "organic" or rigorously metrical—must of necessity signal, however indirectly, a specific social context, even agenda. This is because, historically speaking, one can identify formal attributes that mark the work of poets who seek, by their own account, specific social or aesthetic ends (poets, too, being political creatures). Yet formal content does not *intrinsically* dictate, for example, ideological content, any more than does ideological content stipulate, of necessity, a given form. And the same may be said of formal material, or medium, or mediating action, whether black typeface on white page or multicolored pixels flickering across your computer screen. Advertising firms today regularly appropriate artistic techniques deriving from former avant-garde practices (and, I must add, reap vast amounts of revenue in the process, *unlike* many of their artist-precursors).

71. However occasionally contorted the syntax, however unpoetic the sentences and single-sentence paragraphs, Bob's book *as a book* takes its lead and in some sense its imprimatur from the common public and professional confusion regarding form. Even literate readers are likely to be duped by his presentation, his appearance—are likely, at the very least, sold on the *idea* that he represents something of import. Yet except for the content of Bob's material (authorizing) form—the soft cover, stock, typesetting, even proofreading (to the extent that I could locate no typos) that serve ostensibly as testament to Bob's storied, moneyed *success*—he really has nothing to *say*.

72. If you read Bob carefully, his pages might as well be blank, for his is a bureaucratic tale, full of cautiously modulated sound and utterly devoid of fury, signifying that what words *mean* is of little importance save for the degree to which they reinforce and amplify the platitude, *a good manager can manage anything*—can manage even words, without really knowing how they work. In this mad pursuit of formal appearances, what signals success is the *simple* yet profound capacity to manufacture faith *in* appearances. Arranged on the page with little rhyme and all sorts of reason—or is it vice versa?—words are enlisted in the effort to ensure that even the alphabet as a communications technology will *lead* future leaders/readers toward the mega-objectives of corporate domination and expansion—the way things are meant to be. It's what you *do* that

counts, and finessing words is what those who *can't* do, do. What Bob does (do) is generate billions of dollars of profit worldwide, the bulk of which ends up in decidedly few pockets.

73. Hence, corporate identity as Identity Inc.: the clothes make the man or woman, and with nice teeth, Doc Martens, discreet piercing, a workshop or two under your baccalaureate belt, and unlimited credit, you too can and will attain success success SUCCESS. Content (is) for dummies, and as for you English phuds, you/had better/toe/the line/*here*.

74. Hey, but this can be immensely seductive stuff, especially to an eighteen-year-old who's looking for a way out of financial strife and who's found an acceptable social slot, Professional Engineer, that appears to guarantee her a job—if she's lucky, at Motorola. This helps to explain why so many of my engineering majors envision themselves as engineers for three or four years, with a quick move out and up into management. Not only does this serve to redirect professional (engineering) loyalties and technical passions toward management objectives, but it satisfies Bob's desire to see everyone as a reduced version of the CEO, committed to and dependent upon the corporate being. This is what Bob's *idea of ideas* amounts to, finally, and the only paradox in sight is that this immaterial realm of *ideas* can be so clearly predicated on material entitlement, that a self-professed leader like Bob—the physical Bob—can reveal himself to be such a wishful and irresponsible thinker.

x

75. In 1998, my seventh and final year at IIT, my tenure denial of the prior spring was official—I'd been *fired*, again, but this time with a final year under contract (the industry standard). And this time I'd been fired along with a colleague in Humanities who was also up for tenure—a specialist in African-American lit. But that's his story to tell. The reasons why I'd been denied tenure remained unclear—to some.

76. Even my poker-faced chair had been caught off guard. This typically punctual man kept me waiting twenty minutes, and when he walked into his office his expression was one of deep concern. "The news is not good," he began. And after he handed me the president's letter, in an envelope red-stamped "confidential," he choked out, "It's a shocker." He cleared his throat, tried to be supportive.

77. I was not shocked. I'd been here before.

78. When I pressed him on options, he was at a loss, save for making vague reference to the faculty handbook and recommending that I make an appointment to discuss my situation with our (outgoing) VP. (Discuss my "situation" with the man who devised IPROs?) He also indicated that I might reapply for tenure in the fall. (When the denial had come from the highest level of administration? Or beyond?) He was clearly unprepared for the news himself, uncertain to whom to turn in order to establish the correct, let alone expedient, course of resistance. We left it at him getting back to me, and I asked him to inform the department of the denial (using an online discussion list I founded and ran for my colleagues). In fact most everyone in my department was either "shocked" or "stunned."

79. My chair never did get back to me and had little to say to me in my demoralizing final year. In accordance with faculty handbook standards and procedures and AAUP-recommended policies, I'd asked the president of my university for clarification—in *writing*—of the reasons he denied me tenure; and in the same memo I appealed his decision, whatever the reasons forthcoming. The president's response was as expected: he conceded the "quality" of my scholarship and teaching but reiterated his decision to deny me tenure, admitting "concerns" his deans had regarding my being insufficiently "aligned with the new vision of IIT"—"specifically" with those "contributions needed" to implement interprofessional projects, *writing* across the curriculum, and technical *writing* programs. Naturally he concluded on an ostensibly upbeat note, wishing me "success in finding a position more closely aligned with [my] talents."

80. The tenure process was a closed-door affair. But I had it on good authority that I'd received the highest recommendation for promotion and tenure from all *faculty* committees, and that the sole opposition within my department was from my technology-driven colleague. I had it on good authority, but I'd never have it in *writing*—unless I sued. My mentors often advised me that my situation made for the perfect lawsuit—out of the question, given my finances. But the administration clearly knew nothing of my finances and feared legal exposure; repeated requests for the return of my tenure file were subsequently refused. *When in doubt, surrender no paper.*

81. In the wake of the denials, members of my department and several committees busied themselves distributing memos of their own to the administration, memos filled with polite expressions of distress and dismay. So much writing, so many words words words—collegial sentences of moderate tone configured, no doubt, in compliance with the organizational, "value-added" logic underwriting IIT's newest instructional mission. But I remained *confident* that, my decorous letters included, this was all a strictly *pro forma* gesture: if you read between the lines you would likely have concluded, with me, that my days at IIT were numbered. Academe, like industry, is all about institutional survival, and survive or no, one learns over time to read the writing on the wall. A final meeting the week of Thanksgiving between the president and all faculty committee chairs merely confirmed the administration's adamance.

XI

82. In the same month that I was fired, Bob Pritzker announced to a faculty delegation that he would pull his funding from IIT if the faculty acted to remove our top administrator from his post. If you haven't already guessed, IIT during my tenure—or nontenure—was anything but a happy campus. In a faculty survey conducted in the fall of 1997, no less than 60 percent of the respondents *disagreed* with the statement that the president "is truthful and honest." But if power is relational, both IIT's president and my technology-driven colleague, albeit both in their own ways instrumental in my professional demise, were empowered by their adherence to bottom-line thinking. And my hunch is that, as it proliferates throughout academe, such thinking will continue to profit from the public's poor grasp of ivory-tower policies and procedures, which policies and procedures are complicated further by backroom corporate incursion. Given the arcana and general mystification associated with such practices, I can hardly blame the public. So I suppose (pardon the exhortation) that it's up to profs like yours truly to help the uninitiated to understand that tenure, whatever its inefficacies, is about *academic freedom*—a much-maligned and commonly misunderstood term.[1] Simply put: we faculty need such freedom if the classroom is to remain a place where even the mighty machinations of corporate Earth come under occasional critical scrutiny.

83. So here I am, or was, distributing another exit statement, making my departure from yet *another* institution a matter of public record—my life as the eX-Files. As things stood, and stand—with my bread and butter on the line, and

with students who need to be challenged to develop alternative ways to think and act both as professionals and as responsible social beings—I've had little choice but to continue to struggle with these urgent and conflicting realities.

84. In the meantime, the Department of Humanities elected its first new chair in fifteen years and embarked on a new undergrad major in "Professional and Technical Communication"; the campus also hired a new "vice-president and chief academic officer"—this time *with* faculty input. (And I'm not quite sure what to make of the fact that, during my final semester on campus, Michael Moore used IIT's Hermann Hall auditorium to film episodes of his show, *The Awful Truth*.) But from where I'm sitting, it's IIT business as usual, and it's spreading elsewhere. These days there is little talk of QCEL, and "communication" seems to have become the tried-and-true Humanities buzzword—yet the writing-to-lead/succeed drift prevails. Even the customary teaching-research-service triad eventually found itself under assault, with a proposal on the boards early in 1998 to add an additional tenure category, "impact." Faculty would be granted fifteen points for supervising an IPRO—and from eight to twelve points (depending on the press) for publication of a book. (I am happy to report that most faculty balked at this. But keep an eye out for it—it's liable to stage a comeback.) In fact, since my little trauma, there have been several resignations in the Department of Humanities (all of them English profs) and—lo!—another tenure denial, sadly. Meantime, in yonder corporate sector, the "parent company" of Philip Morris has changed its name to Altria Group, Inc., and has sold Miller Brewing to South African Breweries (SAB) for a cool $5.6 billion in stock (and assumed debt), thus creating the planet's second-largest brewer. And around and around we go. . . .

85. As part of the Introduction to the Professions program, Bob—the physical, Motorola Bob—has made occasional appearances at IIT, lecturing students about those tactics and traits applicable to success (or failure) on corporate Earth. I've never met the guy, and I sometimes imagine that Bob and I might have something to talk about, given that, as Bob notes in his book, he served at one time on Nixon's Foreign Intelligence Advisory Board. (Bob and Nixon, together—the mind reels.) For that matter, I've never met the other Bob (Pritzker), either—he chairs IIT's Board of Trustees, is an IIT alumnus, and—as president and chief executive officer of the Marmon Group, Inc.—is reputedly worth a couple of the Motorola Bobs.

86. But I can't talk with these guys unless they're willing to unclip their word pagers, deactivate their cell phones (I, uh, own a Motorola V600), and do some real listening—and I have my doubts. One of my former students, a computer science major, attended a Motorola Bob lecture some years ago and was courageous enough to challenge Motorola Bob directly as to what seemed at the time ominous threats to the humanities effort at IIT. "I'm an English minor," the student declared, "and you've eliminated the major in English, in History, in Philosophy." Bob observed—quite accurately, if in apparent disregard for how catalyzing agents often come in small proportions—that those disciplines had never managed more than a handful of majors, anyway. And besides, Bob quipped, he'd managed himself to get a whole lot more reading done once he'd gotten himself a chauffeur.

XII

87. Picture this: on the thirtieth anniversary of his father losing a twenty-year union job with General Electric, university professor with a decade of teaching and seven years of industrial experience files Chapter 7—and shortly thereafter, as incredible luck would have it in this job-depleted profession, finds gainful employment on academic Earth.

88. Imagine.

89. But wait. Academic Earth? Or corporate-academic Earth?

90. Picture cloudy.

How to Tell the Difference between Life and Art
A Grant Proposal (Take 3)

.1 $100,000,000 to a single poetry organization might not be an entirely good thing for poetry or poets.

.2 Writing books—of whatever kind—does not in itself make one good or competent or wise. Not writing books doesn't, either.

.3 There are writers, and then there are writers. There are thinkers, and then there are thinkers. There are teachers, and then there are teachers. There are students, and then there are students. There are magicians, and then there are magicians. *Capisce?*

.4 Advocating for the workplace does not in itself compensate for a lack of imagination. Not advocating for the workplace doesn't, either.

.5 Where would we be without our ideals? Only, put them to practice.

.6 You just *know* something is out of kilter when oracular declaratives substitute for sober and considered thought, when postmodern reflexivity undercuts each and every assertion.

.7 Standing Rule #15: We need on a regular basis to turn our attention off campus.

.8 There are two major problems facing writers today: (1) the onslaught of new media and mediations; and (2) the stubborn persistence of second-wave Industrial Revolution conceptions of literary value. With the possible additional complication that 400 people in the U.S. are worth (as of this writing) $955,000,000,000.

.9 Why don't you count all of those zeroes all over again. I will too.

.10 I'd rather work as a writer for the *New York Times* than as a PR man for Dow Chemical. I'd rather work as a teacher for Harvard than as a writer for the *New York Times*. I'd rather write what I want to write than teach what I want to teach, provided I can pay for health benefits and treat myself, my wife, and my friends to a pizza and beers every other Friday night. I'd rather be hired than fired, but I've been fired nearly half as many times as I've been hired. Why is that?

.11 Oh—Molson Golden. Or, conjunction and disjunction are in the eyes of the—*whatever*.

.12 I've neglected to mention children and chicken and Giorgio Agamben.

.13 When you hear the word *digital*, you should:
    A. Step on the gas

.....B. Unplug
.....C. Buy something
.....D. Sign your name in ink
.....E. Some of the above

.14 To listen to some poets talk about digital art, you'd think they'd never read poetry. To listen to some poets talk about poetry, you'd think they'd never got out. To listen to some poets talk about poetry and digital art, you'd think the two naturally (1) have nothing whatever to do with each other, or (2) have everything in the world to do with each other.

.15 Looking to the fringes of art for guidance can be fruitful and can be a waste of time. Looking only to the mainstreams is potentially fruitful and always wastes time.

.16 Artists need to work harder at not being artsy-fartsy. Have some fun, for christsakes.

.17 Suffer only fools who suffer fools. It's form fools win.

.18 The small presses in this country, local success stories aside, are struggling. What are we going to do about this wretched situation? And please don't tell me that things have always been this bad. Fuck you if you think that things have always been this bad.

.19 The mainstream publishing world produces some good work, even some great work. But mainstream writers all too often exhibit woefully little knowledge of their small-press counterparts, many of whom can write their mainstream peers into the shade. This makes some of us very, very angry. In order to channel our anger in constructive directions, I propose that we work harder to be more inclusive and not operate in such tight-knit circles.

.30 Drawing oneself and one's friends into a tight-knit circle constitutes an institutional survival skill.

.31 Repeat after me: *not not Adorno, not not Adorno, not not Adorno.*

.32 We ought all to be better educated about the terrible consequences of pedigree. Especially those of us without a pedigree as such.

.33 Failure is often more instructive than success. If it doesn't kill you. The aim of teaching then—scratch that, the aim of our educational system should be to find ways not to punish failure while at the same time rewarding success. Not being rewarded for mediocre performance is hardly a form of punishment, and those who think it is should be placed under house arrest.

.34 (Long) Standing Rule #11: Deleted.

.35 "A good home is happiness," my fortune cookie advises, and I suppose this is true even if home comprises a tent and a dinner companion.
.36 Everything in dialogue with everything else, got it.
.37 Beware of that word *service*.
.38 Risk is necessary, but not if it means possibly destroying all life on this planet as we know it. How to formulate a conception of risk that people will gravitate toward.
.39 Scholars really need to get off it and stop treating language as though it's exhausted by their virtuosities. Most of them could stand to read more contemporary poetry, too.
.40 Even a man who is pure in heart
And says his prayers by night
May become a wolf when the wolfbane blooms
And the autumn moon is bright.
.51 Learn how to roll those r's.
.52 Poets really need to get off it and stop treating themselves as operating independently of public opinion, the media, the corporation, etc. Where's your ecology? Show it to me.
.53 That old U.S. Navy ad copy had it right—a job should be an adventure. If a job *were* an adventure, I'd call poetry a job, and not just because I'm a sloganeering academic.
.54 Fuck leaders, fuck professors, fuck professionals, fuck callings.
.55 No—I take that back: I *would* like to be thought not a prof, but a pro. So I'll settle for "pro(f)"—long "o," silent "f."
.56 Fuck pro(f)s.
.57 Poetry is a job. Or so say all of us.
.58 And in saying so poetry ends up constrained in some ways, you see, liberated in others. If poetry *were* a job, wouldn't some "we" have to be earning a living wage from same? (Well—a chosen few do, but this is not what I have in mind.) As a pro(f), and a sometime poetry pro(f), it's clear to me that poetry helps establish my market value, both monetarily and in more cultural terms (in which regard my market value goes up and down depending on the fish—I mean, poet, I'm talking to). A sticky matter, then, to align labor with symbolic work, but perhaps worth pursuing, if only to see what turns up.
.59 One thing that turns up: everyone has bread and butter issues, and poets are no exception. Even if you're living off the fat of the land, no exception. Which suggests that labor has a necessary relation to art.

.60 I've said that already.

.61 Standing Rule #9: Deleted.

.62 Making justice is a wild and woolly affair, boofuckinghoo.

.63 One thing: the universe may be expanding more and more rapidly, but it's entirely unclear whether the same may be said of poetry.

.64 Spirituality: a long walk for a good loaf of bread.

.65 Always take your art more seriously than you take yourself. This way, if you put on weight, your art won't suffer the consequences.

.66 Poets ought to be at least as well read as prose writers, who ought to be at least as well read as actors. But reading goes only so far, as any actor will tell you.

.67 All art should aspire to the condition of hootenanny.

.68 And then we have the plastic arts.

.69 And then we have matrimony, and domestic politics, and gaming, and African violets.

.70 This, *this* is one way to campaign for political change.

.71 Most people seek some measure of autonomy in their works and days. Most people want, somehow, to belong. Even "temporary autonomous zones" must be structured so as to balance these competing human tendencies. Without a generative principle of some greater good that opens beyond the boundaries of the given, most collectives will founder on the brink of self-absorption.

.72 Mind your manners, make ends meet, but please don't succumb to *that* kind of precision.

.73. I know what you're thinking, punk: isn't it a contradiction to suggest that some presumed "greater good" will open beyond what we know?

.74 Depends. At least not to the extent that we're willing, finally, to permit our ideals and *a priori* values to bump up against the probable. How to proceed both tentatively and with conviction. How to make a contribution without mucking things up further.

.75 How to be portable? And how easy it is, when the forms of life are manufactured in modules, to forget about trial and error. Ask dada.

.76 We know what's good for us, we don't know what's good for us.

.77 But we all know that they shouldn't be awarding Nobel Prizes for dramatic irony. Or assonance. Or screeching.

.78 We know that textbook publishing is Big Business.

.79 And that there's no such thing as a free brunch.

.80 And that looooove iiis the answer er err.

.91 I'm sure you've detected by now the enormous male ego at work hereabouts, cloaking its formulations in drag-strip humor. If you haven't, time is running out.

.92 Digital as in alternative modes of distribution, alternative modes of distribution as in alternative, possibly capital-intensive networks. Capital as in an important aspect of political change yadda yadda yadda. There were 62 lobbyists in Washington, D.C., in 1968. Today there are approx. 21,000. Surprised?

.93 Help me out here: authorship is the rub, yes? So finding the cost of authorial freedom would be up to . . . *authors?*

.94 For starters: this royalty and copyright arrangement is for the birds. It's not that I'm looking to make a killing, you understand. And I suppose I might (might) be talked into giving my (pseudo-scholarly) work away for free—preferably, with shared copyright—*provided* my campus picked up, say, the postage and copies. Otherwise I'm working at a perpetual per diem loss, and with zero assurance that my financial woes will pay off professionally.

.95 Think, for instance, subvention. Consider our nationwide state budget crises, courtesy of the RNC. Go offbeat. Or apply brewer's yeast.

.96 Willow, weep for me.

.97 Writing that appears to focus on the ethnicity, gender, etc., of the writer is not for that reason any better or any worse than writing that appears not to focus on the ethnicity, gender, etc., of the writer. I write "appears" because we know, or should know, that all writing is, at some level, ethnic writing, gendered writing, etc., regardless whether it's written under the sign of ethnicity, gender, etc. It's not enough to make one's ethnicity, gender, etc., legible, but it could be a start. Writers who write without any regard for their ethnicity, gender, etc., are probably making a big mistake.

.98 Standing Rule #12: You bet your sweet ass collective bargaining. Nontenure track *and* tenure track. Motion: that labor unions rethink the labor-talent relation.

.99 There is little question but that the world as we have come to know it in these World English, WTO times has fallen more and more under the sway of technological solutions to what are in essence nontechnological problems. We have engineered ourselves into and out of all manner of civic quagmire—and the solutions at this point will likely demand both larger-scale socioeconomic revaluations and smaller-scale reengineering.

.100 And of course corporations changing the way they do business. Call the question.
.101 [Molson Golden] Rule #13: Deleted.
.102 Don your sandwich boards, let's hit the bricks. That goes for you too, Larry Summers.
.103 Burp.
.104 There is no such thing as pure Rasputin.
1.291 Hey, we all find ourselves adrift once in a while. And btw, most scholars could stand to be better journalists. A deadline is a deadline, dammit.
.108 Experimental fiction/prose writers have a tougher go of it generally than do experimental poets—until their "experiments" catch on.
.109 But honestly, we really ought to find ways to permit English majors to grow up and be—English majors.
.110 Beeman's Aids Digestion.
.111 The function of Žižek at the present time is not to say what should be said, but to say what should *not* be said. He's doing our dirty work for us. Don't argue with me, I know I'm right.
.112 It's generally easier to dislike someone's work when you dislike that someone. This behavioral fact should serve as ample encouragement to approach the work with generous mind, and the worker with generous heart. Try to be nice as pie.
.113 Apple pie. But evaluate with headset on, principles intact, courageously.
.114 When is the U.S. public going to wake up and realize that, in general, a necessary (but not sufficient) condition for great teaching at the university level is great research?
.115 When is the U.S. public going to wake up and realize that taxpayers have an obligation to fund the arts? I'm keeping score.
.117 When is the U.S. public going to wake up and stop acting like the U.S. public? When are academics going to wake up and realize that some aspects of their professional culture are rotten to the core? When are poets going to wake up and realize that thought is not enough?
.118 Maybe I should be investigating high-end Italian food chains? Or inquiring into why the Wisconsin cheese industry insists on producing such awful Camembert?
.119 Practically speaking, poetry is zoned, ergo you must either be in a zone to produce poetry, or struggling to get out. Further, all language

transactions abound in surplus meaning. So for instance, good Hollywood screenwriting is also good technical writing. Do the math.

.120 In some circumstances you need to think rhizome. Not infrequently, a simple hierarchy will do just as well.

.121 Where's Eli Wallach when you need him? And Red Buttons? And Capucine?

.122 What works in one medium may not work in another. Timothy Leary *is* dead.

.123 Poets should read more nonfiction. Even conventional, theoretically squeamish nonfiction.

.11101 (Yes, after .99 we started over again. Sorta.)

.11102 Look, John Waters is simply more interesting than his films, period.

.124 We could stand another generation gap. (Explanation: youth culture [YC] is, as of this writing, more invested in bottom-line thinking than is aging boomer culture [BC]. It's difficult to blame YC, but post-BC will likely require millennial YC in order to move beyond cultural FUBAR.) And we could stand a retooled geometry of value. And better belles lettres. And fewer clerics, and clerks. And more Carole Kings. Tell me: do you actually find that the online MLA Job Information List saves you time and trouble?

.125 Occasionally I prefer to wallow in cliché, but oftentimes I like to pretend I have a mind.

.126 The air in these parts is decidedly thinner, and rated ILP: *in loco parentis* is advised.

.128 The arts, all told, are constitutive of an alternative reality. This reality, whether understood as a concession to the virtual or as a spin on the actual, is often more real than what many take to be reality. Go on—make something of it.

.129 Or don't, it's up to you—but if you don't, don't expect us to be happy with you.

.133 And I'll say it again: the cultural work performed by criticism and theory and philosophy is not a matter only for critics and theorists and philosophers to deliberate. So there.

Thank you for your patience.
If it's all right with you, we'll take our money now,
preferably in unmarked tens and twenties.

Track 3

Labor, Manufacturing, Workplace, Community
Four Conclusions in Search of an Ending

Conclusion the 1st: Labor

> The chief cause of false writing is economic. Many writers need or want money. These writers could be cured by an application of bank notes.
> —Ezra Pound, ABC of Reading

Pound's characteristically matter-of-fact counsel, published in 1934, will, I imagine, force a knowing smile even in today's market-weary and Pound-leery scribes. Money, it would seem, has everything and nothing to do with literary quality (whatever *that* is). On the one hand, to the extent that writers produce shabby work for profit or as a consequence of material duress—to the extent, that is, that they "need or want money"—quality is, for Pound, inextricably linked with money, or more properly, to income (and by extrapolation to today's economy, with access to credit or assets). On the other hand, once a writer has found a way to bankroll his work—a gift, an inheritance, a job, a patron? (patronage clearly Pound's preferred option)—quality will presumably take care of itself. Writers must in effect be insulated from the effects of capital; otherwise, they may fall prey to less savory or more pressing motives. "More writers fail from lack of character than from lack of intelligence," Pound observes (*ABC*, p. 193), and we are left to conclude that character—whatever *that* is, especially coming from Pound—stands its best chance when it doesn't have to concern itself with those workaday experiences that, as they used to say back in Pound's day, *build* character.

But if money, as they used to say back in Pound's day, doesn't grow on trees, poetry, by today's standards, clearly does. I have in mind here the burgeoning electronic sphere and the hyperproduction that greets those of us who ply this sphere on a daily basis. I write "hyperproduction" when, in light of recent developments, I'm tempted to write *clinical hypergraphia*. To take an extreme example, witness August Highland's Worldwide Literati Mobilization Network (WLMN). Early in 2003, Highland forwarded to the SUNY/Buffalo Poetics list the following from the WLMN "secretary," one "gazelle friedman":

> The sixty members of Worldwide Literati Mobilization Network are pleased to announce that in the year 2002 they collectively produced

> over 70,000 volumes of Hyper-Literary Fiction!! I don't know if they are zealously trying to become the Golden Arches of the literary world (i hope not) or if they just love making honey and nothing can stop their buzz (i personally favor the latter interpretation). (Highland, "70,000")

As we learn at Highland's "Muse Apprentice Guild" site, "gazelle friedman" is, like the other sixty members of WLMN, one of "august highland's multiple personas."[1] The "volumes" have meanwhile increased—by the tens of thousands—and one begins to wonder whether money is, as we still say today, no object.

There are at least a couple of ways to read this development. Clearly, the entire escapade of hundreds of thousands of unread volumes written and published (and publicized) by a single person smacks of something like Žižek's *interpassivity*—upon which, as Žižek would doubtless aver, the frenzied excesses of theory itself depend (viz, "you do the theorizing so that I can get on with my business"); which in the present context suggests a dialectic of sorts in which the hyperproductive subject presupposes its regulating other, a passive audience. It's much as if there is so much material out there now that there is no longer the need for anyone to read any of it, if by "reading" we mean specifically an (ethical) act of verification and support (i.e., of writing, and of writers). I certainly don't have the (life)time to wade through all of that WLMN stuff myself, and more to the point, I may suppose that I am no longer *supposed* to read through that which is presumed to prevail regardless of my attention.

If one endorses instead the more old-fashioned notion that attention *is* required, then the hyperproductive/hyperactive scribe would seem to be someone who imagines that attention span is an endlessly renewable resource. But whether attention is or is not the presumed response—indeed, whether a response is presumed as such—perhaps we would do better to turn our . . . attention from reception (including simple receivership) to the terms of such momentous *generation*. And in fact there are a number of generative precedents.

In his "Epilogue" to Duke UP's *Cultural Institutions of the Novel*, Clifford Siskin interrupts his excursion through eighteenth-century British "novelism" to draw an analogy between that development and the current proliferation of writing and writers that marks the digital boom of the past decade:

> When we keep in mind the historical sequence I've described above—the rise in writing [in the eighteenth century] occurring after the rise in the literacy rate—we realize that one fundamental form of change was

> the transformation of reader into writer. To grasp its impact, a comparison of technologies is again useful. The current heightened concern with the behavioral consequences of electronic media is occurring—not surprisingly—at the moment at which more people are becoming more behaviorally invested in them. (p. 427)

"The middle decades of the eighteenth century," continues Siskin in his major chord, "saw parallel forms of investment in writing, particularly in the form that was proliferating most substantially at the time: periodicals" (p. 427). In essence, writing begets more writing, and its "capacity to produce change"—in particular, to encourage readers "to behave as writers"—renders it "historically crucial" to the "proliferation" of writing (p. 427). Writing, that is, enjoys a *causal* relation to its proliferation; rising literacy rates hardly explain rising publication rates (p. 426). Hence for Siskin, when we turn to the history of the novel—or for that matter, to our histories of disciplinarity—we might regard these latter practices as situated squarely within a history of writing as such. Further, and before writing was "naturalized" (Siskin uses Raymond Williams's term)—converted from a "potentially threatening prescriptive technology" into a "cypherlike tool"—the growing volume of published materials made "writing as much an object of inquiry as a means" (p. 428). "Writing about writing produced more writing in a self-reflexive proliferation," observes Siskin of the eighteenth-century English literary scene, and "all writing became, in that sense, critical" (p. 428).

Siskin goes on to note the "critical self-reflexivity" evident in the developing genre of fiction and the "experimental mixing of creative and critical features" of lyric poetry (pp. 428–429); ultimately he advances the expected nationalistic link between the "domesticated," if stubbornly heteroglossic, (British) novel and his working concept of "novelism": *"the discursive site on which the naturalism of writing is negotiated"* (p. 425; emphasis in original). For Siskin (after Certeau), novelism has, or can have, all to do with "fiction's generative role for modern disciplines"; in particular, novelism underscores the "fictive nature of science and the constitutive power of writing" (p. 438).

Readers who become writers, and writers who write about, among other things, writing: it would likely prove difficult to find a more apt parallel to today's postmodern condition.[2] But what's missing here is a sense of the contemporary context of hyperproductivity. And given the mutually cavalier attitude in evidence in the interpassive configuration—"you may produce literary volumes at your leisure, and I may consume them, or not, much as I consume data archives, or Miller Beer"—the question of reception, this time as *consumption*, enters again into the picture. Is one variety of hyperproductivity matched, in a material world and interpassivity aside, by another variety of hyperconsumption? I am posing this question not to inquire into those libidinal energies that, surely, circulate throughout the fantasy of an enduring textual-authorial legacy; I am interested rather in establishing a political-economic datum. I am intrigued by the idea that the realities of capital have been only superficially deferred in the hyperproductive transaction, for money may yet be "an object," even or especially in an age when robotics would displace human manufacturing labor (see Jeremy Rifkin's *The End of Work*).

Paul Krugman has referred to our current economic era in the U.S. as a "second Gilded Age," with the top .01 percent of households (13,000 families) earning nearly as much as the poorest 20,000,000 ("For Richer," p. 65). This has happened not least because, as Krugman indicates in an e-mail exchange with James K. Galbraith, "if productivity is up and wages are down"—which has been the case now in the U.S. for a quarter century—"this must mean that labor's share in income has fallen" (see Krugman, "Letter"). Clearly, the digital boom, and the emergence of what I've been calling hyperproductivity, coincides very nearly with that nineties economic hysteria which resulted in this new Gilded Age. So if writing productivity is up—*way* up—then, to draw a simplistic parallel (which I will redraw at some length in note 6), is attention down—*way* down? How does one measure "attention"? And whose attention?

First: what about the larger parallel, this question of a "second Gilded Age"? The first Gilded Age gave us the novel of social protest (and of arguable artistic merit), even as New York gradually emerged as the center of U.S. trade publishing—a reality that still persists, even during these globally conglomerating times. In fact, today's Gilded Age is far more materially, if not materialistically, disparate, as Krugman indicates, and this situation prevails not simply (and catastrophically) between haves and have-nots, but between numerous social and public institutions and, most pertinent to our concerns here, between the massive publishing-entertainment complex and the small presses, presses that must struggle for each and every newsprint smudge and shimmering pixel of public attention.

Those invested in online production and overproduction seem, at first glance, to have bypassed such press woes. But if the rich have gotten richer and the poor poorer, the middle classes have gotten—access. (Along with oodles of spam.)[3] And as most writers in the U.S. hail from the middle classes these days, middle-class writers have decided to take publishing matters, as it were, into their own hands. As that student in the Xerox commercial for print-on-demand (POD) publishing technology rebuffs his prof: "So now everyone here—can get published." Followed by a vigorous round of applause. You need simply own a computer, and have online access, and be able to type, and be able to find the spare time—all of which latter attributes are generally attributed to middle-class agency, with its associated money and literacy and material (albeit spare time, we are told, is on the wane). Those so outfitted can flood the broadband with their (computer-generated or soul-searched or—) output. Thus, almost as if in miraculous answer to Pound's (dated?) concerns regarding a dearth of "bank notes," online scribes can now see their work distributed far and wide without regard for budget woes or editorial interference. You too can be an author, never mind having to worry about, what, *readership*? The point is to *get your work out there*, whether or no there's a there there.

What has been glossed here of course is the question of the editorial function, which itself implies an economic datum of sorts. If, unlike the trades, small presses (digital or POD or letterpress) are not driven by profit, they are nonetheless bound by budgets, labors of love notwithstanding. And budgets translate to material limits, which translate to some form of editorial mechanism. Peer review in the small presses is rarely in fact "peer review" in the more formal sense (recall those thermoregulating subcommittees of Track 1), though a peer (not infrequently an acquaintance or friend) may well be the person reviewing your work to see if s/he digs it enough to bankroll it. We might want to turn this around in fact, etiologically speaking: a small press publishing enterprise may commence with editorial concerns—a publisher wanting to see such and such work in print—and end with budgetary considerations. This underscores the fact that, while the small presses are generally viewed by unconventional writers as the necessary antidote to the trade empire, they are often viewed askance by any number of indie (let's say) writers who have turned to the electronic platform to stage their productions.

Thus we needs must turn, for a paragraph or two, to the question of what sort of "cultural field" (to borrow from Bourdieu) we're talking about in the first place. If in fact the more ambitiously avant contours of the online literary "field" constitutes, from production to overproduction, one of Bourdieu's "anti-institutional institutions"—or in Libbie Rifkin's deft elucidation, "paradoxical sociotextual universes . . . in which freedom from institutions is inscribed in those institutions"—then we may want, with Rifkin, to understand better what Bourdieu says is the "logic of homology" that obtains between fields of "large-scale" and of "restricted" production (See Rifkin, *Career Moves*, pp. 10, 17). But as Rifkin rightly (to my way of thinking) concludes, Bourdieu's "map of the cultural field—drawn . . . according to rigidly economic coordinates—cannot be truly responsive to the 'flux' that he finds within it," and this despite that fact that Bourdieu is willing to acknowledge the role played by his own meditations in what he calls the "semantic flux of notions like writer or artist" (ibid., p. 17).

There may be another, more fundamental problem with Bourdieu's influential theorizing, however, having to do with the conceptual sway of the terms employed. We might want to ask, with Bill Readings, "why a thinker whose analytic mode is conservative and normative (the mapping of social positions as algorithms of deviation within a closed national cultural field) should have been so attractive to those in Cultural Studies" (Readings, *University*, p. 106). Readings's answer is that Bourdieu's geometry of social capital, relying as it does on "the model of center and periphery," permits us to treat the "relation between each peripheral position and center *as if it were* a vertical one" (ibid., p. 106; emphasis in original). In Readings's view, this "allows the analysis of power to proceed as usual," hence there is consequently "no way out of the game of culture" (ibid., p. 106). We are left with the rather dire implication that "all cultural games are part of the great game of cultural capital" (ibid., pp. 106–107). Resistance is futile, or pretty much so, except perhaps for a soupçon of insouciance here and there.

Well: we all have our terminological crosses to bear, certainly. It's just that it becomes more than a little difficult to understand an avant-garde, or post-avant, or even, heck, good old-fashioned postmodernism, in such closed (some would say *tightass*) terms. We (postmodernists) begin to look not a little like we're kidding ourselves to think that we might, of all things, actually intervene in meaningful and lasting ways in a world with savagery to spare.

Perish the thought.

We know, at any rate, that power *is* at play on a newly globalized scale today—and globalization has been with us long before anyone used the term QCEL or drove a point across with a sledgehammer—and we may expect to find structural similarities at work between smaller online arts collectives and, say, Tinseltown. How best to gauge the nature of resistance, then, to status quo practices?

Holland Cotter has argued, for example, that we may be witnessing the incipient contours of a new counterculture (emphasis on *culture*) thanks to virtual art collectives that are helping to catalyze the cultural moment via the conjunction of digital media with slam poetry, visual art, performance work, and so forth. Is this mere hyperbole? And what kind of "map," what kind of cartography, can do justice to the sorts of online developments about which Cotter (like me, in my more optimistic moments) might wax enthusiastic?[4]

I stray a bit though from my economic musings. To mitigate those theoretical overdeterminations that would make of every "outsider" move a symptomatic "insider" strategem, imagine a quasi-autonomous transactional sphere—say, a gift economy—that works at some remove from more vigorous circulations of (social, symbolic, cultural) capital. Poetry, anyone? The attendant difficulty is abundantly evident in this way of stating the matter (I wrote "imagine"), for it is customary now to assume that the "private" realm itself—whether construed as the imagination or the unconscious or simply the solitary and suprarational mind—is fully subject to the effects of social power. Indeed, social power as manifested in our symbolic practices is routinely posited as constitutive to some uncertain degree *of* that realm. And if poetic inspiration is tainted by institutional leeching of one sort or another, how are we to *imagine* a poetry that is not subsidized at some level by Fortune 500 attenuations?

Still, there may be qualitative differences to keep in mind when interrogating artifacts and practices whose use value falls far, far below the security analyst's radar screen. Now, no matter how many dollars I (and my publisher, and my partner) actually *lose* in bringing a book of poetry into print, I am not *myself* inclined to an understanding of my poetry in terms of gift economies; for one, my academic-bureaucratic standing, albeit highly tenuous as of this writing, ensures that every "document" I produce has a corresponding line-item value, vita-wise. This is not to suggest, either, that I view the associated (material) losses and (symbolic) gains as *ipso facto* a zero-sum game. Whatever symbolic/cultural capital has accrued to me to date by virtue of poetry publishing—and as an academic poet, I've probably enjoyed more than my fair share—my household has nonetheless suffered, in my view, a disproportionate loss of capital, and credit, and assets. However idiosyncratic my experience may be, the point is that no "theory," economic or otherwise, can predict the outcome of such highly individuated circumstances.

One way around, or through, this empirical impasse, or landscape, may be to argue, with Murat Nemet-Nejat, that poetry is not productive labor as such, with a corresponding exchange value, but a *consumption*; therefore, that the value of poetry is a function of its value *to the poet* as a writing activity (see Nemet-Nejat, "Is Poetry"). "A poet is an anti-productive consumer of time," Murat has written, "similar to an addict" (Nemet-Nejat, "Re: about"). If the response to a poem is utter silence—which, I regrettably report, is often the case—this only serves to point up the incompatibility to poetic practice of a productivity-based value grid (or econometric "cultural field"). And in some sense this squares with old Ezra's pseudoeconomic theory of patronage, which, as Cary Wolfe reminds us, is not a production-consumption arrangement at all, for "the permanent goods of art are not really consumed at all" in Pound's commodity-resistant brand of Modernism—"their value is not dissipated by use" ("Ezra Pound," p. 38).

Yet to observe as much might be to miss an additional possibility, viz, that the artifact may be endlessly expendable, and in some sense consumable, by virtue of its *nonproductive* effusions. I'll return to this question of economic (use-exchange) value in *Conclusion the 4th*. For now, let me note that Nemet-Nejat's notion of poet-as-word-addict seems a literalization of sorts of the subject position (and cultural condition) that Avital Ronell calls "Being-on-drugs" (*Crack Wars*) and takes us back, phenomenologically at least, to our hyperproductive scribes, whose voluminous outpourings may now be digested (or not) simply and profoundly as the trace of an addictive practice, and of an overriding middle-class freedom. This echoes those "libidinal energies," above, that I'd wished to sidestep, only here we should with Ronell recall Freud's speculation about the "apparent libidinal autonomy" of the druggie (Ronell, *Crack Wars*, p. 25).

Anyway. There are so many other factors to consider. We have not examined, for instance, that market niche represented by the gallery system, which continues to foster conceptual work in the visual and plastic arts, despite its debt to connoisseurship and its resiliently *haute* appeal, to a degree that easily rivals whatever such support is in evidence in the trade (and particularly trade fiction) publishing industry (see Steve Tomasula's bracing dance through this minefield, from which I crib this sentence). But if for our purposes here we *have* addressed adequately, or troubled sufficiently (albeit by a variety of circumlocution), Pound's economic problematic of "bank notes," what of his concerns regarding "false writing"? One likes to imagine, too, *pace* Pound, that "working for a buck," however much an impediment in terms of actual writerly output, helps writers to grapple with the workaday realities their writing will necessarily plumb, if only in terms of a readership invariably confronted with such realities; helps writing, that is, become "truer." (This may be another way of addressing Pound's orientation toward "character.") One *likes to imagine* this is so, and doubtless it helps, whatever one's aesthetic convictions, to be able to draw from diverse experiences. But the workaday world, whether salary or hourly or temporary, neither, on the one hand, automatically legislates (and authorizes) the modality of one's articulations (whether one is to embrace realism, for example, or surrealism, or hyperrealism), nor, on the other, automatically locates the assembly line, or time clock, or office cubicle of workaday experience as the originary locus of the poem. On-the-job or on-the-picket-line experience need not translate directly into compositional aspiration and need not be the driving force of same (though in my worldview, they obviously have a helluvalot to do with things).

This is why I find Cary Nelson's recuperative efforts on poetry's leftist-labor front, much as I admire the work, to be somewhat out of step with the poetic of a fully engaged contemporary praxis.[5] This is why, for instance, I am occasionally put off by how seldom literature itself is accorded the status of work in Philip Levine's poetry, much as I admire the *work*. And this is why, at the same time, I am much taken by Paul Metcalf's nuts-and-bolts, prose-poetry interventions into literary history and historical place, his refusal to force facticity into tidy little experiential packages. And this is why Sharon Doubiago's epic (and lyrical) *Hard Country* seems to me a crucial text in bringing personal, on-the-road narratives of hard-won wisdom abruptly into collision with feminist convictions regarding labor (in all of its manifestations), social and historical repression, and the constraints and possibilities of authorship operating under the sign of postmodernity.

Authorship: faced with the factorylike inventory of online hyperproductivity—and there are print variants, to be sure—it may prove advantageous to consider "false writing" from the vantage point of author function as such. In fact, a related writing history is at work when one turns to the mix of U.S. authorial motives, having to do with a divide that emerged in the late nineteenth century. The late postbellum period in the U.S. saw rapid population growth; a continued increase in literacy rates; the introduction of new typewriter, typesetting, and printing technologies; and, by 1890, the consolidation of U.S. publishing in New York City. (International copyright came to the States in 1891.) Most importantly, and as D. G. Myers details, "two different ideas of writing emerged in conflict with one another": the first was "writing conceived as a social practice," either "as a profession (in connection with journalism)" or "as a basic proficiency . . . (in connection with college writing instruction)"; the second, "writing conceived as an art" (*Elephants Teach*, p. 59).

Unlike (public) writing culture of eighteenth-century Britain, then, writers of the Gilded Age and its aftermath were struggling with the ideological distinction not between the critical and the creative exactly—U.S. critics, according to Myers, in fact lamented "the rivalry between art and journalism" (ibid., p. 59)—but between writing (often for money) that appealed to the multitudes and writing as a more refined "literary" activity. Enter a character like Pound.

And this sets up the distinction, even more prevalent today perhaps, between readers who read primarily as a means of entertainment and escape (and infotainment) and readers who read primarily for other purposes, other effects. (If we have difficulty articulating what these "other purposes, other effects" may be, this itself underscores the contemporary ferment.) Historically, writers have responded accordingly, depending on who their readers were and on who they thought their readers were.

Flash forward to the past decade of the digital era: following at least a partial collapse of the old categories of high and low culture—owing to the advent of ever-more-popular culture, for one—the primary fault line today in the symbolic arts would seem to fall neither between the creative and the critical nor between entertainment and (noncommercial) art. If readers and writers have become (let's say) producers and receivers, then generic and formal and career distinctions—poetry v. prose v. codework, blog v. LiveJournal, scholarship v. journalism, fact v. hearsay, amateur v. professional—fall by the wayside as the emphasis lands more on *potentialities* of reading and writing. Whether you choose to read (receive) this or write (produce) that, what's most important is that you *can* receive and produce this and that, Dear Producer/Receiver.

It is in the midst of these historical determinants and encroaching economic disparities, or sets of disparities, that hyperproduction arises. Given my own digital inclinations, I must confess to a certain ambivalence in the face of what might simply be a self-editing problem. Still, it's possible that in parsing the real into the actual and the virtual, we've sacrificed the conceptual leverage which obtained when the imagination was positioned vis-à-vis reality, and along with this leverage, a discourse sensitive to the limits of the imagination. The imagination and its attendant discursive machinery, up to and including the magical (see *Conclusion the 4th*), might be rooted in a romantic (or as some would say, in a different context, primitivist) fiction, but it was nonetheless a useful fiction. Even in its mimetic proportions it provided us not simply with a means—a technology—for modeling alternative realities, but with an awareness of the real as a matter of resistance to the given.

Do our newly energized digital and print performances bear witness, then, to a certain abrogation *of* the real? Have we reneged on a venerable aspect of poetic endeavor, that purposive response to, or reach toward, an outside?

I am reminded here of Robin Blaser's sterling assessment of Jack Spicer's work in "The Practice of Outside," a text which has achieved cult status in the poetry circles (niches?) in which I move. For Blaser, poetic practice is a matter not simply of generating words, but of how we "perform the real" (p. 319). To say that the alphabet participates in the real, then, may be to say very little; likewise, to posit good old-fashioned Baudrillardian hyperreality may be to wallow in the signifying glut (an empirical nightmare)—but at least it pinpoints the problem(atic). If Loss Pequeño Glazier is correct in asserting that "the innovative in digital literature can diversify and pluralize our relation to the text and to the world," I would want to understand better the terms of this diversification and pluralism vis-à-vis our performances (*Digital Poetics,* p. 178). While I have no desire to return to the old class-based hegemony of taste and aesthetic contemplation and the like, it's difficult to see how even the best of sheer performative zeal (I have in mind, for instance, Artaud's *détournement* of writing as "pigshit," or to take a blue-collar, polis-centered example, Michael Moore's documentary *oeuvre*) can redirect the U.S. public's seemingly endless appetite for ever more pulse-quickening, bloodcurdling, and in most cases, mind-numbing productions.

(An odd coupling, I know—but I appreciate Artaud's verbal incitements and Moore's cinematic polemic. And then too, it's fair to say that Moore has given the U.S. political arena quite a jolt. Some performances would seem to defy the more sober appraisals of critical inquiry.)

Walter Benjamin's 1934 lecture, "The Author as Producer," seems in many ways to have anticipated our hyperproductive (and for that matter, productive) scenario. Benjamin would "define a hack as a man who refuses as a matter of principle to improve the production apparatus and so prise it away from the ruling class for the benefit of Socialism" (p. 496). "I further maintain," Benjamin continues, "that an appreciable part of so-called left-wing literature had no other social function than that of continually extracting new effects or sensations . . . for the public's entertainment" (ibid., p. 496). Thus, "the New Objectivity as a literary movement . . . has turned *the struggle against misery* into an object of consumption" (ibid., p. 497; emphasis in original). Benjamin proposes instead that the author-as-producer "will never be concerned with products alone, but always, at the same time, with the means of production" (ibid., p. 498). For Benjamin, "a writer's production must have the character of a model: it must be able to instruct other writers in their production and, secondly, it must be able to place an improved apparatus at their disposal. This apparatus will be the better, the more consumers it brings into contact with the production process—in short, the more readers or spectators it turns into collaborators" (ibid., p. 498).

Benjamin's preferred "model" is "Brecht's epic theater," and if Benjamin were still alive, he would likely find great promise in today's communications technologies, with their unprecedented production (and reproduction) potential, recombinant "aura," and capacity for consolidating collaborative (textual, artistic, corporate) agencies. But he would doubtless be disturbed by the mediating influences of immediacy itself. One's screeds and scrawls can now be distributed far and wide and with relatively little effort, and this enables, practically speaking, all manner of what the poet Anselm Hollo might call "pathos & farce transmitters" ("Canto," p. 222, l. 4). For Benjamin, on the other hand, lecturing only six years after the publication of Edward L. Bernays's *Propaganda*, the "organizational usefulness" of written products "must on no account be confined to propagandistic use," and further, "*a writer who does not teach other writers teaches nobody*" ("Author as Producer," p. 498; emphasis in original). Thus, the author-as-producer adopts (today we might say, cops) an "attitude which transforms him, from a supplier of the production apparatus, into an engineer who sees his task in adapting that apparatus to the ends of the proletarian revolution" (ibid., p. 498). (Shades of Archibald "Harry" Tuttle [Robert De Niro], the renegade HVAC engineer of Terry Gilliam's *Brazil*.)

Here the issue of literary-aesthetic quality smacks dead up against political-ideological (-pedagogical) expediency. Benjamin could not foresee that producers with access to the requisite technological (digital) means might detour around this aesthetic-ideological bind simply by forgoing quality control outright in favor of sheer quantity, and plenty of PR. The quantities entailed can be so vast that one might well wonder whether such producers are reading much of anything—even or especially their own productions.[6] Here, what one means by "reading" comes to the fore (along, of course, with "writing"), and we may catch a glimpse of an emerging parallel between those who read insatiably without doing much writing and those who write compulsively without doing much reading. Pathological or not, however, isn't the phenomenon of readers consuming text to produce meaning and affect equivalent, push come to shove, with writers producing text to consume meaning and affect? Never mind whether reading ought to be construed not as consumption *or* as production, but as a vital form of *creation*; the poet Adonis has argued, for instance, that reading "is not an act of consumption," but "an act of creation," in order to provoke a break from what he regards as the repressive conventions of Arabic discourse (see Adonis, *Poetry*, p. 182). Consumption or production *or* creation, isn't our (waning?) *épistème* of discourse as such—I am thinking here of the widespread appeal, even for today's world-weary literary and cultural theorists, of Foucault's "archaeological-genealogical method" (see Poster, "Foucault")—grounded in the notion that such activities, whether individually or collectively realized, are largely interchangeable operations constituting a juncture in the discursive force field that determines the conditions *of* textuality?

Well, this may be to understate the gravitational reach of a thinker (Foucault) to whom I have often been drawn, despite my text- and auteur-centered leanings, not least because *his* work is so often caught up in actual textual practices and their historical deposits. It is worth remarking here, in contradistinction to the drift of the prior paragraph, that there persists among writers—Pope, Hazlitt, Emerson, and others—a venerable tradition of railing occasionally against the dogma of reading for reading's sake. These writers would derogoate readers who read (pablum, masterpieces) without applying their individual lights to the matters read (see Nehring, "Books"). Can the same now be said of writing? How is the text/meaning/production/consumption matrix modified by the hyperproductive moment? Or does this moment simply throw into relief the extent to which reading and writing are merely twin halves of a bipartite metaphor that underwrites (underreads?) the cultural mythology of authorship?

What to do, finally, about "true" (as opposed to "false") writing; and, as I have suggested in exploiting an untrue if provocative binary, about "true" (as opposed to "false") reading? As Michael Joyce conjectures, what may be at stake in our heavily commericalized online sphere is nothing less than the capacity of new media to "shrink the cyclic into the momentary," thus "deny[ing] and depos[ing] our sense of mortality, which is nothing less than our awareness of how the cyclic gives meaning to repetition" ("Persistence," p. 137). For which Joyce proposes, as cultural-user antidote, that we "set aside any fascination with the merely lasting in favor of conserving the lasting power of reflected and reflective moments" (ibid., p. 137). We must attend, that is, to that ordinary and memorable persistence one finds amid such audacious and audaciously divergent effusions, "all gone   & going things" (Hollo, "Canto," p. 222, l. 26).

Conclusion the 2nd: Manufacturing

A TREATISE OF WHOLE NUMBERS

> *That is, in prose you start with the world*
> *and find the words to match; in poetry you start*
> *with the words and find the world in them.*
> —Charles Bernstein, "Dysraphism"

0

Because we use our heads, we forget ourselves.
Because we forget ourselves, we forget our bodies.
Because we forget our bodies, we use our heads.

—Overheard at a gathering held at U of Notre Dame, early twenty-first century

1

Because it's not abstract, it's not just anybody.
Because it's not just anybody, it's somebody.
Because it's somebody, it's somebody like you.

Because it's somebody like you, the screen came between us.
Because the screen came between us, we came together.
Because we came together, I said so.

Because I said so, we might have.
Because we might have, it's not abstract.
Because it's not abstract, it's concrete.

Because it's concrete, we advance to the plot.
Because we advance to the plot, I rest my hand on the cold red granite.
Because I rest my hand on the cold red granite, the sky was cloudy.

Because the sky was cloudy, the sun is out.
Because the sun is out, we looked ahead to the plot.
Because we looked ahead to the plot, I don't know why.

Because I don't know why, you flew to Chicago.
Because you flew to Chicago, we poets think we're little gods.
Because we poets think we're little gods, poetry becomes synonymous with language.

Because poetry becomes synonymous with language, all prose is poetry.
Because all prose is poetry, not all poetry is prose.
Because not all poetry is prose, we tried to escape.

2

Because it's raining out, they tell me to.
Because they tell me to, I'm melancholy.
Because I'm melancholy, the narrative progresses.

Because the narrative progresses, art reveals itself as the artifice of patrician splendor.

Because art reveals itself as the artifice of patrician splendor, you fly to Chicago.
Because you fly to Chicago, we fall in love with a mysterious third party.

Because we fall in love with a mysterious third party, time stands still for a moment.
Because time stands still for a moment, eternity beckons.
Because eternity beckons, we return to our senses.

Because we return to our senses, Chicago becomes a small fishing village on the Mediterranean.
Because Chicago becomes a small fishing village on the Mediterranean, we're only one click away from a conversion of the real.
Because we're only one click away from a conversion of the real, we're instantly wealthy.

Because we're instantly wealthy, we have not a care in the world.
Because we have not a care in the world, the plot thickens.
Because the plot thickens, it's more difficult for the author to stir things up.

Because it's more difficult for the author to stir things up, you're quickly aroused.
Because you're quickly aroused, we have sex without protection.
Because we have sex without protection, you feel safer.

Because you feel safer, it's easier for me to do my job.
Because it's easier for me to do my job, I raise the hem on my skirt.
Because I raise the hem on my skirt, they think I'm a femme fatale.

3

Because you think you're white, you think she's white.
Because you think she's white, she says she's Latino.
Because she says she's Latino, I think I'm African American.

Because I think I'm African American, they must be Iraqi or Native American.
Because they must be Iraqi or Native American, a small fishing village on the Mediterranean becomes a country the size of Florida populated by young retirees.

Because a small fishing village on the Mediterranean becomes a country the size of Florida populated by young retirees, we demand new maps.

Because we demand new maps, we're viewed as demanding.
Because we're viewed as demanding, they might have been poor at one time.
Because they might have been poor at one time, they may never be wealthy.

Because they may never be wealthy, we won't notice the body.
Because we won't notice the body, he'll get away with it.
Because he'll get away with it, we'll buy his book.

Because we'll buy his book, we'll visit his website.
Because we'll visit his website, we'll send him an e-mail or two.
Because we'll send him an e-mail or two, he'll discontinue his website.

Because he'll discontinue his website, she'll question his fortitude.
Because she'll question his fortitude, he'll lose faith in Merriam-Webster (an Encylopædia Britannica company).
Because he'll lose faith in Merriam-Webster (an Encyclopædia Britannica company), she'll abandon the plot.

Because she'll abandon the plot, we'll have far too many explanations on our hands.
Because we'll have far too many explanations on our hands, they'll have room for far too many answers.
Because they'll have room for far too many answers, magic will become indistinguishable from cliché.

4

Because it's not ideological, it's aesthetic.
Because it's aesthetic, it's momentary.
Because it's momentary, we're confused.

Because we're confused, we hyphenate our word-images.
Because we hyphenate our word-images, we forget what we mean to say.
Because we forget what we mean to say, we lose our physicality.

Because we lose our physicality, the sky is blue.
Because the sky is blue, they blew my mind.
Because they blew my mind, we tried to escape.

Because we tried to escape, the screen goes blank.
Because the screen goes blank, the printer stopped.
Because the printer stopped, the bookshelves emptied.

Because the bookshelves emptied, people stopped reading.
Because people stopped reading, the days grow shorter.
Because the days grow shorter, the Earth spins faster on its axis.

Because the Earth spins faster on its axis, lightweight humans drift away from terra firma into geosynchronous orbit around the Earth.
Because lightweight humans drift away from terra firma into geosynchronous orbit around the Earth, the average weight of a human increases.
Because the average weight of a human increases, the average Joe sits more.

Because the average Joe sits more, the days grow longer.
Because the days grow longer, the Earth spins more slowly on its axis.
Because the Earth spins more slowly on its axis, lightweight humans return to terra firma.

5

Because we stopped trying to escape, the sun went in.
Because the sun went in, it began to rain.
Because it began to rain, we understood that the short duration of the aesthetic provides a glimpse of patterned timelessness.

Because we understood that the short duration of the aesthetic provides a glimpse of patterned timelessness, we felt a sense of calm wash over us.
Because we felt a sense of calm wash over us, we shuddered in the presence of an archaic ideology.
Because we shuddered in the presence of an archaic ideology, we took a bath and returned to the plot.

Because we took a bath and returned to the plot, she finds the body.
Because she finds the body, the authorities were called in.
Because the authorities were called in, the two are married on 1 July.

Because the two are married on 1 July, they fall in love.
Because they fall in love, eternity beckons.

Because eternity beckons, lullabies yield high returns on investment.

Because lullabies yield high returns on investment, the hem on my skirt needs to be lowered.
Because the hem on my skirt needs to be lowered, he requires an alternative syntax.
Because he requires an alternative syntax, they grow interested in him.

Because they grow interested in him, he tried to escape.
Because he tried to escape, they grew even more interested in him.
Because they grew even more interested in him, he forgets how to speak.

Because he forgets how to speak, he learns to sign.
Because he learns to sign, he makes new friends.
Because he makes new friends, as of this writing he coauthors children's books for adults.

6

Because the body is old, the authorities think old age had something to do with it.
Because the authorities think old age had something to do with it, the real cause of death remains a mystery.
Because the real cause of death remains a mystery, he becomes melancholy.

Because he becomes melancholy, he rests his hand against the cold red granite.
Because he rests his hand against the cold red granite, it begins to rain.
Because it begins to rain, it begins to pour.

Because it begins to pour, he remembers the past.
Because he remembers the past, he forgets about the future.
Because he forgets about the future, he picks up a cold.

Because he picks up a cold, she cooks him chicken soup.
Because she cooks him chicken soup, he loves her even more.
Because he loves her even more, she cooks him even more chicken soup.

Because she cooks him even more chicken soup, they grow old together.
Because they grow old together, they watch more television together.
Because they watch more television together, they buy a new sofa.

Because they buy a new sofa, they can't travel to the gravesite.

Because they can't travel to the gravesite, he begins to grow melancholy again.

Because he begins to grow melancholy again, his biographer surmises that he led an unhappy life.

Because his biographer surmises that he led an unhappy life, people refused to read his books.

Because people refused to read his books, his posthumous reputation suffered.

Because his posthumous reputation suffered, she spent her last years rebutting his critics.

7

Because there is nothing more anyone can do for them, it might be wrong to ask why.

Because it might be wrong to ask why, we ask why.

Because we ask why, we fail to advance the plot.

Because we fail to advance the plot, it's more difficult for the author to stir things up.

Because it's more difficult for the author to stir things up, you're quickly aroused.

Etc.

Because you feel safer, I felt less safe.

Because I felt less safe, I keep writing.

Because I keep writing, you kept wanting me to explain myself.

Because you kept wanting me to explain myself, I began to think that you don't value the singular expression.

Because I began to think that you don't value the singular expression, you begin to think that I can't theorize my work.

Because you begin to think that I can't theorize my work, you devised a theory that accounts for all such work.

Because you devised a theory that accounts for all such work, I begin to think that you're not sensitive to the particular work as it articulates the universal idea.

Because I begin to think that you're not sensitive to the particular work as it articulates the universal idea, you began to think that I didn't appreciate the sweep of your theory.

Because you began to think that I didn't appreciate the sweep of your theory, you and I stop talking to each other.

Because you and I stop talking to each other, we stopped playing games with each other.

Because we stopped playing games with each other, aliens take over our institutions.

Because aliens take over our institutions, we had less time for our work.

Because we had less time for our work, we have more time for cooking.

Because we have more time for cooking, we conclude that beauty is a matter of taste buds and taste buds alone.

Because we conclude that beauty is a matter of taste buds and taste buds alone, they tried to escape.

8

Because I'm a logician at heart, this might not be logical.

Because this might not be logical, you may submit to the murmur of language.

Because you may submit to the murmur of language, you might divine a higher power.

Because you might divine a higher power, I may be accused of having religious affectations.

Because I may be accused of having religious affectations, I might reclaim spirituality for nonreligious beings.

Because I might reclaim spirituality for nonreligious beings, we may be happy if and only if we're atheists.

Because we may be happy if and only if we're atheists, some devout beings might give us the creeps.

Because some devout beings might give us the creeps, some of you will be disappointed in us.

Because some of you will be disappointed in us, I will give you money to get off my ass.

Because I will give you money to get off my ass, they will tell me to stop.
Because they will tell me to stop, I will give you more money.
Because I will give you more money, and not because you need it.

Because and not because you need it, you will probably find him
    aggressively repetitive.
Because you will probably find him aggressively repetitive, he inserts
    because it's there here just because.
Because he inserts *because it's there* here just because, you may not
    understand your own class or cultural bias.

Because you may not understand your own class or cultural bias, you might
    very well treat him like some people treat foreigners.
Because you might very well treat him like some people treat foreigners, he
    may withdraw into the privacy of his own thoughts.
Because he may withdraw into the privacy of his own thoughts, she will
    forget to send him a Valentine's Day card.

Because she will forget to send him a Valentine's Day card, he will develop
    strange habits.
Because he will develop strange habits, religious beings will think him
    competitively religious.
Because religious beings will think him competitively religious, he will seek
    only those truths that cannot be expressed as the quotient of two
    integers, and Bertrand Russell will smile.

9 [SPAM, OR SPICED HAM]

Because she was accustomed to proving mathematical theorems, she just
    could not understand how a literary theory might be advanced
    without a thorough assessment of related axioms.
Because a thorough assessment of related axioms would be the only way to
    advance the plot.

Because a thorough assessment of related axioms would be the only way to
    advance the plot, the function of criticism at the present time seemed
    suddenly to have rendered tacit those quality judgments pertinent to
    the articulation and dissemination of ambitious critical and
    theoretical discourse.
Because to have rendered tacit those quality judgments pertinent to the
    articulation and dissemination of ambitious critical and theoretical
    discourse would permit some critics and theorists to neglect issues of
    aesthetic merit when scrutinizing the marketplace of ideas.

Because to have rendered tacit those quality judgments pertinent to the articulation and dissemination of critical and theoretical discourse would permit some critics and theorists to neglect issues of aesthetic merit when scrutinizing the marketplace of ideas, much ambitious artwork would be overlooked on the basis of its low popularity, apparent inaccessibility, or modest cultural work.

Because low popularity, apparent inaccessibility, or modest cultural work may or may not be measures of cosmic import.

Because low popularity, apparent inaccessibility, or modest cultural work may or may not be measures of cosmic import, those artists with food and drink sufficient to drawing an easy breath would find it to their occasional advantage to give some critics and theorists the raspberry.

Because to give some critics and theorists the raspberry seems to be the only way to draw attention to certain kinds of functional disparities.

Because to give some critics and theorists the raspberry seems to be the only way to draw attention to certain kinds of functional disparities, one may begin to wonder how far away that tiny star really is.

Because one may begin to wonder how far away that tiny star really is, we may assume that we have touched upon a hopeful grammar, and Bertrand Russell will smile.

10

Because he said everyone has their reasons, nobody made a move.
Because nobody made a move, nothing happened.
Because nothing happened, Mark Wallace wasn't there.

Because Mark Wallace wasn't there, Laura Mullen decided to take his place.
Because Laura Mullen decided to take his place, Tom Raworth RSVP'd.
Because Tom Raworth RSVP'd, Mark Wallace attended anyway.

Because Mark Wallace attended anyway, Anselm Hollo got to meet Charles Alexander.

Because Anselm Hollo got to meet Charles Alexander, Lisa Jarnot met Laura Wright.

Because Lisa Jarnot met Laura Wright, Lance Olsen claimed he saw the ghost of Primo Levi.

Because Lance Olsen claimed he saw the ghost of Primo Levi, Marjorie Perloff was elected president of MLA.

Because Marjorie Perloff was elected president of MLA, rumor had it that Pierre Joris translated into Esperanto Aldon Lynn Nielsen's indictment of Clear Channel Communications.

Because rumor had it that Pierre Joris translated into Esperanto Aldon Lynn Nielsen's indictment of Clear Channel Communications, Don Byrd dreamed he was at a séance with Robert Duncan and Judith Johnson.

Because Don Byrd dreamed he was at a séance with Robert Duncan and Judith Johnson, Anne Waldman hired Bhanu Kapil Rider as her personal masseuse.

Because Anne Waldman hired Bhanu Kapil Rider as her personal masseuse, Joe Amato sent a bottle of champagne to the North Pole, where Kent Johnson had been spotted.

Because Joe Amato sent a bottle of champagne to the North Pole, where Kent Johnson had been spotted, Kass Fleisher balanced the household budget without Kristin Dykstra's help.

Because Kass Fleisher balanced the household budget without Kristin Dykstra's help, English departments started behaving themselves.

Because English departments started behaving themselves, Nick LoLordo borrowed money from Art Linkletter and the Steve Katz-Ron Sukenick Dance Troupe to open his own Italian restaurant featuring dishes from Sicily.

Because Nick LoLordo borrowed money from Art Linkletter and the Steve Katz-Ron Sukenick Dance Troupe to open his own Italian restaurant featuring dishes from Sicily, someone dropped Cole Swensen's name right alongside Jody Swilky's and Ralph Berry's.

Because someone dropped Cole Swensen's name right alongside Jody Swilky's and Ralph Berry's, everyone dropped everyone else's name in the pasta with fennel and sardines.

Because everyone dropped everyone else's name in the pasta with fennel and sardines, nobody knew who anybody was.

Because nobody knew who anybody was, somebody looking like Kent Johnson stood up and said, "I'm Walter Cronkite, and that's the way it is."

11

Because Charles Bernstein never met Sam Spade or Ricky Nelson, but knew Hannah Weiner's brother and a fountain pen aficionado named Gabe Gudding, Bernstein could not be invited to 10.

Because Bernstein could not be invited to 10, Beowulf entered stage right holding Donald Rumsfeld in his left hand.

Because Beowulf entered stage right holding Donald Rumsfeld in his left hand, readers exited center stage.

Because readers exited center stage, naming became of less consequence to Jack Benny and Octavio Paz, or an MFA student reading Steve Tomasula or Jed Rasula, or Rita Moreno with the London Philharmonic, with Andrew Levy on drums.

Because naming became of less consequence to Jack Benny and Octavio Paz, or an MFA student reading Steve Tomasula or Jed Rasula, or Rita Moreno with the London Philharmonic, with Andrew Levy on drums, writers flocked to the balcony.

Because writers flocked to the balcony, the performer quoted from Ron Silliman's blog.

Because the performer quoted from Ron Silliman's blog, the fiction writers left in protest.

Because the fiction writers left in protest, there was a shortage of material in Hollywood.

Because there was a shortage of material in Hollywood, poets now place more scripts.

Because poets now place more scripts, the price of boxed macaroni has gone up and Sheila Murphy reports that F does in fact = ma.

Because the price of boxed macaroni has gone up and Sheila Murphy reports that F does in fact = ma, Nick LoLordo closed his restaurant.

Because Nick LoLordo closed his restaurant, someone at Yale published an essay about racial and ethnic stereotypes and how damaging they can be to entrepreneurial enterprises.

Because someone at Yale published an essay about racial and ethnic stereotypes and how damaging they can be to entrepreneurial enterprises, knowledge was advanced about the nature of sexuality.

Because knowledge was advanced about the nature of sexuality, the plot, as Michael Joyce put it, "succumbed to its lyrical excesses."

Because the plot, as Michael Joyce put it, "succumbed to its lyrical excesses," the author was bored shitless.

Because the author was bored shitless, she begat a family with pets.
Because she begat a family with pets, the sky was cloudy.
Because the sky was cloudy, the granite was cold and wet.

Because the granite was cold and wet, his fingers grew numb.
Because his fingers grew numb, he whispered her name.
Because he whispered her name, the poetry reading was canceled forever and ever.

12

Because we are older now, the trees seem more beautiful.
Because the trees seem more beautiful, they speak to us in whole numbers.
Because they speak to us in whole numbers, we have no way of knowing what they mean.

Because we have no way of knowing what they mean, we will write about it.
Because we will write about it, something may be advanced.
Because something may be advanced, little may be learned.

Because little may be learned, we will write about it.
Because we will write about it, the young will know exactly what we mean.
Because the young will know exactly what we mean, insight may be gained.

Because insight may be gained, cognitive evidence may be lost.
Because cognitive evidence may be lost, we must be comforted.
Because we must be comforted, we will write about it.

Because we will write about it, we will draw numerous conclusions.
Because we will draw numerous conclusions, we will approach the end.
Because we will approach the end, we will grow anxious.

Because we will grow anxious, we will write about it.
Because we will write about it, the young will grow increasingly aware of certitude.
Because the young will grow increasingly aware of certitude, they will stop being what they might be.

Because they will stop being what they might be, they will grow more finite.
Because they will grow more finite, the trees will seem more beautiful.

Because the trees will seem more beautiful, mortality will continue to accumulate in whole numbers.

*

[A NOTE ON PROCESSING]

Because we wanted to create a machine made of words, we selected a word resembling "because" to initiate processing.
Because we selected a word resembling "because" to initiate processing, we anticipated minimal deviation from the norm.
Because we anticipated minimal deviation from the norm, we expected a response proportional to any such deviation.

Because we expected a response proportional to any such deviation, we were somewhat surprised to receive complaints regarding signal-to-noise ratio.
Because we were somewhat surprised to receive complaints regarding signal-to-noise ratio, we forgot how to conjugate several common French verbs.
Because we forgot how to conjugate several common French verbs, we immediately grasped Roland Barthes's observation that "it is the misfortune (but also perhaps the voluptuous pleasure) of language not to be able to authenticate itself."

Because we immediately grasped Roland Barthes's observation that "it is the misfortune (but also perhaps the voluptuous pleasure) of language not to be able to authenticate itself," we went back to the drawing board with our Mars plans.
Because we went back to the drawing board with our Mars plans, Jack Spicer's name will appear on the Democratic presidential ballot in 2008.
Because Jack Spicer's name will appear on the Democratic presidential ballot in 2008, members of the Republican National Committee will propose a constitutional amendment prohibiting thought in public places.

Because members of the Republican National Committee will propose a constitutional amendment prohibiting thought in public places, it is strongly advised that non-enemy noncombatants seek shelter in a nearby bookstore.

Because it is strongly advised that non-enemy noncombatants seek shelter in a nearby bookstore, bookstores nearby may sell more books.
Because bookstores nearby may sell more books, machines made of words may become more popular, especially among the heard.
Because machines made of words may become more popular, especially among the heard, we have begun work in our studio on a new, more efficient model that we call "The Barbasol Argonaut: A Guide to the Better-Known Species," or BA for short.
Because we have begun work in our studio on a new, more efficient model that we call "The Barbasol Argonaut: A Guide to the Better-Known Species," or BA for short, we are asking that you feed us back at jamato2@ilstu.edu.
Because we are asking that you feed us back at jamato2@ilstu.edu, we are requesting further that you initiate feedback with a word resembling *because* and that you please keep all comments to ten words or less.
Because we are requesting further that you initiate feedback with a word resembling "because" and that you please keep all comments to ten words or less, we anticipate plenty of pluck and pith.
Because we anticipate plenty of pluck and pith, we expect our author to submit his resignation on the morrow.
Because we expect our author to submit his resignation on the morrow, kids under twelve not accompanied by a parent or guardian will get a chance tonight to see the cow jump over the moon.

Conclusion the 3rd: Workplace

Noun: A skill in doing or performing that is attained by study, practice, or observation. art, technique, knack, expertise.
?

Noun: Deceitful cleverness. art, cunning, artfulness, artifice, guile, craftiness, foxiness, wiliness.
?

Noun: Lack of straightforwardness and honesty in action. dishonesty, chicanery, indirection, slyness, underhandedness, craftiness, deviousness, shadiness, sneakiness, trickery, trickiness.
?

Noun: Natural or acquired facility in a specific activity. ability, skill, command, mastery, knack, expertise, proficiency, adeptness, expertness.
?

In her provocative analysis of work and power, *In the Age of the Smart Machine* (1988), Shoshana Zuboff argues convincingly that "action-centered" manufacturing environments of the past, with their reliance on the instrumental and tactile capacities of the human organism's sensory equipment, are rapidly being replaced by a contemporary information workplace in which "intellective" skills gain primacy. Informating technologies, as Zuboff has it, result in increased *textualization* of the process at hand—the production and dissemination of symbol-ridden form, not to say forms—which development in turn requires smart workers who, located now at a physical remove from industrial production processes, are able to grasp the overarching organizational insights afforded by smart machines. Zuboff is careful not to privilege in any inherent way either action-centered or intellective skills. For instance, she is quick to concede that "the knowledge associated with doing cannot be reduced to talking or writing about doing" (p. 175). But because intellective skills depend upon a knowledge of symbolic form—a knowledge, that is, typically associated with the educational system, with *book learnin'*—Zuboff is led toward the end of her book to make a rather surprising claim: "The informated organization is a learning institution, and one of its principal purposes is the expansion of knowledge—not knowledge for its own sake (as in academic pursuit), but knowledge that comes to reside at the core of what it means to be productive" (ibid., p. 395).[7]

Describing the corporate workplace as a "learning institution" is at once suggestive and problematic—and recall that Benjamin assigned the author-producer the explicitly pedagogical function of teaching other author-producers—but I want to take this alignment at face value. To wit: how might Zuboff's analysis be applied to creative writing in general and to "craft" in particular? As writers use the term, "craft" has become a catchall that can designate everything from acquired, programmatic skill, or technique—as in arts and crafts—to careful attention to detail. "Craft" implies a practice-makes-perfect approach to writing, an approach that generally presumes, at some point, the pedagogical presence of a master. But "craft" invokes, too, a certain ingenuity, a *crafty* form of, say, hands-on-the-keyboard *know-how* as well as intellective knowledge.

Unlike many of the craftspeople Zuboff interviews, then, most writers are already aware of their commitment to things and thoughts as mediated through language. So "craft" tends to function as a category by which writers, the once-and-future information workers, preserve the time-tested conception of the laboring body, of action-centered work. The writer's embodied presence is thereby emphasized, generally through the convention of *voice*, the figurative manual labor of writing. Figurative or no, the physicality of the writing act is quite literal, in fact "cannot be reduced to talking or writing about doing." But here, "talking or writing about doing" can be taken to mean "talking or writing about" *talking and writing*—or, articulating the various assumptions and constraints guiding one's work, what some might call *theorizing*.

Which explains in part why "craft" has become a primary means by which writers, sometimes unwittingly, render legible their practices while preserving the unsayable of their processes, metabolic and otherwise.[8] Again, if creative writing is viewed in terms of the information workplace, where "intellective" skills are focal, "craft" in creative writing instruction may be understood as part of a voice-based holdover from "action-centered" thinking; that is, here, the body manifests itself through *voice*. And in managing the intellective associations that their own textual practices require, writers—who may understandably wish to refrain from submitting to the (institutional) authorities—often resist theorizing their subject positions by positing *voice* as unassailably unique. Yet at the same time, it is through the institutionalization of "craft" that the uninitiated must pass in order to stand on the verge of what thus becomes, for all intents and purposes, the ineffable. Because *craft*, you understand, is trial by error, or trial by ordeal, but as so many writers and critics will be quick to tell you, *craft* can take you only so far, for true art is anything but knowable—poets *are* born, not made, as one of my more craft-oriented instructors, a Pope expert, once assured me. Hence *craft* is the best we can do, and the best is not teachable anyway—talent, inspiration, genius are necessarily mysterious (not to say mystified), obscure, beyond the ken of those who are not so endowed. In so much *classroom* practice, developing one's voice merely affirms one's limitations—*except* for those chosen few who manage, according to good authority, to sing "beyond the genius of the sea."

Let me be clear about what I'm saying: talent *can* be enigmatic, just as "craft" *can* be a useful way to think about practice—especially, in educational circles, the practice requisite to shaping well-wrought urns. (I set aside here the question of whether such urns constitute the desirable end products of poetic endeavor.) As I've seen it customarily administered in the classroom, the notion of "craft" is simply not the most effective means of drawing out a variety of writing talents; it's not even practice leading to improvisation. It serves instead primarily as another gatekeeping mechanism, generally to maintain one or two aesthetic camps, when a student-centered critical pedagogy (see Amato and Fleisher) might be used to more diverse aims, might help to situate artistic practice on a continuum with other social practices. Based on my own classroom experiences, exposing students to the full panoply of writing practices means putting less emphasis, say, on the rules of prosody, and more emphasis on what *students* might want to do once they see what has been done. And once you let go a bit, no telling what might happen. The results can be remarkable—and certainly no more dismal than twenty odes to instructional authority.

In any case, safeguarding the sanctity of art in this way, within an institutional setting as overdetermined as the university, ensures that more and more books will be written that expound more and more tricks of the trade—all of those "the craft of" books that are filled with partial insights (or "Craft Quickies," the title of a session at the Charleston Writers' Conference); unwritten laws (now writ); and experiential testimony. Such are the rules and, ultimately, the regulations of a thereby reduced, if not decimated, art form. The irony of course is that all of this serves to obscure even further what so many writers are about, and this because the more we develop our "craft" in such terms, the more we formalize our "voices," the more likely the conventional Self becomes the signpost of our various practices. Any question of play, or for that matter, of a more aleatoric conception of creative rules, remains off-limits. It's not surprising, then, that those who speak of "craft" as though it were the *sine qua non* of creative endeavor are often very orthodox writers. No surprise at all that poetry, in particular, once sentenced to "craft," is often sentenced as well to well-formed *sentences.*

A bit harsh, I know. But if the point is, in part, to resist the sometimes debilitatingly programmatic influence of academic and other social structures, there are more bracing ways to go about doing so. And besides—"craft" will take you only so far, as I've indicated, and then—LOOK OUT. Consider Frank Lentricchia's (self-alleged) conversion some years ago, in the pages of the now defunct *Lingua Franca*, into a born-again Platonic rhapsode. Lentricchia apparently shut the doors of his undergrad classrooms and then ensured they were "shut tight" ("Last Will," p. 65) before he took to lip-synching (i.e., "reciting") various literary works, possessed of *furor divinus* and confident that his apparent transformation within would become, at least for his target students, a transformation without. "We're out of our minds," he cheerfully and notoriously proclaimed.

Not all that much different than British poet David Whyte holding retreats for corporate executives in which he reputedly recites poems committed (and I mean *committed*) to memory in order presumably to inspire our managerial ilk to hold themselves, their very *souls*, accountable to a sustainable ecological reality. Whyte manages to employ both chaos theory and New Age spiritual thinking in this new and improved role for poetry and, perhaps, for the poet (articulated at length in his book, *The Heart Aroused: Poetry and the Preservation of the Soul in Corporate America*), and I daresay that Lentricchia's students, some of them, may well possess the right stuff for the job (which appears to turn on *self-possession*). For Whyte, evidently, the path to a corporation's soul is a detour around the body politic and through the healing power of poetry. Not surprisingly, much of the poetry Whyte uses by way of detour—selections from Blake, Wordsworth, Yeats, Eliot, Frost, Stevens, Williams, Auden, Sexton, Bly, Snyder, Walcott, and himself (very male, very white, hence very like this item you hold in your hands)—employs the narrative, experiential "I," often to natural-meditative ends, the sort of poetic quest one finds celebrated in Camille Paglia's writings (which latter Whyte cites approvingly). Readers will be hard-pressed to find reference to contemporary work that might properly be termed *avant-garde, experimental, unconventional, radical*—let alone an understanding of poetic practice as, all told, mounting a challenge to the standard canonical impulse toward art-as-self-actualization (if permitting for that too). Perhaps most telling, though, is that I found Whyte's book in my local bookshop shelved not in the poetry or self-help sections, but under business/economics. (For mild metrical send-up of the financial districts, see Silverstein.)

Now hold on a second! I don't have anything against poetic quests (I love Blake, and Wordsworth, and Whitman), or convention *per se* (I still find the time to reread *Four Quartets*), or traditional form (especially when it's playfully altered, as in Ted Berrigan's or Bernadette Mayer's sonnets). But I *do* have something against the use of natural science and the like to support a hierarchy in which classical form emerges as somehow tacitly, or *naturally*, superior, as Paul Lake managed some years ago in his lead piece for the *AWP Chronicle*, "The Shape of Poetry."[9] The point here is that the institutionalization of "craft," whether in the graduate or the undergraduate classroom, permits for all forms of mystification to emerge at its presumed limit, on the verge of genius, or insanity—which suits quite well Lentricchia's classroom antics, or Whyte's corporate soul-searching, or Lake's metered hierarchy.

Now in some sense, Lentricchia's musings and Whyte's exhortations may be viewed as the post- or pre-literary-theoretical equivalent of bringing poetry to a wider audience, and vice versa (and notwithstanding Whyte's and Lake's quasi-scientific theorizing). So in effect I'm suggesting that current after-theory shocks, as described, for instance, in Kurt Spellmeyer's "After Theory" piece in *College English*, are likely to encourage some to turn toward poetry and our other arts as an antidote to the textual obsession of English departments and as a means of making it "back" to "the world." Unfortunately, "the world" thus rendered will likely be given over to the same old same old experiential voicing, and Spellmeyer's almost-poignant attempt to recuperate the arts as embodiment, and "art as experience," is a case in point. In fact Spoken Word/slam poetries often suffer in my view from a similar ordaining of the experiential and from a collapse of distinctions between poetic artifice and poetic persona, but at least a goodly number of slam practitioners manage to transcend the poignancy and preciosity both of our latter-day converts and the tweedy academic set.

As "craft" has rendered poetic practice nearly incomprehensible to the nonpracticing lay public—by definition, "great" writing transcends craft—I regard it as responsible in part for the popular mystification of the poet and as perfectly congenial to what I like to call the Telefon School of Embodied Poetics. The Telefon School takes its name from the Don Siegel film *Telefon* (1977), starring Charles Bronson, Lee Remick, Tyne Daly, and Donald Pleasance. A group of fifty-odd Soviet agents have been subjected to drug-assisted hypnosis, given new identities, and distributed around the U.S. in random locations to live out their lives. These otherwise ordinary, peaceful citizens have but one little glitch: when they hear their given name coupled with a few lines from a certain poem by Robert Frost, they click into preprogrammed mode and are immediately entranced into, oh, blowing up a munitions dump and themselves with it. And this can happen to the nicest folks—good ole Hank down the street, say. All it takes is a single phone call from your friendly vindictive Soviet clerk-gone-wacko bad guy, Donald Pleasance: "The woods are lovely, dark and deep, but you have promises to keep, and miles to go before you sleep. Remember, Nikolai, miles to go before you sleep." Bang, just like that, and they blow.[10]

Notwithstanding the possibility that exposure to a Frost poem at an early moment in one's poetic *Bildung* might result in a post-traumatic creative disorder (sorry!), my main point here has to do with the fact that poetry and madness are once again aligned, à la Plato; that poetry is again made a matter of self-search, a search that, however lacking in dramatic closure, is sentenced to end-rhymes; that poetic license is reworked, in effect, as license to kill, via a *voice*-activated network. OK, but we might have expected our poetic terrorists to be triggered by a few lines of Gertrude Stein, or (my favorite choice here) Williams: "So much depends, Sergei, upon a red wheel barrow, glazed with rain water, beside the white chickens."

I can hear the squawking already: What's wrong with Frost? (What was it Stevens said to Frost?—that his poems "had subjects"?) Even, what's wrong with *Telefon*? (Answer: nothing, really, nothing at all. It's a solid action flick.) Harp on issues of quality as one may, I am suggesting here why a few lines from Frost (our first Inaugural Poet) seem to resonate so well with madness and civilization. I am suggesting why one must be crafty, indeed, to ignore the implicit popularity of poetry as explicitly depicted in *Telefon*—where poetic inspiration meets *and* exceeds all acceptable social criteria. And craftier, still, to presume to *teach* such inspiration on the basis of formal rules, especially rules divorced from their social moorings.

And to call my own bluff: if poetic inspiration *is* in fact a matter of sublime or ecstatic apprehension (coming up in our fourth and final conclusion)—if it demands that one lose one's "voice" in order to *give* voice—how on earth might one articulate such reaches through the secular modalities of "craft"? And where is the necessary discussion of what one might *do* with such a voice once plumbing such rarefied regions, regions in which one can be hard-pressed to know the dancer from the dance?

There must be other ways of preserving a measure of autonomy for the institutionalized writer than by maintaining, as a matter of curricular custom, the crypto-policy of writing-as-voiceprint while advancing programmatically the distinction between "mere" craft and "true art." Which distortion further encourages the popular proliferation of pedagogies (and plots) that link creative inspiration (and aspiration) to iconoclastic genius, romantic pining, entranced madness, *poète maudit* posturing, poet *manqué* raving, author mal-function, witchcraft, and so forth. Thus scleroticizing poetic practice in the process (thank you, Charles Bernstein). Human bodies are, after all, *social* bodies. How then—in an academic workplace gone more and more corporate, in a public sphere that would put privacy itself at the mercy of privatization—how to elicit that fire down below, that "strange spirit of fire" (Whitman, "To Those," p. 508, l. 6)? How to keep the faith? And how to let go?

And how.

Conclusion the 4th: Community

There's nothing surer:
The rich get rich and the poor get poorer.

In the meantime, in between time,
Ain't we got fun.
—Gus Kahn and Raymond B. Egan, "Ain't We Got Fun" (1921)

You attend a poetry reading because (check all that apply):
   A. You like poetry.
   B. You like poets.
   C. You like people.
   D. You want to be moved.
   E. You want to be provoked.
   F. You want to learn something new.
   G. You want to be made to think.
   H. You enjoy performances of any sort.
   I. You feel it's your duty to support the arts.
   J. You want to support the work of your peers.
   K. You enjoy social outings of any kind.
   L. You want to be seen in public.
   M. You wonder.
   N. You have nothing better to do.
   O. You are required by your teacher to attend.
   P. You want to have fun.
   Q. You want to be part of something greater than yourself.
   R. You owe someone.
   S. You hope your attendance will somehow result in your work being published.
   T. You want to meet new people.
   U. You want people to come to your reading.
   V. You think it's the fashionable thing to do.
   W. You think it's a good way to build community.
   X. You find comfort in numbers of like-minded people.
   Y. You want to be reassured as to the value of your own work.
   Z. You want to get laid.
(I left out the word "entertainment." Oops.)

*

Gerald L. Bruns opens his panoramic essay on "poetic communities" with a nod toward Hesiod—"from Hesiod we ... learn that poetry itself is not a kind of learning but a species of ecstasy"—concluding with the conjecture that the "sociality" of such "series or tradition of communities" is perhaps best understood as "theatrical and performative rather than civil, economic, or even ideological" ("Poetic Communities," pp. 1, 38). First, note Bruns's "poetic" instead of "poetry" community: this clever bit of business puts us one notch closer to the poem (or poetic event), as opposed to the poet, as the proper locus of community. For Bruns, the poet is less a creature of sheer expressivity or polemical élan than an ecstatically-charged being whose poetry facilitates the collective present by drawing group (readers', listeners') attention to the continuously unfolding poem-event as a fully historical (f)act. Working through Plato, Bataille, Benjamin, Blanchot, Olson, Cunningham, Cage, Fried, Nancy, Antin, Middleton, and a host of others, Bruns positions the poem-event as a saturation point of (let us say) mad historicity, dispersing its "nonproductive expenditure" via words that become "like images of fascination—moments of reversal that displace the logical or cognitive subject from its position of sovereignty or control" (ibid., p. 9).[11] Given this orientation toward performativity and Nancy's *partage*—"a sharing or division of voices in which the divine voice ... is multiplied by being passed from one singularity to another like rumor or panic" (ibid., p. 3)—one might have imagined Spoken Word/slam poetries to surface as the chief *performative* moment of such a contemporary pantheon. Instead, L=A=N=G=U=A=G=E writing emerges in Bruns's conceptually-charged, very male, very white (hence very like this item you hold in your hands) lineage as chiefly illustrative, along with Antin's talk-work, of this ecstatic-anarchist complex, largely due to the latter poets' "self-conscious" grasp of history and tradition and their treatment of poetry as "a condition of *language as such*" (ibid., p. 24).

Aside from the, well, grand entrance of the most ostensibly text-intensive of our contemporary poetries, what troubles me here—and troubles me a great deal, my knee literally jerking during my first cursory reading of the piece—is the degree to which Bruns's *formal* grasp of the poem *per se* as a contagious event ultimately gives him *carte blanche* to read, quite literally, poetic community as circulating about the poem's various edicts, "poetry open[ing] up a mode of existence in which poems appear" (ibid., p. 13). The "self-identity" of the poem, as Bruns coaxes, "entails the multiple communities that it generates through those whom it fascinates" (ibid., p. 28). Among the many things presumably projected (ejected?) from such a poem-event—a happening that, as Bruns has it, "is accessible only through layers of social mediation" (ibid., p. 15)—are (ever-altering) reading contexts (e.g.), poetic personae (e.g.), cultural effects (e.g.), marketplace dynamics (e.g.), etc. etc. etc. Bruns cites Peter Middleton's conception of the poem as a "heteroclite entity" to point to the vast network of effects leading away from this singular, henceforth "radically socialized" and diversified event (ibid., p. 27).

But heteroclite entity or no, situated at the *center* of its corresponding flux is the poem-event, enduringly stable only in the perpetual aftereffects it puts into motion, community being either one of many such effects or a reciprocating partner in the heteroclite transaction. And once the poem is invoked as the paradoxically hermetic (i.e., selflessly self-sufficient) yet distributive instigator of community, imagined community is likely to follow. Bruns's may thus be viewed as an austere (if caffeinated) conjuring of transitory (if persistent) poetic community, actuated by a crowd's (say) varying capacity for (at least) discrete euphoria when in the (must be) rarefied enunciation of the controlling substance, viz, poetry—which puts one in mind perhaps of Robert Duncan's "psychotic," soul-in-transit theory of poiesis. (See O'Leary for helpful discussion of Duncan's and others' gnostic ambitions, a creative effort that would conjugate "a language of illness" [*Gnostic Contagion*, p. xiii]).

And which austere view may account for Bruns's having extolled the L=A=N=G=U=A=G=E moment, for Charles Bernstein's early essay/interview (with Cris Cheek), "On Theatricality," ends with Bernstein arguing for a mode of performance, poetic and otherwise, that "is experienced more like a text," one amplifying (in the audience) "self-consciousness about the artifice" (p. 206; Brecht and Richard Foreman are offered as salutary examples, but Pirandello's "theater within the theater" would seem to loom large here as well). However, Bernstein is wary of performance art in its "'amateur and proud'" forms, with their correspondingly live or "'spontaneous'" audience overtures; hence he concludes by advocating "a theatre that resists theatricality"—which squares perfectly with his earlier remarks regarding poetry readings, his sense that "a sharp break is needed both from the shamanistic incantation of neoritualistic sound poetry and from the presentation of personality as a projected cohering force" (ibid., pp. 200, 205, and 207). It's only a small, if profound, step from these remarks on performance to the conjecture that a *community* predicated on something like self-consciously performative mediation would share, first and foremost, a *text*, or imagine its theatrical (i.e., *sans* theatrics) communion largely in such terms. But in light of Bernstein's emphasis on *awareness* (of artifice), Bruns's description of the response to similarly shared (poetry) texts in terms of *ekstasis* seems an almost ironic rendering of the self-conscious experience thus posited.

Now whether this riff on Bernstein speaks to Bruns's agenda, well—it speaks rather directly, at least, to the performative-phenomenological complex that Bruns evokes.

If Bruns's lead is instructive, then, it is likewise sporadically abstruse. And as I have in mind to pursue here my own extravagances, I must diverge from Bruns by observing, first, that in order for *any* community, however anarchic or "underground," to be communal—if by "communal" we mean having anything at all to do with community as this latter word applies to, or arises from, actual gatherings of writers—something more may be required than the mere registration of shared fascination by the attentively disembodied, those projected "outside of themselves" ("Poetic Communities," p. 4).[12] Perhaps because of my professional duties, I would like to think that the working knowledge of communities of *interested* parties—communities in which the broader social sphere is understood, however tacitly, as shaping the conditions for community in general—generally attends to Vico's learning principle, the *verum ipsum factum*, or "knowledge is equipollent to operation"; which is to say, knowledge is fully engendered not by passive reception, but by *doing*.[13]

Even the more avid among us have been bored shitless at readings—*be honest now!*—and poetry momentarily languishes, becoming little more than what Bierce skewered as that "form of expression peculiar to the Land beyond the Magazines" (*Devil's Dictionary*, p. 101). Sometimes background noise—*that cell phone in the third row, that screaming brat in the second*—drowns out vital inflections, and sometimes ambience is complementary. "The reader of poetry performs authorship," as Peter Middleton has it in the expansive essay that Bruns himself cites, and this holds whatever the performative particulars ("Contemporary," p. 268). But readings that tease out the *possibilities* of authorship are generally the preferred venues for writers of my ilk—and to admit as much is to foreclose on one kind of value, verily.

*

Still, part of what complicates any discussion of "poetic community" is that it's extraordinarily difficult to align the performative aspects of a poetry (or prose) reading with more popular performance venues. Of course theater itself is hardly awash in demotic aspirations alone. And the language of unconventional theater—from the basics of dismantling the proscenium (an "alienating effect"), to active interrogation of the spectacular (often through pointed *intensifications*), to establishing a critical and participatory distance (Artaud's Theater of Cruelty)—may prove difficult to apply to a poetry forum dedicated to unconventional practice and so often populated by amateur performers who are no less for that talented scribes.

Yet even amateur theatrics are theatrical, and commentators as diverse as Lester Bangs and Pauline Kael have been happy to acknowledge the legitimacy and use, for instance, of the trash aesthetic.[14] That is, there may be some pragmatic purchase in exploring alignments between unconventional poetic practice and the most *conventional* of theatricalities. One gets the rather distinct impression that Bruns would dismiss out of hand all media-energized mediations, from rock/pop concerts to the more confrontational solicitations of Russell Simmons's *Def Poetry Jam*. Yet there are dances of the intellect and there are dances, and (to swap discourses rather too enthusiastically) one need not be mad to effect or to suffer something like a Barthesian *punctum*.[15]

There are, to be sure, some specifically poetic circumstances that inform (perform?) the poetry reading. Since sound recordings rarely serve as a draw, and ever-circulating theories of performance aside, readers are never entirely certain how a poet has scored her text *for* performance; prior to performance, then, the text-as-score will coincide with a reader's silent reading habits—inner speech phenomena, say—or, alternately, with one's neighbors' tolerance for hearing one declaim.

Countless other factors contribute to that performance of authorship we call the poetry reading, factors having to do with the poet's person, his personality, or ethos, general appearance, reputation, punctuality; and with the venue itself—architecture, A/V services, and so forth. And the substantial sound archives currently under assembly at sites such as UbuWeb and PENNsound may be altering the soundscape for prospective listeners. But the little temporal drama played out while hearing a poet read-perform (hyphenated without apology), even a poet one has heard read-perform a half-dozen times, is generally one of attention to sonic/bodily/ambient presences alternating, or better, overlapping with attention to the formal attributes of the poetry.[16] One is not exactly listening for meaning at all times; rather, one often surfs the crests of meaning (a phenomenon most in evidence, in my view, when listening to expert speed performer and ace poet, Tom Raworth).

For most listeners of poetry, the customary absence of (melodic-harmonic) musicality heightens awareness of the words and their articulation, prolonging a singular listening experience that lacks the datum to which so many recording artists aspire (or from which they defiantly depart). Even technically inspired—and, with due regard for Stein's objection to "pure repetition," ostensibly repeatable—poetry performances are rarely greeted by their audiences as sing alongs. Their performative energy, precariousness, and live-wire instability emerge from the interplay between the aleatoric qualities of the speaking body—diction, certainly, but the gestural too in all of its culturally ramifying glory—and sound's sometime echo, sense (and nonsense). Thus the musical is rendered, as Zukofsky intuited, an upper limit of sorts, and one that poets would do well to maintain as such. Unless, that is, they're prepared to be greeted as experts in vocalization (as some are), or as singer-songwriters; in which event, they might listen carefully when Joni Mitchell discusses what she calls her "chords of inquiry," i.e., chords that ask questions (see *Joni Mitchell*; see note 14). It's clear, too, that some oral performance genres—hip-hop, dada-driven poetry—relieve or provoke listener anxieties primarily through sonic quality (rhythm, stuttering, etc.). Sense here becomes, in a sense, the gravy on the mashed potatoes.

In any case, even were we to accept Pater's dictum, *how* poetry might aspire to the condition of music is indeed a complicated affair. And the resistance of potatoes to their mashing might provide a clue, as well, as to the material resistance at stake in poetry readings. As Jed Rasula deftly elucidates (borrowing from Foucault's conception of the "raw being" of language in *The Order of Things*), "the subterranean rumble of language" might offset the regulatory signifying practices of the social order ("Understanding," p. 252). By "rumble," Rasula is denoting a specific (radical) aesthetic effect (pertaining to sound poetry in particular), one that can be voiced. I daresay you can hear this rumble to varying degrees in *every* poetry reading, if you listen closely. I daresay you can hear this rumble watching Peter Cook sign.

But to what extent can the poetry reading be understood as comprising, in effect, an industrial moment, a moment in and of our industrial (and postindustrial) culture? Short of embarking at this point on a history of the contemporary poetry reading—which group phenomenon is often imagined today, with some justification, as sanctuary from the edicts of the corporate (and technocratic)—perhaps we might simply observe that in posing this question, we are asking after the idea of community in an industrialized age. In which light we might ask, additionally, whether and to what extent community itself may be manufactured, or better, remanufactured?

*

Likewise one may question that which would permit one to speak without equivocation of the community of lovers. . . . Is it a question of the love (happy or unhappy) that forms a society within society and from which the latter receives its right to be known as legal or conjugal society? Or is it a movement that cannot abide any name—neither love nor desire—but that attracts the beings in order to throw them towards each other (two by two or more, collectively), according to their body or according to their heart and thought, by tearing them from ordinary society?
—Maurice Blanchot, The Unavowable Community

Thus far I have probably been arguing against a community that, as Blanchot puts it, "has as its ultimate goal the destruction of society" (*Unavowable*, p. 48). These may be matters of degree, but Bruns's understanding of "poetic communities" is clearly much closer to what Blanchot is struggling toward than what I am rather taking for granted in terms of (let's say) everyday motivations. And in fact I *was* playing it rather fast and loose a few pages prior in my thumbnail sketch, and critique, of Bruns's (thirty-eight-page) essay, an essay jam-packed with erudition, in order to tease out some core concerns. Standard critical practice, no? Bruns's essay may instead be approached, in all of its sweep, as a sophisticated interpolation of a lettristic and nuanced call-and-response, for Blanchot and Nancy are in effect responding to each other (see Bruns, "Poetic Communities," pp. 29–30n, on this point). And these three thinkers—Blanchot, Nancy, and Bruns—are themselves clearly united by their attention to the work of "The College of Sociology," a series of lectures organized by Georges Bataille, Roger Callois, Michel Leiris, and Pierre Klossowski, "whose purpose was to investigate the nature of such social structures as the army, religious orders, secret societies, brotherhoods, companies, salons," and the like, and which purpose would later include, thanks to Bataille, analysis of "the community of lovers and the artists' community" (ibid., p. 7).

We'll begin this time 'round with Bruns's gloss on Nancy, which comes near the beginning of his piece: "This ecstasy is what poetry communicates, not a vision or a revelation; the sharing of ecstasy rather than of mind or spirit, language or myth, is the essence of poetry and of the poetic community" (ibid., p. 3). The College of Sociology would have us treat such structural "essence" as a category of the sacred. But, as Bruns indicates, this has nothing to do with theology, for the sacred here is a "social concept" (ibid., p. 7). "Sacred communities," writes Bruns, "are not part of the productive economies of modern capitalist states; or rather, whatever function or goal might be assigned to them in the bourgeois order of things, they are defined by what Bataille calls 'nonproductive expenditures of energy [*depense*]'" (ibid., p. 7).[17] "A nonproductive expenditure of energy," Bruns continues—I provide a fuller excerpt this time 'round—"is one in which there is no return on investment. It is a gratuitous expenditure, absolutely outside any economy of exchange or use value. It is predicated upon a principle of loss rather than on the accumulation of capital. It belongs, if anywhere, to the economy of the gift" (ibid., p. 7).

Whereas Bruns has suggested, then, that such sacred communities may well have a "function or goal" in capitalist economy, by the time we get to "economy of gift" we've been given to understand that the related "expenditure" resides "absolutely outside" of such social functions, whether by fiat (the intrinsic nature of the "gift" itself) or choice (how we would prefer to view things) is not entirely clear. Bruns goes on to emphasize the following snippet from Bataille as "the thesis of modern poetry": "'poetic expenditure ceases to be symbolic in its consequences'" (ibid., p. 8).

This sets up the rationale by which Bruns argues for an avant-garde whose history belongs to that of the "anarchist group," and he settles upon "a minimalist event such as Cage's 4′33″" as most emblematic of those avant-garde efforts that are "accessible only through layers of social mediation" (ibid., p. 15; and minimalism seems so often to pass as the paradigmatic conceptual thrust among avant poets these days, no?). A community predicated on such language practices would be one attentive to "the conditions that make the work a possibility in the moment at hand" (ibid., p. 15). "In the avant-garde," Bruns writes, "the production of the work cannot be separated from the formation of the group, and vice versa" (ibid., p. 19). The notion that a social formation is the subsidiary work (but is it *work*?) of symbolic parsing buttresses Blanchot's concept of *desoeuvrement*—"worklessness" or "unworking" (ibid., pp. 14, 26)—leading Bruns to conclude that the avant artwork initiates what is predominantly an interactive theatrical event: "the work is folded into an event in which one is a participant and not simply a beholder, at least not a critical observer whose job is zoning and assessment" (ibid., p. 17). For Bruns, the "purse" of such performative events "is entirely exhausted by what takes place" (ibid., p. 17). Thus again we find, even in the case of Olsonian energy transfers (ibid., p. 12), that a poetic *desoeuvrement* or (again) "nonproductive expenditure" characterizes the *modus vivendi* associated with poetry happenings and get-togethers.[18]

And with this second (or third, or fourth) gloss on "nonproductive expenditure," the gist of my belabored scrutiny will, I hope, become evident: to my way of thinking, far too much emphasis has been placed of late on the more austere functions, if indeed they can yet be called functions, of conceptually informed art—its vaunted and inherent purposelessness or uselessness, its anti-utility—which itself has led, in some post-avant writing quarters, to undue valorizing of austere, even precious artwork and theories of art and, as I have suggested in my reading(s) of Bruns, all-too-insular appreciations of community. (Pardon me if I don't name names as far as the artwork goes. As for Bruns, his work is tough enough to stand up to substantive critique.)

There are equally problematic artworks and theories of art (and insular arts-based communities) circulating throughout popular culture—for instance, in my more curmudgeonly moments, I would voice skepticism as to the kind of cultural work performed by those gaming communities cropping up around the globe—but at least the art | commerce divide (or rather, lack of same) is generally foregrounded as such. We would seem to be caught, then, betwixt and between: on the one hand, an economic model of poetic production and associated community development [cough] entailing a "cultural field" that would make little room, as discussed in *Conclusion the 1st*, for theorizing career maneuvers, among so many other things (Rifkin); and on the other hand, an ecstatic intervention into the local that would make just about anyone feel small [ahem] who selected three or four of the A through Z motivations with which I opened this final movement. (Me, I selected eight.) The controversy here is not merely a matter of insisting on use value in the absence of exchange value. We can probably agree that poetry and its byproducts, community interaction chief among them, while not always or solely a gift, are not strictly speaking a matter of commodity exchange—like oil or pork bellies. But to situate poetry in "nonproductive" terms is to raise serious doubts as to its use value.

I suppose I *am* being too hard on my peers, and I certainly need to make good on my beef with Bruns. OK then: I need to show how an approach grounded in "nonproductive expenditure" may not be the best way to conceive of poetry or poetry community.[19] To put it another way, nonproductive expenditure may not constitute the best *magic* to employ in talking about (what I will now refer to as) rhetorical constructs such as "poetry" and "poetry community" (which constructs correspond, empirically, to actual social practices). Given the entrenchments in various arts quarters, the fact that poets and artists generally have so little to work with in the way of cold hard cash, and the difficulties associated with getting by with a little help from one's friends, well: it's not unthinkable that artists working under unremitting peer (and self- and market-imposed) pressure to produce their art *no matter what* might take solace in a variety of conceptual magic as a means of fostering community. And by "magic" I certainly don't mean hocus-pocus—I mean a shared conviction that such and so discursive or visual or aural practices are vital to art and its future, which conviction serves as a form of communal glue. Thus the magic I have in mind is, at one level, broadly rhetorical but not rhetoric alone, as I will discuss shortly.

First though: what kind of community tekhnē helps to bring us, apart, together?

*

As a representative USA con man, I offer a partial disclosure: if at times I'm beside myself at a poetry reading—and this doesn't happen often, mind you—it's likely that the poet and audience have managed, somehow, to dignify the occasion, or—to paraphrase a nice bit of thought by director Sydney Pollack—have managed to discover together a truth in the art experience that is true of all art experiences (no panic attack or theatrical absorption implied or intended).[20] It's an essence I'm after, I must confess, and if I can't say exactly what it is, I *can* say that I know it when I see it, or feel it. Such truths—commonplace human insinuations of joy, love, grief, loss, and so forth—have to do neither with the passionate impositions of groupthink nor with the ideological supersaturations of "community spirit." They inhere in an enduring virtue of migratory subjects, subjects who migrate to what they love: their willingness to be transported together, consensually if too infrequently, to the precincts of experience-for-happiness'-sake. Happiness of this sort permits for the freest of inquiry and constitutes an out-of-time temporality, a felt proximity to something of more than passing duration, a thing . . . eternal (and see *Conclusion the 2nd*). Now, "eternal" may not be the best word in light, for instance, of Blanchot's *le pas au-delà*—such a negation of the negation of time may suggest, more precisely, a time *out of* time—but I can offer this much with some certainty: if time flies while you're having fun, time in retrospect stood still when you had fun (see Blanchot, *The Step*, and Lycette Nelson's Introduction). Ergo, such happiness is founded on a transitory apprehension of the real—the really meaningful—and in all, it bespeaks an ordinary, if in our times less and less accessible (let alone evident) sense of *wonder*.

Hey, I've never suggested that there wasn't a downside to the outsourcing industrial, but insufficient attention to wonder may be, contrary to Luddite thought, more the fallout of sweeping epistemic change than of industrial revolutions as such.[21] I am in any case much taken by Hakim Bey's formulation: "Let us admit that we attended parties where for one brief night a republic of gratified desires was attained" (*T.A.Z.*, p. 134). I see (with Bey, I would think) a liberatory ethics at stake here, an ethics of liberation. And I would want to ask, do we have an *obligation* to pursue same? Because if so, we're back to a renewed sense of social responsibility, but this time with utter regard for the figure of the Other.

And this is about as close to *ekstasis* and its implicit negations as this poet gets.

And heck, I'm not even sure that "writing community" isn't something of an oxymoron, since, of late, too few of my poet-artist-friends would, alas, have me over for supper.

This predilection on my part for the true might comprise an incipient motoring toward some mutually felt sense of—some will say, despite my naysaying, Habermasian—community, but wait just a moment: if the enemy of your enemy is not necessarily your friend, the friend of your friend is not necessarily your friend, either. We don't all discriminate equally, and it is all too common to find that what draws people together, "two by two or more, collectively" (Blanchot), can prove to be precisely that which pulls them apart. I can attend a reading and register a favorable reaction—and we all register reactions of one sort or another, let's be honest—and meet *post facto* someone who feels similarly. And yet on a closer encounter still, that person might be at work on work that I find just . . . abysmal.

I'm sure you know what I'm talking about, you artists or scholars or engineers out there. Speaking as a poet, I would certainly admit that it's nice to make new poet-friends, but it's a whole lot easier when your prospective poet-friends are doing work that you (can) like. Check that: it becomes damn nigh impossible, over the long term, to hang out with poets whose work you find absolutely positively *bogus*. And this is quite apart from feeling sick and blunted with smiling, chatty poetry people.

How's that for a glitch in the community of (poetry) lovers?

But lest we become a tad too frivolous in bandying without definition a term as loaded as community: we need not be so fastidious as to stipulate, categorically, all of those attributes that social scientists might routinely apply to a discussion of community, but focusing on one such attribute might prove fruitful to our inquiry. Let us examine, then, a term that emerged during the early sixties and has to my knowledge caught on in literary studies only in the past two or so decades: *dissensus*.[22] Here I would turn to the work of Bill Readings, who has himself followed the lead of Nancy and Blanchot (and Agamben) to propose, as a matter of academic praxis, a "community of dissensus." "Our obligation," writes Readings, "is to explore our obligations without believing that we will come to the end of them" (*University*, p. 190). For Readings, "the community of dissensus that would propose nothing in common" would, as well, "have to be understood on the model of *dependency* rather than emancipation" (ibid., p. 190; emphasis in original). Readings maintains, rightly I think, that we are "addicted to others," and since "there is no freeing ourselves from the sense of the social bond," we will likewise never "emancipate ourselves from our dependency on others" (ibid., p. 190). "The thought of community that abandons either expressive identity"—you creative writers out there, listen up!—"or transactional consensus as a means to unity"—ditto you department chairs!—"seems to me to refer to what the posthistorical University may be" (ibid., p. 192).

I sympathize with Readings's desire to put aside any notion of autonomy or "emancipation" from others on the basis of our inexorable primate addictions, and I am impressed by the meta-deontological platform he would have us follow, our obligation to "explore" obligation itself (which, stated in such terms, would seem to partake of a Kantian premise, despite Readings's avowed departure from Kant's *concordia discors*; ibid., p. 191). I am struck too by the leverage Readings's ideal (let's say) community might have in pulling us toward "ethical probity," as opposed to what, only paragraphs above, I described as an ethics of *liberation* (ibid., p. 192).[23] But I am left wondering whether this idea that we share "nothing in common" doesn't amount to too weak a heuristic gesture, finally, one lacking the teeth we need to chomp through the stubbornly commonplace material realities that greet us on our way to our workplaces, whether shop or workshop.[24]

Isn't it possible that we might fare better in our engagement with the common, including the public commons, by running right at it? (This is a lesson I [think I] learned from watching the old NFL rivalries.) Communities of writers, for instance and among other things, *write*. What does it mean, then, to be so preoccupied with the alphabet? How do we speak of the *common* when we live in a world, as Pierre Joris observes, "where accident is rule" ("one moment," p. 54, l. 15)?

Hmm. Looks like we need us one more detour before we can get us back to magic. Sorry about this . . .

*

In his "unapologetic modernist essay," *The Poetics of the Common Knowledge*, Don Byrd has launched a sustained attack, from the standpoint of a poetic practice wedded to philosophical inquiry (and vice versa), on what he regards in sum as the foundational (Western) "epistemological pathology" (ibid., p. 15)—viz., the West's obsession with epistemological abstraction. Byrd's opposing concept of the "common knowledge" has nothing to do with "common sense," or what Byrd calls "the lore of compromise" that sustains cultural mythologies (ibid., p. 23). "*The common knowledge*," he writes, "*might be properly contrasted with disciplined knowledge*" (ibid., p. 23; emphasis in original); such knowledge emerges "only when contingent beings come into contingent relationship" (ibid., p. 23). Byrd is keenly aware of the challenges that arise in positing such contingent knowledge in a world chock-full of pre- and overdetermining mediations. "In order to constitute an effective community rather than a symbolic machine for social production," he writes, "organized beings must orient themselves in their mediascapes" (ibid., p. 23). No longer resembling Information-Age signal transmission, then, knowledge in such a community thus becomes "the condition of action that permeates the space of the community" (ibid., pp. 23–24). This is the knowledge that "makes speaking possible," a knowledge "perpetually made manifest in the acts of creation" (ibid., p. 24). Take poetry, for (prime) example.[25]

And it is upon such a "common knowledge" that Byrd finds his way to an alternative grasp of human temporality itself:

> A describing system may include itself in its descriptions of the world—that is, take its own activity as the background for itself. As soon as one does, however, the event, a thing that has reference only to itself, is transformed into an example. . . . The background may be more or less extensively articulated as a cosmic schema, a Weltanschauung, an archetype, a paradigm, a history, a society, a natural or artificial language, an aesthetic canon, or an electronic circuit. When an important background suddenly appears, it is a sun burst, illuminating the features of a New World—or what *seems* to be a new world because each event becomes an *example* of an entire world. . . . Now we know that we cannot bring reason to the world, not because our reason is weak but because the world is not that kind of place. We must welcome the fragmentation, not because a new sunburst awaits us but because, legitimately, we should never have hoped for knowledge as more than a way to "get by" with a little grace. (ibid., p. 383; emphasis in original)

For Byrd, even words "are not *examples* of words." "The design we cut in time," Byrd continues, "we cut once and once only" (ibid., p. 384). And this has implications not only for our ecologies of mind, but for our inhabited environments (ibid., p. 338). For finding our ways (back?) home.[26]

So: Are Byrd's finely tuned conclusions a matter simply of reason reasoning its way toward a form of faith, a faith in practical particulars as against the power of abstraction? Is Byrd's book appropriately shelved, not under "literary criticism" but under theology? What to do with bardic thinkers like Don Byrd, or indeed with the quasi-religious, if not outright doctrinal, convictions of so many poets identified with the Black Mountain and the San Francisco Renaissance schools? How do we negotiate (if that's the proper word) the mélange of convictions—about love, life, liberty, and the pursuit of happiness—that our bardic minions would force upon us? In particular, how do we square Byrd's singular take on earthly singularities with something as variously received, yet as vital, as community?

*

Presto! Back to magic, whose office may be understood in this context as that of resisting, affirmatively, instrumented reason (*mea culpa*), and may well be the only surefire means of doing so. Building on the work of Daniel Lawrence O'Keefe, William A. Covino has argued that "magic is not the instant and arhetorical product of an otherworldy incantation: it is the process of inducing belief and creating community with reference to the dynamics of the rhetorical situation." (I cite from the electronic version of Covino's essay, "Magic and/As Rhetoric.") For Covino, magic has all to do with discursive power, and he illustrates how the new "mechanical" and increasingly scientific cosmologies of the Enlightenment—the originary locus of Byrd's "epistemological pathology" and the historical bugbear for so many Continental theorists—displace both "classical conceptions of rhetoric" as well as "occult symbolism." Whereas the rhetor of old was attentive "to the Greek doctrine of logos as magic," the Enlightenment rhetor is a "technician fixed on clarity and precision, for whom words are lifeless"—anything, that is, but a technician of the sacred. As Covino has it, even "the Romantic effort to reconstitute magic/rhetoric in the Western imagination" is itself undone by "what De Quincey recognized as the sterile and non-magical rhetoric of 'public business,' with its reliance on 'external facts, tangible realities, and circumstantial details'"; ultimately, this produces "an ostensibly non-magical 'plain rhetoric'" that informs "discourse prepared for mass consumption."

"What is at issue then," Covino writes, "is not whether rhetoric is magic, but what kinds of magic/rhetoric produce what kinds of effects." He goes on to discuss in brief how Mary Daly's *Wickedary* comprises one way to counter the "sorcery" of commercial and authoritarian discourses. "Magic rhetoric" and its counterpart, "magical consciousness," augur a more "participatory, exploratory, generative" social discourse. To understand rhetoric in such terms is to motion the collective toward an "open source" rhetoric, and while the magical thus seems clearly preferable to the plain vanilla versions, this leaves open the question of what kinds of magics are likely to be used to unsavory ends (but see notes 7 and 21, above, for some ideas).

I'm sure it's not lost on my readers that Covino has provided an intriguing way to think about that species of magic that mad bards presumably wield (*Conclusion the 3rd*). Interestingly, Covino seems much drawn to George Kennedy's conception of rhetorical practices as a form of energy—

"the *energy* that attends communication" (Covino, "Rhetorical," p. 47, and see his *Magic, Rhetoric, and Literacy*), perhaps because Kennedy too views magic as "one of the first rhetorical genres to emerge" (*Comparative*, p. 40). As Covino indicates parenthetically, rhetoric-as-energy "is part of a larger argument that rhetoric is inherent in the natural world" ("Rhetorical," pp. 47–48). Kennedy finds energy at work in the entire circuit of rhetorical give-and-take: "the emotional energy that impels the speaker to speak, the physical energy expended in the utterance, the energy level coded in the message, and the energy experienced by the recipient in decoding the message" (ibid., p. 48; see also Kennedy, "A Hoot").

Full stop.

With this nod toward physical-rhetorical "energy," and in light of Bataille's "nonproductive expenditures of energy," it would seem that "energy" has become something of a key word in these proceedings. It's a word that brings us, in a roundabout way, back to Byrd's example (if we can yet call it an example). Consider first that, as a poet, Byrd is speaking not only on behalf of poets, but on behalf of the poetic function—in which, to be egalitarian about it, all of us participate to some degree. On behalf of poetry, then.

And it is on behalf of poetry that I would like to ask, in the spirit of co-workmanship: what is the alchemy to which Byrd, or—with due respect for associated discrepancies of thought—Bruns, or Blanchot, or Bataille would have us subscribe?

On the one hand, in light of Byrd's advocacy and demonstration of the nonrepeatable and contingent nature of the world we inhabit, one might summarize his (hypo)thesis with a (1969) lyric courtesy of Jay and The Americans: "This magic moment/So different and so new"—so different and so new, that is, right alongside this next magic moment. And this next. And so on.[27] Byrd's is an extrapolation from, refinement of, and rationale for a new performance model (or vision) articulated most succinctly by Jerome Rothenberg in 1977: "The response-as-creation thus supersedes the response-as-criticism, just as the maker/particularizer comes to be viewed (or to view himself) as the superior of the interpreter/generalizer. It is this which Charles Olson had in mind when he saw us emerging from a 'generalizing time,' etc., to regain a sense of the poem 'as the act of the instant . . . not the act of thought about the instant'" ("New Models," p. 643). Rothenberg regards "an exploration of the boundaries of the mind" (he cites Snyder and Duchamp) as marking an alternative "area of performance" in which "extended time techniques toward actual transformations (of the self, of consciousness, etc.) parallels that of traditional meditation (*mantra, yantra*, in the Tantric context)" (ibid., p. 644). We see echoes here of

Heller's disquisition on poetics (see Track 1); perhaps of Bruns's performance-based poetic communities; perhaps even of Blanchot's unavowably "elective" community, insofar as the latter would seemingly forgo social hierarchies and spreadsheets in favor of what Rothenberg calls, with regard to the poet or artist, "the right to self-definition" (ibid., p. 644). In the works and days of poets and writers, "the right to self-definition" has often been a matter of prying open the relationship between words and things to expose, and expand, the horizon of definition, of the descriptive as well as the prescriptive functions.[28] But perhaps most importantly, we get a glimpse here too of the foundational impulse requisite to a poetic practice having the shamanistic muster to resist the dictates of unbridled reason. Magic (theorized as above) mobilizes human and social energies to *manufacture* time-sensitive alterations in behavior and feeling.[29]

My use of *manufacture* is no accident. The word has gotten a bad rap among humanities intelligentsia, and for some very good reasons. I certainly wouldn't wish to push the factory analogy too far, not least because, after seven years in factories, I'm no fan of factory "life" in its current manifestations. But factories are, after all, places where some important things happen, manufacturing chief among them. In factories, one set of material things is converted into another set of material things via human labor and machine action. In some cases, the material things that are manufactured in factories are conspicuously inessential, sure, but in many cases they're absolutely essential to social life as we've come to know it. In go raw materials, out come air conditioners (and air-conditioned nightmares). Just like magic—only there's sweat involved, of course, and wear and tear, and the threat of outsourcing, and the exaltation of silly organizational algorithms, and a welter of acronyms (not unlike the welter of citations with which I manufacture these rangy conclusions).

Factory life is life directed to reducing variability in end product—with the preordained aim, today, of boosting profits *no matter what*—and such (manufactured, yes) objectives may result in QCEL-type managerial mystifications, as we have seen; whereas social beings generally strive to incorporate into their daily and weekly off-the-job activites a more open response to contingencies of one sort or another. When it comes to bread and butter issues, you do what you gotta do. Still, the industry of our actions is no less for that committed to producing quality of life (no apologies for the buzzword), and this means, among other things, that we seek in our experiences with one another some counterpoint to a contingent planet; thus would we preserve an elemental proportion of the routine, the stable, the reliable, the time- and road-tested. (Eliot's "still point" is much less repressive seen in this light than as poetic first, or last, principle.)

We just don't like it when our friends don't call.

Community is when your friends call. When they make an effort. When they keep a close eye on the industry of their ways not least because they're looking out for *you*. Not to make too much of it, but: you work 8 to 5 with someone for five or ten years helping to manufacture something that people want or need, you really do get to know what makes your coworker tick. And if, out of a felt kinship, a number of coworkers build upon such daily familiarities to see each other off-the-job on a regular basis, why then they've got something approaching on- and off-the-job community. A labor union, even. Just like magic, only—

Community can be manufactured, then, under the auspices of manufacturing, whether widgets or poetry; it can also be decimated under such auspices (see *Roger & Me* and the perennial poetry wars, respectively). But more importantly, it may be no coincidence that in manufacturing things together, we learn what togetherness means. Might we divine, then, in the designation *Homo faber* the rational creature's collaboratively cosmic reckoning? Could it be that meaningful making, from steeple to song to colander, inspires us to look past our inviolable solitudes? That solitary souls—and I presume only that "soul" points to *something* palpable, if numinously so—may be as difficult to bring into happy union with one another as some elements of the periodic table itself suggests that making things happen together, courtesy of industrial magic, can but jump-start the magic bus.

The rest is work and play, play and work, night and day and day and night and sleep. Tired eyes, and limbs, and backs. And sleep. Sleep.

It may well be, too, that magic (as above) is the ostensibly mysterious substrate at work in the production of Raymond Williams's "structures of feeling." And it's probably a factor, to varying degrees, in the substance of things hoped for—in all formations of faith, all varieties of religious experience (James)—to the extent that the faithful are granted sufficient noetic agency and energy to enjoy (again) the participatory, exploratory, and generative aspects of associated rhetorical and spiritual practice (and admittedly, so many religious communities are simply not prone to offering this kind of intellectual-emotional freedom).[30] Magic (as above) summons us, then, to contribute to the discursive slop, requiring on the part of its practitioners only a willingness to fall away from the harsher edicts of ratiocination; if we're willing, magic (as above) can serve as an antidote to the dictates of common sense, received wisdom, the doctrinal. Magic (as above) can allay the inhumanly analytical, the remorselessly principled, the dumbly instrumental, permitting reason its fair share, but not the entire share, of input into our ceaselessly remanufactured, energy-intensive environs; and generating a reasonable discourse in the process, a discourse attentive to local, seasonal variations. As Rothenberg and Joris put it in their concise "commentary" on the work of Blake: "And it's Blake who turns transmitted Wisdom on its head, working out a poetics of oppositions, a new dialectic in which energy (= 'desire') can have a central place alongside 'reason'" ("Commentary," p. 24).

*

As an engineer at heart, if not *of* the heart, I am drawn (if I may) to construction projects of the soul (as above); hence I feel compelled to ask how we might best go about "building community," elective or industrial or otherwise, with such magics at our disposal. If building is construed as a form of labor, of work, of activity; and if activity of any sort—productive, hyperproductive, linguistic, interpersonal—constitutes, in quantitative terms, an energy expenditure; then we would likely want to worry the nature of the community production that results.[31] Clearly, recourse to magical energy does not come without associated costs: one must give of one's time and attention, one's biological and cerebral *energies,* and communities must give of materials and facilities and collective time, in order for a simple poetry reading to take place.

In light of which, Bruns's decision to center his community deliberations on the performative seems prescient. As Steve McCaffery observes in his brilliant elaboration of what he calls "paleotechnic sound poetry," the "complex machinic assemblage generating performances" may be construed as a "community-in-process . . . constantly positioned in that double estrangement between a signifying social organic called 'the group'" and "a performed expenditure by numerous bodies in occasion—in performance 'without organs'" ("Voice," p. 169). With and without organs (i.e., with and without Deleuze and Guattari's prompt), such expenditures suggest that "the paleotechnic poem was conceived as a communal performance at the outset" (ibid., p. 170). It may well be that, as McCaffery suggests, this energy-based "performance of expenditure" capitulated ultimately to Debord's "spectacular society"; or it might comprise instead a "failed radicality of the subject" (ibid., p. 171). McCaffery himself elects to locate in this "extreme mission" for (vocalic) poetry an ineluctable modicum of resistance to "capitalistic embodiments" of speech, a resistance that exploits sound-silence collusions (ibid., p. 172). I would imagine that similar collusions extend, latently and to varying degrees, to all performative community wagers, to all such magics.

In all, we might understand magical energies as facilitating the *quid pro quo* of a dynamic social process that consumes (variously renewable) resources of time and material. We each receive, among other things, some quotient of faith—in poetry, its corresponding communities and community actions—in return for what we've put "into" poetry, together and singly. And if, as I have suggested, magic (as above) might be one path to an alternative and participatory conception of spirituality, "community spirit" may be nothing more, and nothing less, than those collective material and spiritual energies circulating throughout a community and dedicated to preserving space and time for free communal inquiry. It takes more than a village, and more than mere didactics (although see note 33, below).

Further, my hunch in fact is that such poetic evocations of community, or evocations of poetic community, rely on an *apparent* communal-semantic surplus, a kind of surplus value, emanating from symbolic action.[32] I type

The magic of poetry

and my readers (provided I still *have* any), from outside reader to editor to copy editor to blurb-er to John Q (in print and, if I'm lucky, during a public reading), are forced to negotiate what I mean by these words. Like magic!—though we should bear in mind that all manner of material transaction has to take place in order to get these words "across." *The magic of poetry*, then, enables productive, unproductive, *and* nonproductive energy transfers associated with cultural, spiritual, and emotional *work*. Poetry works its magic despite the many trade-offs—to which, for instance, my postal bills may attest—that accompany the I-give-I-give of publishing, of going public; or in more ideational terms, poetry works its magic whatever the banter and barter and bickering that accompanies community events, which corresponding transactional activities eat up so many carbs (if not as many as some of us might wish). While there may be little or no modification of community value(s) during a poetry reading, for instance (it depends on the reading), such events routinely become an active part of communal memory.

"I guess you had to be there."

I wrote "apparent" surplus, above, in order to be sure to give conservation of nonnuclear matter and energy its due. If there are (energy and other) costs associated with such language "surpluses," my point is they seem at times to "cost" us virtually *nothing*. And that they seem so comprises but one aspect of their magical aura, however difficult it may be in actuality to speak of symbolic energies in thermodynamic, zero-sum terms. Then again, though—and not to be too awful Marxist about it, but—it's all real *labor*.

*

The subsumption of so many activities under the rubric of magic, or magical work, much like my industrialized retooling (or appropriation) of such terms, presupposes the belief that there are, in a word, *consequences* at stake in our word-actions, our productions, our accretions and indiscretions. Readings, book signings, gatherings, and the like are, like so many consequential things, *valued*, and value is assigned accordingly, good and bad and in-between (see note 31, above). Such activities can exhibit customarily formal profiles—"Would you review my book for me?" (Would you?)—or can be highly informal. Regardless of the accidents or machinations attending thereto, though, (re)valuations of this sort are not simply informational—they can and do result in rumor, gossip, and mild exercises in internecine warfare, both *inter vivos* and courtesy of more remote mediations. "Art/aesthetics is one of the carriers of both secrecy and difficulty," wrote the late Fehta Murghana, "and of course conspiracy theory/rumor as its correlate in the body politic. (Virtual computer space and paralogical space—the space of poiesis—'public' secrets)" ("Puncture," p. L). Poetry communities are open to what magicians call "misdirection": they intuit the potential, and potentially disruptive, energies of deception and play, the capacity of the ludic for accessing, if not enabling, what Cassirer calls "the mythic mode" of language, a "substantive being and power," which "Word Magic"—a "hypostatization" of language, to be sure—Cassirer identifies as the "first form" in giving language its "fundamental function in the construction and development of spiritual reality" (*Language*, p. 62).

While Cassirer is chiefly interested in expositing on the (gradational, global) development of spiritual thought, his remarks suggest that the mythic residue of language must at least condition the communal glue. "For it is language that makes his existence in a *community* possible," observes Cassirer of the social animal (ibid., p. 61; emphasis in original). Whereas "logical reflection tends . . . to resolve all receptivity into spontaneity, mythic conception shows exactly the opposite tendency, namely, to regard all spontaneous action as receptive, and all human achievement as something merely bestowed" (ibid., p. 60). Cassirer's language may be too anthropologically assertive for the contemporary thinker, but apropos of his observation, any number of gift-driven and "given"-driven poetic formulations, my own included, would thus appear to harken to the mythical-magical mode. It is not my intention to collapse distinctions between Cassirer's "myth" and magical rhetoric; neither do I envision artistic communities as phalansteries whose childlike members fall prostrate at the mere sight of top hat and wand (although I find myself yearning at times for a little prestidigitation). It's clear, however, that if rhetorical magic itself has any sway over us, it may be owing to the baggage that comes along with our language practices, and in particular, the archaic "physico-magical power" with which we once endowed the word (ibid., p. 61). Power is everywhere at stake in such disseminations. But if, with our words, we cast spells on one another, shouldn't we wish, as well, to *break* such spells?

Sometimes. Doubtless we can't, always, for words cast a spell on *us*. Our words may capture our encrypted judgments and "interprofessional" desires, but language is less about codes and coding, digital and communications rhetorics notwithstanding, than about McLuhan's mediated "massage" or Lorca's *duende*, the magic formulae (see Ayto for the etymology of "spell") by which we workers negotiate value, by which we reconfigure community energies in our pursuit of art and its mysteries, conflicted beings though we are even about our own feelings and perceptions. An industrial poetics foregrounds the instrumentalized conditions that underwrite such reconfigurations of selves and others, but not without offering homage to the associated energetic, synesthetic, and performative possibilities of such magical processes.

Or such would be the community fiction I would foist upon my peers. It would be a mistake, surely, to propose a hard-and-fast, value-added lineage as the regulating *telos* of community transformation. At the risk of stating the obvious: the reckless if calculated pursuit of enhanced product, and increased profit, that characterizes globalization—the built-in fad-ability of a "better" hamburger, a "better" novel, a "better" employee, a "better" teacher, a "better" student, a "better" citizen, a "better" hex sign, a better mousetrap—points to a professional-managerial demographic that would preserve little public space or time for the brash, often oracular provocations of art.[33] So a plea, I suppose, this attempt to limn the communitarian workplace, a workplace knee-deep in intellective labor, its products manufactured without apology, its raw materials worked and reworked by hand, by machine, by hymn. In my view, our hyperproductive combines in particular (see *Conclusion the 1st*) ought to pay (note: *pay*) attention here—says a teacher who would himself hazard the didactic to teach other teachers, those most in need of instruction: a small alphabetic measure may be all that is needed, in principle, to catalyze a rather startling, even lasting poetic effect in texts and in people.

My would-be exorcisms aside, there persists a mystery at work in poetry, finally, a mystery in what brings its makers to it, and a mystery in what permits its recipients, each of us, to carry it away, making it our own through our finite comings and goings. It is this mystery that comprises a truly radical practice, a practice rooted, as are we each, in the turning Earth, which "gives such divine materials to men, and accepts such leavings from them at last" (Whitman "This Compost," p. 370, l. 47). For the sake of a humane and ecological poetic practice, but also for the sake of a practice that can move us, together, beyond the tried and true, we would do well to acknowledge fully the industrial and industrious energies at work in this common and communal and ever-useful mystery. Not only on behalf of poets, but on behalf of the poetic function. On behalf of poetry, then.

"I have nothing at all to say. But I wanted to say it anyway." Fellini's sublimely absurd gesture in *8 1/2* reminds us that most art haunts the peripheries of the orthodox, the administrative, the organizationally competent. If this has nothing to do with an aversion to thought or theory or intellectual work or even technique, neither does it suggest a reluctance to say what needs saying, even under the pretense that "nothing" need be said. Industrial mojo bids us stay tuned and attuned to the present moment, *this* moment in and of form, somewhat at the expense of so much that has come before, and may come after. Communities of poets and artists do what they can with the storehouse, the library, the archive, the authorized versions—this much they must do—but their overriding aim is to contribute, whether through makeshift make-believe or mundane magic, to the buzz under the big top.

And ain't we got fun?

*

Industrial Magic Lite © 2007
A New-Old Project for the 21st century™
(Batteries Not Included)
SOME ASSEMBLY REQUIRED

Notes

Track 1

1. As a practical matter, engineers treat their designs as if communicative transparency were the objective. Symbols are regularly viewed as opening a window onto the world of things, and the aim is generally to ensure merely that the window is clean. Of course, to thus shortchange the life of symbols has potentially dire consequences for a society or an institution governed by "technology-driven" management practices. "Nothing in the world, however, guarantees the assumption that the force of sentiment and the clarity of logic can be harnessed, that communicative transparency is possible," Bill Readings has observed (*University*, p. 183). For Readings, the presiding claim of culture is that "it can provide such a guarantee in that it is both the *object* of communication (what is communicated) and the *process* of communication (something that is produced in communicative interaction)" (ibid., p. 183). Culture presents itself, in Readings's view, both as "*Wissenschaft* (what we talk about) and *Bildung* (the very act of our talking together)" (ibid., p. 183); hence engineering culture (and community) might be seen as amplifying this ur-cultural gesture by resisting the implications of mediation. With every blueprint for a (re)design, engineers transmit to one another a *prêt-à-projeter* world. An awareness that knowledge is situated, and mediated, and that all knowledge claims reinforce discursive limits—marking out the domain of what can, and can't, be said or known—might serve to offset the cultural impositions of communicative transparency. But are such limits, properly speaking and all told, epistemological, or does the notion of limits as such have ultimately to do with the terrain of the human, the anthropological shorn of its disciplinary mediations? Is there a human limit to human limits, and if there is, how might we talk about such a limit without risking all manner of mystification? See also Track 3, *Conclusion the 4th*.

2. Petroski discusses Joyce's *Ulysses* and *Finnegan's Wake* in terms of "the process of successive revision," which is likewise, as he has it, "the successive elimination of faults and error," and common both to writing and engineering (*To Engineer*, p. 79; see his chapter, "Design as Revision," pp. 75–84). While Petroski acknowledges that "the analogy between books and engineering structures" is not "perfect," he gives short shrift to those highly disparate contingencies of literary value at work in deciding which (canonical) works have "stood the test of time" (ibid., p. 70). His chief concession in this regard is that "the failure of a book may be arguable whereas the failure of a building collapsed into a heap of rubble is not" (ibid., p. 70). Arguable indeed! As Christian Moraru observes in

developing his concept of "narrative rewriting," *Ulysses* may represent, "in effect, the stumbling block of any effort to sift out modern from postmodern forms of renarrativization" (*Rewriting*, p. 23). And that's just for starters. *Ulysses* has "stood the test of time" due to all manner of institutional shenanigans, certainly—not least among which, the special dispensations of the New Critics—yet it remains a successful novel for so many of us, if not for Dale Peck and his brood. The book would seem thus to embody a collapse of the familiar success-failure binary by presenting us with a *de facto* literary success that is peppered throughout with willful communicative failures of one sort or another—aporias, lacunae, the nonsensical, etc. I must confess to having only recently gotten through *Ulysses*, if not entirely "gotten" it; and much of what I did manage to "get" was owing largely to *The New Bloomsday Book*. But if I was at times frustrated by Joyce's lexical conceits (yes) and exhausted by the text's semantic supersaturations (yes), I nonetheless enjoyed the ride, the heady immersion in sense and sound. In fact a chief "failure" of such late Modernist works, at least for today's literate set, may reside in their apparent disregard for our expectations—a disregard for what we are able to ask of them, a disregard for what we can *imagine* ourselves asking of them.

3. I'm all for renovating corporate charters, redirecting obscene profits into public works projects, renewing federal oversight of infrastructure repair and upgrade (the U.S. railroad system, for instance) and, while we're at it, instituting new, comprehensive environmental programs. But if you think the book you're holding in your hands is *not* part and parcel of the industrial-manufacturing private sector (including the publishing industry), you must be banking on a free print run. The problem for the industrial sector today may be summed up in a handful of statistics: of the top ten U.S. employers in 2004, half are low-wage retailers, with Wal-Mart and McDonald's leading the way. And it's in the largest companies where deunionization is occurring fastest (see Labor Research Association). So while "the Democratic Party of the machine age" (Bai, "Wiring," p. 35) may be dead in the gray water, as Matt Bai reports, those entrepreneurial "progressives" and left-wing philanthropists who hope to mount an alternative to the old party machine had better think, and think hard, about restoring the relationship between making things and making happiness, a challenge that industrial-age thinkers and workers have been caught up in for decades now.

4. I.e., will not block the ducts of your sebaceous glands. Has nothing whatever to do with funny bones.

5. My use of "poem-event" is itself hardly original; it relies on the pathbreaking work of Gerald L. Bruns, who advised long ago that "poetics [must] seek not only to explain how poetry is made but also how its design is fulfilled by the presence

of the world." For Bruns "the poem must be understood both as structure and as event... both object and utterance, both a thing made and a thing spoken" (*Modern Poetry*, p. 262). My (perhaps nontrivial) amendment to Bruns's both/and imperatives can be grasped immediately by asking, *Understood by whom?* The generative (uttered) and symptomatic (structured) aspects of poetic production owe much to the often-antagonistic institutional sites of uttering and structuring. Mallarmé could perhaps theorize the "presence of the world" in poetry without troubling institutional presence. Alas, my sense is that we have no such luxury today, unless we are willing simply to ignore how the vast landscape of design that greets us each waking instant "fulfills," inexorably, the design of the poem. I will have occasion in Track 3 to consider the limitations of Bruns's more recent poem-bound formulation of "poetic" community, but for now let me just say that I could not have advanced (?) to this point in the absence of Bruns's astute solicitations (see Bruns, *Modern Poets*).

6. See Amato and Fleisher, "Reforming."

7. The Situationists were after something like this in regarding poetry as an occasion for revolution, and not the other way around (see Debord et al., "All," p. 418). One objective in doing so was to safeguard the contingent nature of the creative act against programmatic and potentially alienating agenda. The U.S. highway system, the interstate branches of which have so often facilitated my zigzagging across the lower forty-eight, may itself be a metastatic exemplar of such programmatic agenda when understood as a material network by which the nation-state regulates the dispersal of migrating subjects and subjectivities. *Rhizomes* 8, "Retro-Futures," features two articles of special relevance: see Kuswa for a theory-rich romp through the "machinic rhetoric" associated with this exceptionalist labyrinth of asphalt and concrete, and its consequent "body-as-accident"; and see Burgess for a concise history of the Interstate system, including a discussion of its more sinister realities (environmental damage, civic disruption, loss of human and animal life) as fallout from what J. G. Ballard termed "Autogeddon." Clearly the highway has served as the travel paradigm for my figural motions in this track, but moving at this speed, I'm emboldened to make a bid for unalienated agency.

8. Contrary to appearances, then, there is no conservation of advanced knowledge (which can be created and destroyed). Knowledge-bodies vetted out of the KIA system, once returned to the respective owner-operator, may be retrofitted for resubmission (typically this requires a new Modulating Emission Armature [MEA]); alternately, they may be scrapped. As an individuated, if not individualized, system in its own right, the owner-operator can, if so equipped, utilize Poetry Overpressure Protection (POP), which under certain conditions may

also be used for Peer Pressure Protection (PPP). As to the question of dizzy (aka giddy) form: Gerhard Richter has rather painlessly, and a wee bit facetiously, described *form* in the following terms: "My approach to form is very simple. Whatever is real is so unlimited and unshaped that we have to summarize it. The more dramatic events are, the more important the form. That is why people marry in a church and why we need a priest for a funeral" ("A Picture," p. 26). Dizzy knowledge and form may be understood, then, as a dramatic response to a vertiginous real.

9. Or everybody's autobiographical (some would say confessional) criticism, especially criticism in which critical agency exudes the very conditions that deny such agency its unmediated access to selfhood (to gloss a fine bit of thought by Charles Altieri). Perhaps, as David Simpson argues, a bourgeois "conversational ideal" haunts our every academic attempt to talk turkey—i.e., we literary scholars cannot quite overcome the feeling that, like research scientists and technicians, we too are specialists, members of an elite; hence we presumably resort to anecdote and the like in an attempt to give a more commonplace sheen to our highly professionalized chatter. I trust it's not lost on my readers, appearances to the contrary (and witness my titular "Chautauqua"), that I have zero intention of "modeling" a discourse for future, what, fan edits? I am perfectly aware that I am dancing among a variety of different discursive, even esoteric codes—codeswitching, as it were—in order see what might be teased out in the way of conceptual openings and closings. It's a gambit. There are other ways to proceed, to be sure, other performative approaches or techniques that may be even more impervious to the po-faced forces of instrumental reason.

In particular, Charles Olson's refreshingly blunt, clipped patois raises implicitly the question of representational, and ideational, seamlessness. With regard to which, the word *elegant* has an established public valence in this latter rhetorical regard (though the word is rarely used to describe the U.S. public domain *in toto*, with its oratorical frills and incessant jibber-jabber). As Ayto remarks, "elegant" might initially have denoted fussiness and the like, but it's become the book reviewer's fallback locution for lampooning, by contradistinction, the clunky, the mechanistically contrived, the routinely serviceable, the (pardon me) *flatulent*. "Successful" poetry and fiction are generally held to have aspired to the polished, the refined, the sophisticated, the beautiful. Splendid even. Or elegant, as Edward R. Tufte might say of visually enhanced displays of information.

Which is fine as far as it goes. But ambitious artworks may or may not be inelegant in refusing to succumb to rigid formulae or guidelines. I have of late settled upon *ambitious*, in fact, as my preferred tag for describing the difficult writing, produced by more *and* less ambitious writers, of which I've grown fond; the word *ambition* itself, as Ayto indicates, is derived from *ambire*—or "go round"—but came nominally to mean "seeking favor or honor" (or votes), hence it seems a capacious enough term to capture the range of pertinent motivational logics. Even the post-avant curries favor. While they work against the public appetite for instant-satisfaction froth—which appetite itself is a matter of some social engineering, and may signal ever-more-frivolous apprehensions of belief and disbelief—ambitious artworks often appear to the uninitiated as partial or "experimental" gestures. But the art of juxtaposition, just for instance, while surely benefiting from improvisational (and contextual) synergies, is no less for that shot through with premeditation.

Choke me in the shallow water/before I get too deep. And *ambitious* suddenly seems a mouthful—maybe I should simply have used, in this context, "drive"? To bring this rambling superscript appendage to a close: oddly or appropriately enough, "elegant" comes to us from the Latin *elegans*, a derivative of *eligere* (pick out, select), which in fact ties it to the verb "elect," hence with collect, eligible, elite, lecture, legible, neglect, select—all of which operate in the margins and at the center of these decidedly ragged, raggedly dysfunctional, stop and go tonal proceedings.

10. Jed Rasula's regenerative effort in *This Compost: Ecological Imperatives in American Poetry* is at once so broad and so deep as to give even this industrial "wreader" (I can only hope) pause. But the foundational differences one might imagine to inhere between the revitalized organic as surveyed by Rasula—in his able hands, a bioconceptual complex characterized by terms such as *proprioceptive* and *autopoietic* (anything but back-to-unmediated-nature)—and the technological—a *telos-* or design-driven grasp of creative volition—are hardly irreconcilable. This is worthy of extended discussion. I would observe here only that more speculative work in the biological sciences seems, to speak far too loosely, to have recycled that age-old mythos of the "self-made man" to yield the self-made (or self-making) *organism*, even as the new technologies of the mind (AI, NLP, neural networks, and the like, in conjunction with robotics) are serving up something like a "man-made self." (I borrow the latter from Tetz Rooke's discussion of Arabic literatures and autobiography.) Those cultural figurations attendant to the trope of the cyborg may thus be seen as manifesting a mediation between such metaphorical and material poles of self-construction and identity (and aversion to the social?), though in the case of the cyborg in particular, the popular fusion that results, while biomechanically (cybernetically) futuristic, often invokes an older, more stable conception of the biological, "natural" component (which tendency Haraway, in her seminal treatise, clearly tried to anticipate as an aspect of her

"blasphemy"; for more on pertinent issues of interiority, see Rasula, *This Compost*, p. 169n). Further such mediations are doubtless inevitable and may prove indispensable to our prosecutions. More and more I find that conceptual purchase obtains in recognizing how our organic, temporal boundedness is pushed and pulled toward closure and possibility by our relentless longing for some quotient of structural (if lived) certainty and purpose. Mechanics *are* bricoleurs (the term upon which Rasula hinges his closing exposition at p. 199), for they must be sensitive both to system (the trial and trail of cause and effect) and circumstance (the rusty bolt); and to the extent that this bifurcated mechanical poetic presides over our language practices—Rasula's stylized footnotes and his argument *for* footnotes; or my gesture, alternately overheated, ironic, and deadpan, toward an industrial synthesis—we will find ourselves busy constructing, while constructed by, our habitats.

11. "The essay strikes me as unexplored territory in English" (Eliot Weinberger to Kent Johnson in a 2001 interview). In which regard, see for instance the collection of innovative essays edited by John D'Agata. But "the essay" is only part of the story. Building on Giorgio Agamben's *The Coming Community* (1993)—specifically, Agamben's articulation of a "whatever" singularity—Robert C. Thomas eloquently makes the case for intellectual-artistic life that falls outside of official purviews: "This essay is not simply about the fact that 'I' exist, but that intellectual ways of being *radically different* from those taking place within established forms of association *do exist* and that such forms of intellectual existence (and the type of belonging they imply) are extraordinarily important for thought, for politics, for individuation, for life; in short, for becoming-intellectual. The whatever intellectual *does* exist, even if its direct expression remains wholly suppressed" (Thomas, "Whatever").

12. Especially in light of receptivity to reception theory, the working distances and meadows must be maintained. (Jerry-rigging permitted, natch.)

13. See note 23, arf, arf arf, of my *Bookend: Anatomies of a Virtual Self* (to which this volume is something like the prequel). There's an old joke goes something like this: mechanical engineers build weapons, civil engineers build targets. Does this mean that mechanical engineers are *uncivil* engineers? This former ME can only hope he's not designing more matériel, but matter has, in any case, proved itself such a sticky matter, resisting my designs at every turn. Ergo my corresponding resistance to materialist thought that would underestimate its material effects and affects. There may be more than a hint here too of that "double curse" Thomas J. Ferraro has helpfully detailed, that effort of ethnically marked writers (myself included) both "to prove to the world at large that one's

people have what it takes" and "to prove to the ancestors that one has not assimilated" (Ferraro, "Ethnic Passages," p. 193).

14. Gone vertical/to accrue interest/and could use some slop/ to reduce the risk of/art disease.

Track 2

1. Many readers are likely familiar with the tradition of tenure (under siege at present), its working assumption of academic freedom and the somewhat controversial corollaries attending thereto—for instance, that truth seekers are obliged to set aside personal considerations in their free investigation of the truth. The term *academic freedom* makes its way into English around the turn of the twentieth century, and there is continuing speculation as to the German term that would seem to prefigure it, *Lehrfreiheit*. Two related touchstones: in 1884, the National Education Association (NEA) proposed tenure as a solution to U.S. educational problems, and in 1940, the AAUP issued its Statement of Principles on Academic Freedom and Tenure. Academic freedom may find its precursor in the medieval university, where censorship of several of Aristotle's texts (on theological grounds) was paradoxically undercut by the scrupulous study of these selfsame texts. Some have argued, alternately, that our current understanding of academic freedom is directly linked to the increasing dissemination of scientific method during the Enlightenment and to those more secularized institutions that followed in its wake. For helpful discussion, see Michael Davis, "Academic Freedom, Impartiality, and Faculty Governance," *Law and Philosophy* 5 (1986): 263–276.

Track 3

1. Many thanks to Damian Judge Rollison for pointing me to this site. As of this writing, Highland's output continues to increase by the thousands of volumes. See, e.g., www.muse-apprentice-guild.com.

2. This may have as-yet-unresolved consequences for professional writing fields too, such as journalism. As Mark Glaser reported in a 2003 newsletter, technology columnist and blogger Dan Gillmor (*San Jose Mercury News*) "loosed the hounds of hell, so to speak, by opening up his upcoming book-in-progress, 'Making the News,' to input from his blog's readers." "It makes sense," Glaser observed, "because the book's subtitle is 'What Happens to Journalism and Society When Every Reader Can Be a Writer.'" According to Glaser, "Gillmor says he's trying to work out the crediting scheme, but plans to quote contributors or acknowledge their help in some way." See *Glaser Online*, a feature of the *USC Annenberg Online Journalism Review*. With sufficient numbers of authors, we approach the state of

compositional anonymity, and this raises the literary-critical question of whether anonymity might allay any number of judgmental biases. In which regard, see Clements *et al.* for a "symposium"-style review of H. L. Hix's attempt (in *Wild and Whirling Words*) to employ a species of anonymity in an effort to develop a less partisan and more candid evaluation of poems.

3. Clive Thompson's Collision Detection blog featured discussion of a "poetry of spam" just as SpamAssassin and similar virus protection packages were gaining acceptance on mail servers nationwide (see Thompson, "Poetry of Spam"). Thus does the poetic function continue to enjoy a symbiotic relationship with all technologies of the word, even those markedly driven by market forces.

4. Rasula has delineated "four zones" of the contemporary American "poetry world": the Associated Writing Programs; the New Formalism; language poetry; and "various coalitions of interest-oriented or community-based poets" (*American Poetry*, p. 440). Rasula is careful to observe that these four zones are "utterly disproportionate" in resources and the like, and that the fourth zone is "more heterogeneous and fluid than the others" (ibid., p. 440). More recently, Mark Wallace has identified five "major networks of poetry production," two of which correspond roughly to Rasula's "AWP" (Wallace uses the MFA designation) and "New Formalism" zones (for Wallace, "traditional form"); his remaining three "networks" comprise identity-based poetries (with a strong MFA component), speech-based poetries, and avant-garde poetries (see Wallace, "Toward," p. 193). Whether "zones" or "networks"—and note that there is substantive semantic difference in the choice of terms—poetry production in the U.S., however balkanized, is thus provided with a kind of practical territorial unity *as* poetry. Without taking exception either to Rasula's or Wallace's helpful efforts, I would ask whether any attempt to distinguish poetry from, say, prose, regardless of the *de facto* perceptions or publishing realities that prevail, constitutes at its core the imposition of imagined (at the very least, conceptually hermetic) community or communities. Perhaps slam poetry has more to do, for instance, with theatrical production than with poetry *per se*.

5. See my review of Nelson's *Anthology of Modern American Poetry* (Amato, "It was"). See also Nelson's helpful exposé of the editorial quandaries he faced while trying to bring his volume into print, especially as regards this very question of reprint fees. Though I sympathize with Nelson's labor-intensive plight and have great admiration for his contributions to the poetry archive (in print and online)—and against his "felt" conviction that he was indeed "resisting the aesthetic of political correctness" (p. 326)—he seems ultimately unwilling to stray too far from the experiential-representational line that guides his anthology selections and his research in general. Still, I need to thank (we *all* need to

thank) Nelson for his tireless efforts to reform our institutions of higher learning for the better—which is, I suppose, simply another way of offering an olive branch. And while I'm tossing around olive branches, I'll toss one at Philip Levine, whose *7 Years from Somewhere* remains a key influence on my own poetic sensibility.

6. This warrants an extended digression: As reported by the *Guardian* (online)—and I think it's important here to give some sense of the media flux responsible for disseminating such news—the NEA survey of U.S. reading habits, *Reading at Risk*, indicates that "the number of non-reading adults increased by more than 17 million between 1992 and 2002"; less than half, or 47 percent, of U.S. adults read (books of) poetry, plays, or fiction, "a drop of 7 points from a decade earlier" (see Italie, "Report"). "The likely culprits" for this decline in reading, according to the *Guardian* piece, are "television, movies and the Internet"; the "drop in reading was widespread" and "was especially great among the youngest people surveyed." But in his op-ed piece in the *New York Times*, Charles McGrath (former editor of the *New York Times Book Review*) would ferret out survey information more pertinent to our discussion here: "While the number of people reading literature has gone down"—and McGrath notes that the survey does not include nonfiction under the "literature" banner yet *does* include mysteries, for instance—"the number of people trying to write it has actually gone up" (see McGrath, "What," and United States, *Report*, p. 22). "We seem to be slowly turning into a nation of 'creative writers,'" he surmises, "more interested in what we have to say ourselves than in reading or thinking about what anyone else has to say." One might want to amend this last to read, "creative writers" more interested in what we have to say *to* ourselves—but hold on. Perusing the study myself, I note that McGrath turns out to be only half right: while the *number* of people doing "creative writing" (all genres) increased from 11.5 to 14.4 millon between 1982 and 2002 (a 25 percent increase), the *percentage* increase was only a tenth of a percent (from 7 to 7.1 percent)—meaning that population increases most assuredly account, in the main, for the upward trend in numbers. Reading (of books) may be trending (way) down, then, but writing of all genres across a broad demographic is trending up only by a little. Even more intriguing is that the number *and* percentage of people who have taken a creative writing class *decreased* significantly in those two decades (29.5 to 27.3 million and 18 to 13.3 percent, respectively). So we might want to ask what it is that accounts for this slight upward trend in "creative writing" and (relatively large) drop in reading, especially in the absence of formal training; and we might want to ask what it is that accounts, too, for the current proliferation of creative writing programs.

The electronic sphere seems a likely explanation—but as one might expect, reading and writing e-mail isn't what is meant in the NEA study by reading or writing "creative writing"; at some point we would want to distinguish, too, between writers who think of themselves as writers and writers who don't. Still, before concluding that our newly or non- or multiliterate (?—I am groping for a term) public may be characterized by its writing of unread (print *or* digital) literature, we may need to develop a better grasp of what kinds of books, read or unread, *are* generating revenue. In *Newsweek*'s piece on the NEA survey, we learn that there was a 58 percent *increase* in the number of titles published between 1993 and 2003 (see Jones, "Waiting"). But in the *New York Times* (online) news release, we learn additionally that, while adult hardbound books and adult and mass-market paperbacks worldwide "all showed relatively flat revenues" in 2003, sales of religious texts were up 36.8 percent over the year prior (see Weber, "Fewer Noses"). Given the tendency of our transnational mediating hosts to feed on trends, we might expect annual transcendence of this already steep increase—and this says something about our collective desire *for* transcendence, never mind whether by nature or nurture.

Discussion of reading habits, in any case, without a working knowledge of how marketplace phenomena reinforce such habits can be highly misleading. Most who trade in some aspect of the book business know that five publishing-entertainment conglomerates are responsible for roughly 80 percent of book sales worldwide: Bertelsmann AG (Random House and its imprints), Time Warner, News Corporation (Rupert Murdoch), Disney, and Viacom/CBS. But how many of us are aware that, as a rule of thumb, these conglomerates will not acquire a title unless projected sales are in the neighborhood of 50,000 copies (see Ross and Ross, "Book News")? Compare this with your standard 500 to 1000-copy small press run (academic presses are frequently in this range as well), or with your average 75 copies sold per title by POD companies that inventory at least 10,000 titles (ibid.), and you get some idea of what small press publishers and self-published authors are up against in terms of market share.

Finally, we would do well to unseat the working conception of literacy upon which the NEA study is founded. In a brilliant exchange that takes the study as its starting point, Stuart Moulthrop and Nancy Kaplan denaturalize older (and historically quite recent) understandings of literacy in order to propose, ultimately, a broader conception of literate practices. While I find myself in essential agreement with Moulthrop and Kaplan, I would nonetheless want to interject something like the market analysis of paragraphs prior and remind everyone that though more staid conceptions of (print-based) literacy may be a relatively recent development (and that it is recent, incidentally, does not *ipso facto* diminish its importance), our collective yearning for the arts—sacred or secular, somber or ludic, page or screen, word or image—is as old as the hills; further, that which poses a threat to the arts poses a threat to all literacies, and then some. Thus to celebrate (say) the diversity and inventiveness of human endeavor—which we humanists often fall back on as the default justification for what we do—seems, to this writer, a necessary but insufficient response to once and future privatizations of the real, especially the version that greets me each morning in my advanced writing (and thinking) classes. How to remain open *and* selective on this increasingly "flat" if stubbornly topographical planet (see Friedman, *The World*)?

7. Before I get all perfervid about this, we might want to ask whether "the informatic organization is a learning institution" by default or by design. Building on the work of Harry Braverman, David Noble, Stanley Aronowitz, Andrew Ross, Tiziana Terranova, and others, Marc Bousquet has done a stellar job of showing how the "casualization" of (commodified) academic labor—the gradual and insidious process by which the everyday (sensual) labors associated with knowledge work and intellection are obscured by the very regulating entities seeking to exploit them—is in fact "the key measure of informatic instruction" ("Informatics," p. 246). Bousquet's point is that, regardless of the various modes of academic production—whether conceived as artisanal, industrial, or entrepreneurial (see Aronowitz, *Knowledge Factory*)—"commodification critique" (ibid., p. 245) requires attention to a distributed workplace informatics, which attention can serve to demystify how the privatization of higher ed is actually managed as such. Faculty unionization may be a case in point, particularly vis-à-vis those casualizations that contribute to the tenured indifference toward the plight of the untenured. "While 44% of all faculty and nearly 2/3 of public-institution faculty are unionized (by comparison with 14% of the workforce at large and 30% of public-sector employees)," adduces Bousquet, "consciousness regarding what to do about the contingent workers of the second tier [adjunct faculty, graduate students, etc.] has been slow to develop in faculty unions" (ibid., 236). As one such (unionized) "contingent worker," I would say that we tend to behave, all of us, as if the effects of casualization were a matter of forces beyond our ken.

8. It's not that there may not be problems, too, with theory, or rather, with theorists. See Eakin ("The Latest Theory") for recent reportage surrounding the controversial claim that, even for many theorists, theory today "doesn't matter." Clearly theory (materialist theorizing in particular) continues to matter, for instance, to Terry Eagleton, but his assault on postmodernist theory is so strenuous as to leave one with the sense that we would do better simply to ignore it

(see *After Theory*). Indifference may be something less than that outright rejection of theory to which I will shortly turn my attention, but it does seem to me that the Critical Inquiry symposium held in Chicago in 2003 (the subject of Eakin's piece) points to something of a collective about-face among the Carnegie I research ranks as to the efficacies of theory. It's difficult for me to believe that those scholars in attendance were not able to anticipate the impact that their apparent (apparent) recantation might have on those who teach out their lives amid much less endowed quadrangles, with a much higher quotient of service-related duties, and who have had to work harder than ever during these penny-pinching times to maintain a curricular presence for challenging intellectual engagement.

9. Lake's somewhat hipper, if polemically similar, essay, "The Enchanted Loom," borrows extensively, and in my view deceptively, from work in information theory, cognitive science, theories of complexity, and so forth in an effort to dismiss postmodern avant-gardism—the very literature that one might expect to coincide with such theories.

10. Revising this passage in preparation for book publication, I am struck by the degree to which this cinematic residue of cold war hysteria parallels our own troubled times.

11. For the etymologically obsessed, "fascination" itself *might* herald potential gender trouble: some ancients believed that penis-shaped amulets honoring the Roman phallic deity *Fascinus* could protect children from bewitchery (see Ayto, *Dictionary*).

12. Expanding on Owen Barfield's work, Susanne K. Langer discusses a variant of the "disembodied" in relation to an artwork's effect on consciousness as such. Langer's "disembodiment" resembles Russian futurism's *ostranenie* ("making strange," and what a strangely convenient term this has become of late); for Langer, this phenomenon illustrates the experiential dialectic of two "functions," the "objectification of feeling" and the "subjectification of nature" (*Mind*, p. 241). See Langer and also, for an unusual, Buddhist-grounded attempt to make cogsci versions of embodiment answer more productively to "everyday experience" (p. xv), Varela et al., *The Embodied Mind*. The prospect of disembodied mortal coils enjoying poetic communion together might prompt us to consider what sorts of textual embodiments aid and abet ecstatic practice. Devin Johnston's examination of contemporary poetry in terms of its embodiment, or "precipitation," of occult doctrine (and dogma) provides a textually explicit foundation for understanding how such poetry might function in communities predisposed to occultist métier—a matter into which we will foray, obliquely, as we proceed. See Johnston's *Precipitations*.

13. See Elio Gianturco's fine "Translator's Introduction" to Vico's *On the Study Methods of Our Time*.
14. Conversations with Susan Duran have persuaded me of a related risk: that of the potential anomie that results from audience identification with the pining performative persona of the "singer/songwriter," which Duran rightly sees as intensified by that "self-referentiality" Michael Dunne has located in pop-cultural artifacts. See Dunne's *Metapop*.
15. There are times when I find myself siding with those for whom academic culture and its drift toward the popular provides abundant occasion for *Weltschmerz*. Here is 2003 MLA president Mary Louise Pratt, a scholar whose work has proved pivotal to my understanding of disciplinary practices, waxing perhaps a bit *too* enthusiastic about the "resurgence of poetry": "Today the premier poetry magazine in the United States receives ninety thousand submissions a year, nearly three hundred a day. At the last wedding I attended, two poems composed for the occasion were performed, one in traditional Urdu by a family elder and the other a rap in English by a friend of the groom. Poetry is alive among us, juices flowing" ("Of Poets," p. 3). For starters, which "premier poetry magazine" does Pratt have in mind? *Poetry*? Surely any such assertion ought to be offered up with a degree of trepidation, especially coming from the topmost ranks of the MLA, if only to reflect just how contested a site "alive" poetry is, and has been—an "art of the contact zone," indeed.
16. In her generally negative appraisal of poetry readings ("these faintly embarrassing speech acts"), Judith Shulevitz glosses Robert Pinsky's remarks on the poetry reading (in *The Sounds of Poetry: A Brief Guide*) as "describ[ing] the tension between the syntax of a sentence and the shape of the poetic line" (see Shulevitz, "Sing, Muse"). It's up to the poet, as Shulevitz reads Pinsky, to maneuver between line breaks ("the flow of the sentence") and the "rhythmical and accentual scaffolding inside" those sentences that (it is apparently to be assumed) make up lines. Not to put too fine a point on it, but there are some serious limitations to this (prosodic, if not harmonic) account of the poetry reading.
17. In *Lipstick Traces*, Greil Marcus details how Bataille himself "seized on" the figure of the potlatch in Marcel Mauss's *The Gift* in order to mount a theory of (non)expenditure and waste to address "humanity's inherent hatred of utility and limits" (see Marcus, pp. 394–395).
18. In a third sweep through Bruns's remarkably fecund piece, I might want to emphasize how his pursuit of poetic community, while steering decidedly clear of philosophical pragmatism, is nonetheless thoroughly pragmatic in its elucidation of those make-do exigencies generated by the "anarchy" of poetic form (see Bruns, "Poetic Communities," p. 28).

19. I've found screenwriting, in fact, and the business of screenwriting, a refreshingly brutal departure from those positively *wack* publishing policies that both small and trade press reps will, given the chance, pontificate in terms of "love." Sometimes it's nice to work with an unambiguous bottom line, and whatever else it may be, "love" is not unambiguous.
20. See Sydney Pollack's introduction to the teachings of Sanford Meisner: "When truths about one art are deep enough, they become true about all art" (Pollack, "Introduction," pp. xiv–xv).
21. If the history of progress as a social precept is indissociable from, and not merely contiguous to, the history of industrialization, then John Berger is correct in attributing to the factory the demise of (a common perception of) historical changelessness and corresponding timelessness (see Berger's *Another Way of Telling*, his chapter on "Appearances"). For a renewed appreciation of wonder, see Fisher, and Rasula's remarks in *Syncopations* (pp. 199–200n). And again, in light of my industrially tooled thematic, Bousquet's commentary on informationalized "car parts, novels, and armored divisions" seems especially pertinent here (Bousquet is building on Mark Poster's notion of "the mode of information"):

> A fully informationalized carburetor is available in the way that electronically-mediated data is available—on demand, just in time. When you're not thinking of your carburetor, it's off your desktop. When you need to think about it, the informationalized carburetor lets you know. When it does manifest itself it gives the illusion of a startling transparency—you have in the carburetor's manifestation the sense that you have everything you need to know about carburetors: how they work, fair prices for them here and in the next state, and so on. ("Informatics," p. 238)

Thus industrial poetics may be understood, at one level, as a demonstration against this facile "casualization" of a car part (see note 7, above), the Rochester versions of which once gave me and my pinkies a great deal of grief. I demonstrate in symbols, of course—the foremost instruments of casualization and (much as I'm with him) the means by which Bousquet can so casually conjure up a desktop carburetor and the illusion by which it comes to pass as the thing itself (much like my use of mechanical tropes). Had he to make his argument to a crowd of onlookers, holding an actual carb in his hands, recourse to the data model would, I believe, appear that much more precarious. Still, it's tough to say whether the carburetors I have "in mind" are, at this point in my knowledge-working life, more material or more Euclidean. The tried and true calibrations are lost on me, the nicks and scrapes have long since healed, and my beloved Rochester carbs have gone the way of typewriters and mimeograph machines.

22. See Trimbur for an early discussion of dissensus in the context of collaborative learning. Ziarek's *An Ethics of Dissensus* represents a bold attempt to forge a modern ethical foundation by synthesizing a wide range of postmodern and feminist theories. While my own inquiry (if we can yet call it that) is guided, broadly, by demonstrations for and against pragmatic (and occasionally utilitarian) principles (or ideals) of ethical thought and action, I would depart from Ziarek chiefly in my desire to develop a non-normative discourse that, often despite itself, registers contingency and (tenured and untenured) otherness *and*, fraught metaphysics aside, attention to the physical, workaday attributes of material reality; hence a discourse that is less wedded to the normative logic and seamless execution of theoretical articulation. This is no small matter, albeit it *could* be a laughing matter, if handled properly. I am probably more prone, as well, to advancing as a practical necessity some working conception of justice. Otherwise, Ziarek is way ahead of what I will offer in the paragraphs that follow. See also Sedinger for a searching review and critique of Ziarek's book.

23. I refrain here—judiciously, I trust—from deploying the term that describes, for some of my fellow travelers, the preferred subject position of the global citizen: cosmopolitan. I like the word, I really do, and I use it on occasion. Really. "Winnipeg is a very cosmopolitan city." OK? I'm just not certain that the word doesn't ultimately work as a kind of crypto-urban, upper-middle-class marker. For cosmopolitanism as a literary-historical construct *per se*, see, for instance, Tom Lutz's *Cosmopolitan Vistas*. As Lutz shows, American regionalist writers adopted a "literary cosmopolitanism" at once egalitarian and elitist in its approach to the public sphere.

24. Not hours after composing the first draft of this paragraph I learned of Marlon Brando's passing. Perhaps it's not too much of a stretch to suggest that Brando's putative talent for "becoming" a character, for inhabiting another's skin—at least, to judge by the reaction so many of us have had to the body of his work—would seem to give the lie to radical alterity, the notion that we are, each to each, ineluctably *other*. It may well be the case that Brando's exceptional "method" cannot be reproduced or packaged for consumption simply because his abilities were very much a part of his person and, as such, nontransferable. But is it possible that his talents, whether owing to genes or to artifice or to improvisational energy, lay less in mimicking a static "human nature" than in remaining open to the differential attributes of the human? I may be out of my depths here, but is it possible that, in radically altering the representational scope of what it means to be human, Brando was anything *but* a "natural"?

25. "We must develop a theory of literary history," counsels Stephen Greenblatt, "that does not inevitably betray the aleatory, accidental, contingent, random dimensions of literary creativity," a theory that would do justice to "the ancient sense of contingency and the still more ancient sense of mobility" in reckoning the cultural and aesthetic work of global literatures (see Greenblatt, "Racial," p. 60). "The task is difficult, but it is not impossible," Greenblatt writes (ibid., p. 60). In my view such a theory is implicit, and often explicit, in the work of so many poets and writers, and two anthologies in particular that bring such theorizing to the fore are Rasula and McCaffery's *Imagining Language* and Rothenberg and Clay's *A Book of the Book*. Also, for a casual and highly "contingent" stroll through decades of lived and living literary culture, see Hollo's *Caws & Causeries*.

26. As Ayto indicates, "ecology" means quite literally "study of houses," but I'm thinking here of that old Blind Faith song, "Can't Find My Way Home." For a nice discussion, complete with samples of student writing, of how ecological thought and praxis might impassion the writing classroom, see Collom ("An Ecosystem").

27. (I prefer the Jay and The Americans version, but having studied with Byrd, I suspect he might hanker for the Drifters' original.)

28. Here is Lyotard on writing, speaking on the more informal occasion of an interview:

> [W]riting is the capacity to resist the network of exchanges in which cultural objects are commodities, and maybe to write is precisely to avoid making a book (or even a small paper or article), but rather to oppose, to resist the simple and naive exchangeability of things in our world. That's to say, to write is necessarily to allude to something else which is not easily communicated. It doesn't mean that a work is difficult to read; it could be very simple, but it alludes to something else. (Interview, p. 145)

29. I am tempted, but only tempted, to draw a parallel here between the sorts of communal energies I am busy reifying and Houston A. Baker Jr.'s erstwhile efforts to situate the blues at the crossroads of cultural studies inquiry and African-American experience.

30. See Robert Corbett's *Experimental Theology* for a useful compendium of assorted writings that motion toward "experimental theology"; see John Corbett's *Extended Play* for a theoretically informed critique of avant-disposed musicians, their music, and the community formations that support such work (Corbett includes a number of marvelous interviews); see Nielsen's *Black Chant* for a groundbreaking inquiry into the imbrications of postmodern African American

poetry and jazz communities; and see Clay and Philips's *Secret Location* for a fine attempt to document the peregrinations of (small press) writing community by foregrounding the little magazines and mimeo productions arising from community interaction.

31. Readers will detect some conceptual slippage here in my emphasis, in particular, of linguistic *work* as against, e.g., linguistic activity, or *energy*. This work-activity (*ergon-energeia*) couple was explored by Romantic savants (such as Humboldt) and later influenced poets such as Whitman—but the issues are complex, wound as they are around the energy conservation law as it was first formulated during the nineteenth century. It pains me to report that while laboring over my labored excursion into competing figurations of energy—see my "No Wasted Words"—I was not aware of Gerald L. Bruns's far more fluid antecedent in *Modern Poetry and the Idea of Language*, namely his splendid chapter, "*Energeia*: The Development of the Romantic Idea of Language" (see Bruns, *Modern*, pp. 42–67). For the purposes of this discussion, I wish only to situate both the work-object itself and the capacity for doing it as potentially unalienated, community-based labor (as opposed, say, to an alien craft); which efforts may be distinguished from so much commercial culture by virtue, say, of their happy power to elicit axiological cogitation, to bring under active interrogation even the performance of community. The abiding emphasis I place on a finite, bounded understanding of *terra firma* work and related energies of production, while anything but a nominal conceit, is not intended, either, as a strategy by which to foreclose on literary form; rather, I wish to establish, with some precision, how certain kinds of human and social activities are integrally related to certain kinds of human and social limits. In Joseph Tabbi's scrupulous analysis of Blanchot's meditation on literary space, for example, a keen awareness as to the "temporal constraints" of life is shown to point up parallel mortal and literary expenditures. Thus despite having espoused the writer's "solitary work" as a process that can resist, through the strivings of writerly interiority, the unwanted noise of mediation ("Solitary Inventions," p. 748), Blanchot must eventually shift his attention from the more arbitrary and endless repositories (of human and social energies) associated with "infinite [literary] 'work'" to the discrete artifact, "the delimited space of the 'book,'" death's analog (ibid., pp. 757–758). See also Rasula's treatment of what he refers to as the "restorative disabling," or "indigence," endemic to encyclopedic narrativization (Rasula, "Technical"). At any rate, it's likely that energy will persist as the word of choice when we materialists of the intellect wish to couch our spiritual druthers in physical trappings (see, for instance, Krishnamurti and Bohm).

32. Whitman's gesture amounts, all told, to a prototypical U.S. variant, the inaugurating vista of ever-renewable, if democratically bound, creative energies.

33. It may be time to revisit the conceptual gist of what, nearly forty years ago and with reference to Montreal's Expo '67, Umberto Eco identified as an "avant-garde didactics"—a "developing pedagogy" that might constitute a "revolutionary way of teaching" (Eco, *Travels*, p. 305). Eco was much taken at the Expo by those "systems of popularized communication" that permitted "both educated and naïve visitors alike" to experience "felt aesthetic emotion . . . that gave them ideas and data to think about, decisions to make, conclusions to draw" (ibid., 305). Eco's excursus into the pedagogical echoes (sorry) his long-standing commitment to "a novel intended at once as a work of entertainment, a consumer item, and as an aesthetically valid work capable of providing original, not kitsch, values" (quoted in Parker, "Eco, Umberto," p. 221; from *Apocalittici e integrati* [1964]). Without wishing to motion toward some final (formalist) resolution of social intercourse and its discontents, I would advance the implicit pairings at work here—education and entertainment, aesthetics and commerce, ethical value and consumption, emotion and communication, demonstration and observation, pull and push—as worthy of any writing community's strivings toward provisional self-definition.

Bibliography

Note: The following list is comprised of items I've read cover-to-cover, items I've read sizable portions of, items I've read around in, items I've read about, items I would like to read, items I have no intention of reading, a few items I wish I hadn't read, items I've seen, items I would like to see, items I've taught, items I would like to teach, a few items that probably shouldn't be taught, a few items that probably shouldn't have been written, items that friends and acquaintances have written, items I wish I'd written, and items I wish I'd written differently.

Adonis. "Poetry and Apoetical Culture." *Poems for the Millennium: The University of California Book of Modern and Postmodern Poetry*. Ed. Jerome Rothenberg and Pierre Joris. Vol. 2: *From-Postwar to Millennium*. Berkeley: U of California P, 1998. 182–183.

Adorno, Theodor W. *Aesthetic Theory*. Trans. and ed. Robert Hullot-Kentor. Minneapolis: U of Minnesota P, 1998.

Agamben, Giorgio. *The Coming Community*. Trans. Michael Hardt. Minneapolis: U of Minnesota P, 1993.

Allen, Donald, and Warren Tallman, eds. *The Poetics of the New American Poetry*. New York: Grove, 1979.

Altieri, Charles. "What Is at Stake in Confessional Criticism." *Confessions of the Critics*. Ed. H. Aram Veeser. New York: Routledge, 1996. 55–67.

Amato, Joe. *Bookend: Anatomies of a Virtual Self*. Albany: State U of New York P, 1997.

———. "It was the best of tomes, it was the worst of tomes: Cary Nelson's *Anthology of Modern American Poetry*." *Jacket* 11 (May 2000). jacketmagazine.com/11/nelson-by-amato.html.

———. "No Wasted Words: Whitman's Original Energy." *Nineteenth Century Studies* 12 (1998): 37–63.

Amato, Joe, and Kass Fleisher. "Reforming Creative Writing Pedagogy: History as Knowledge, Knowledge as Activism." *ebr (electronic book review)* 12 (Summer 2001). 4 July 2004. www.electronicbookreview.com/v3/servlet/ebr?command=view_essay&essay_id=youngend.

America's Best Colleges. 2005 ed. U. S. News & World Report.

Anderson, Benedict. *Imagined Communities*. London, UK: Verso, 1991.

Andrews, Bruce. "The Poetics of L=A=N=G=U=A=G=E." Talk delivered 25 Sept. 2001 at White Box in NYC. Archived at www.ubu.com/papers/andrews.html.

Antin, David. "Modernism and Postmodernism: Approaching the Present in American Poetry." *Boundary 2* 1 (1972): 98–133.

———. "Some Questions about Modernisms." *Occident* 7, new series (Spring 1974).

———. *what it means to be avant-garde*. New York: New Directions, 1993.

Aristotle. *Metaphysics*. *The Complete Works of Aristotle: The Revised Oxford Translation*. Vol. 2. Ed. Jonathan Barnes. Princeton, NJ: Princeton UP, 1984. 243–296.

Aronowitz, Stanley. *The Knowledge Factory: Dismantling the Corporate University and Creating True Higher Learning*. Boston: Beacon, 2000.

Artaud, Antonin. *Watchfriends and Rack Screams: Works from the Final Period, 1945–48*. Ed. Bernard Bador. Trans. Clayton Eshleman. Cambridge, MA: Exact Change, 1995.

Auerbach, Erich. *Mimesis: The Representation of Reality in Western Literature*. Trans. Willard R. Trask. Princeton. NJ: Princeton UP, 1974.

Augustine, Saint. *On Christian Doctrine*. Trans. D. W. Robertson, Jr. Indianapolis, IN: Bobbs-Merrill, 1983.

Axelrod, Robert. *The Evolution of Cooperation*. New York: Basic, 1984.

Ayto, John. *Dictionary of Word Origins*. New York: Arcade, 1991.

Bai, Matt. "Wiring the Vast Left-Wing Conspiracy." *New York Times Magazine* 25 July 2004: 30+.

Bailey, Britt, and Marc Lappé, eds. *Engineering the Farm: The Social and Ethical Aspects of Agricultural Biotechnology*. Washington, DC: Island, 2002.

Baker, Houston A., Jr. *Blues, Ideology, and Afro-American Literature: A Vernacular Theory*. Chicago: U of Chicago P, 1984.

Ballard, J. G. *The Atrocity Exhibition*. Rev. ed. San Francisco: Re/Search, 1990.

Bangs, Lester. Interview with Jim DeRogatis (Nov. 1999). 28 June 2004. www.furious.com/perfect/lesterbangs.html.

Barlow, John Perry. "The Economy of Ideas." *Wired* 2.03 (March 1994): 84–90, 126–129. Available at www.wired.com/wired/archive/2.03/economy.ideas.html.

Barnard, Chester Irving. *The Functions of the Executive*. Cambridge, MA: Harvard UP, 1938.

Barthes, Roland. *Camera Lucida: Reflections on Photography*. Trans. Richard Howard. New York: Hill and Wang, 1984.

———. *Mythologies*. Selected and trans. by Annette Lavers. New York: Hill and Wang, 1986.

Bataille, Georges. "The Notion of Expenditure." *Visions of Excess: Selected Writings,*

1927–1939. Ed. and trans. Allan Stoekl. Minneapolis: U of Minnesota P, 1985. 116–129.

Baudrillard, Jean. *Simulations*. Trans. Paul Foss, Paul Patton, and Philip Beitchman. New York: Semiotext(e), 1983.

Benjamin, Walter. "The Author as Producer." Trans. Anna Bostock. *Art in Theory, 1900–2000: An Anthology of Changing Ideas*. Ed. Charles Harrison and Paul Wood. New ed. Oxford, UK: Blackwell, 2003. 493–499.

Berger, John, and Jean Mohr. *Another Way of Telling*. New York: Pantheon, 1982.

Bernays, Edward L. *Propaganda*. New York: Liveright, 1928.

Bernstein, Charles. "Poetics of the Americas." *My Way: Speeches and Poems*. Chicago: U of Chicago P, 1999. 113–137.

———. "On Theatricality." *Content's Dream: Essays 1975–1984*. Los Angeles: Sun and Moon, 1986. 199–207.

———. "Artifice of Absorption." *A Poetics*. Cambridge, MA: Harvard UP, 1992. 9–89.

Berrigan, Ted. *The Sonnets*. New York: Penguin, 2000.

Bey, Hakim. *T.A.Z.: The Temporary Autonomous Zone, Ontological Anarchy, Poetic Terrorism*. New York: Autonomedia, 1991.

Bierce, Ambrose. *The Devil's Dictionary*. New York: Dover, 1958.

Birkerts, Sven. "Present at the Re-Creation." Rev. of *Oryx and Crake*, by Margaret Atwood. *New York Times Book Review* 18 May 2003: 12.

Blamires, Harry. *The New Bloomsday Book: A Guide through Ulysses*. 3rd ed. New York: Routledge, 1996.

Blanchot, Maurice. *The Space of Literature*. Trans. Ann Smock. Lincoln: U of Nebraska P, 1982.

———. *The Step Not Beyond*. Trans. Lycette Nelson. Albany: State U of New York P, 1992.

———. *The Unavowable Community*. Trans. Pierre Joris. Barrytown, NY: Station Hill, 1988.

Blaser, Robin. "The Practice of Outside." *The Collected Books of Jack Spicer*. Ed. and with commentary by Robin Blaser. Los Angeles: Black Sparrow P, 1975. 269–329.

Blind Faith. "Can't Find My Way Home." *Blind Faith*. Prod. Jimmy Miller. Polygram, 1969.

Bloch, Ernst. *The Spirit of Utopia*. Trans. Anthony A. Nassar. Stanford, CA: Stanford UP, 2000.

Bourdieu, Pierre. *The Rules of Art: Genesis and Structure of the Literary Field*. Trans. Susan Emanuel. Stanford, CA: Stanford UP, 1996.

Bousquet, Marc. "The Informatics of Higher Education." *The Politics of Information:*

The Electronic Mediation of Social Change. Ed. Marc Bousquet and Katherine Wills. PDF e-book. AltX Press, 2004, in conjunction with *electronic book review*. 233–257. Available at www.altx.com/ebooks/infopol.html.

Boyer, Ernest L. *Scholarship Reconsidered: Priorities of the Professoriate.* Princeton, NJ: Carnegie Foundation for the Advancement of Teaching, 1996.

Bramson, Leon, and Michael S. Schudson. "Mass Society." *New Encyclopædia Britannica: Macropædia.* 15th ed. Vol. 11. Chicago: Encyclopedia Brittanica, 1979.

Brand, Stewart. "Environmental Heresies." *Technology Review* (10 May 2005). www.technologyreview.com/articles/05/05/issue/feature_earth.asp?p=1.

Braverman, Harry. *Labor and Monopoly Capital: The Degradation of Work in the Twentieth Century.* New York: Monthly Review P, 1974.

Brazil. Dir. Terry Gilliam. Screenplay by Terry Gilliam, Tom Stoppard, and Charles McKeown. Perf. Jonathan Pryce, Kim Greist, Robert De Niro, Katherine Helmond, Ian Holm, Bob Hoskins, Michael Palin, Jim Broadbent, Ian Richardson, and Peter Vaughan. Embassy International Pictures and Universal Pictures, 1985.

Brickell, Edie and New Bohemians. "What I Am." *Shooting Rubberbands at the Stars.* Geffen/Warner Bros., 1988.

Broderick, Harold M., ed. *The Practical Brewer: A Manual for the Brewing Industry.* 2nd ed. Madison, WI: Master Brewers Association of the Americas, 1978.

Bruns, Gerald L. *Modern Poetry and the Idea of Language: A Critical and Historical Study.* Normal, IL: Dalkey Archive P, 2001.

———. "Poetic Communities." *Iowa Review* 32.1 (Spring 2002): 1–38.

Burgess, Helen J. "Futurama, Autogeddon: Imagining the Superhighway from Bel Geddes to Ballard." *Rhizomes* 8 (Spring 2004). 17 July 2004. www.rhizomes.net/issue8/futurama/index.html.

Burke, James. *Connections.* Rev. ed. New York: Little, 1995.

Burke, Kenneth. *Counter-Statement.* Berkeley: U of California P, 1968.

Byrd, Don. *The Great Dimestore Centennial.* Barrytown, NY: Station Hill, 1986.

———. *The Poetics of the Common Knowledge.* Albany: State U of New York P, 1994.

Byrd, Don, John Clarke, and Susan Howe. "Radical Poetries/Critical Address: The Poetry of Charles Olson." Three panel papers (revised). Ed. David Levi Strauss. *In Relation: ACTS* 10 (1989). 135–173.

Carrier, David, ed. *History and Theory* 37.4 (Dec. 1998). Theme issue. Danto and His Critics: Art History, Historiography, and after the End of Art.

Carson, Rachel. *Silent Spring.* Boston: Houghton Mifflin, 1994.

Cassirer, Ernst. *Language and Myth.* Trans. Susanne K. Langer. New York: Dover, 1953.

Certeau, Michel de. *Heterologies: Discourse on the Other.* Trans. Brian Massumi. Minneapolis: U of Minnesota P, 1986.

Charleston Writers' Conference. Conference flyer. Received 15 Jan. 1997.

Cheek, Chris. E-mail to Imitation Poetics online discussion list. 15 Jan. 2002.

Cixous, Hélène, and Mireille Calle-Gruber. *Hélène Cixous, Rootprints: Memory and Life Writing.* Trans. Eric Prenowitz. New York: Routledge, 1997.

Clark, T. J. *Farewell to an Idea: Episodes from a History of Modernism.* New Haven, CT: Yale UP, 2001.

Clark, Tom. *Charles Olson: The Allegory of a Poet's Life.* New York: Norton, 1991.

Clay, Steven, and Rodney Philips. *A Secret Location on the Lower East Side: Adventures in Writing, 1960–1980.* New York: Granary, 1998.

Clements, Brian, with Charles Altieri, Susan Briante, Elisabeth Frost, Arielle Greenberg, Frederick Turner, and Lorenzo Thomas. "Wild and Whirling Words." Rev. of *Wild and Whirling Words,* by H. L. Hix. *Rain Taxi Online Edition* Summer 2004. 1 July 2004. www.raintaxi.com/online/2004summer/wildwords.shtml.

Collom, Jack. "An Ecosystem of Writing Ideas." *JACK Magazine* 1.2. 3 July 2004. www.jackmagazine.com/issue2/eco.html.

———. *Red Car Goes By: Selected Poems 1955–2000.* San Francisco: Tuumba, 2001.

Corbett, John. *Extended Play: Sounding Off from John Cage to Dr. Funkenstein.* Durham, NC: Duke UP, 1994.

Corbett, Robert, ed., with Rebecca Brown. *Experimental Theology: Public Text 0.2.* Seattle, WA: Seattle Research Institute, 2003.

Cotter, Holland. "Doing Their Own Thing, Making Art Together." *New York Times* 19 Jan. 2003, natl. ed., sec. 2: 1+.

Covino, William A. "Magic and/As Rhetoric: Outlines of a History of Phantasy." *JAC* 12.2 (1992): 349–358. 1 July 2004. Electronic version archived at jac.gsu.edu/jac/12.2/Articles/7.htm.

———. *Magic, Rhetoric, and Literacy: An Eccentric History of the Composing Imagination.* Albany: State U of New York P, 1994.

———. "Rhetorical Pedagogy." *A Guide to Composition Pedagogies.* Ed. Gary Tate, Amy Rupiper, and Kurt Schick. New York: Oxford UP, 2001. 36–53.

"Craft." *American Heritage Electronic Dictionary.* Version 3.0.1. Houghton Mifflin Co.

Crane, Hart. "The Bridge." *Norton Anthology of American Literature.* Ed. Nina Baym et al. Vol. 2. 3rd ed. New York: Norton, 1989. 1674–1707.

Crosby, Stills, Nash and Young. "Suite: Judy Blue Eyes." *So Far.* Atlantic, 1974.

D'Agata, John, ed. *The Next American Essay.* St. Paul, MN: Graywolf, 2002.

Daly, Mary, with Jane Caputi. *Websters' First New Intergalactic Wickedary of the English Language.* Boston: Beacon, 1987.

Damon, Maria. *The Dark End of the Street: Margins in American Vanguard Poetry.* Minneapolis: U of Minnesota P, 1993.

Davis, Michael. "Academic Freedom, Impartiality, and Faculty Governance." *Law and Philosophy* 5 (1986): 263–276.

Davis, Mike. "The Flames of New York." *New Left Review* 12 (Nov.–Dec. 2001): 34–50.

Debord, Guy, et al. "All the King's Men." *Poems for the Millennium: The University of California Book of Modern and Postmodern Poetry.* Ed. Jerome Rothenberg and Pierre Joris. Vol. 2: *From Postwar to Millennium.* Berkeley: U of California P, 1998. 417–419.

Dee, Jonathan. "Playing Mogul." *New York Times Magazine* 21 Dec. 2003. www.sachsreport.com/Playing%20Mogul.htm.

Deleuze, Gilles, and Félix Guattari. *A Thousand Plateaus.* Trans. Brian Massumi. Minneapolis: U of Minnesota P, 1987.

Delville, Michel, and Christine Pagnoulle, eds. *The Mechanics of the Mirage: Postwar American Poetry.* Liège, Belgium: Liège Language and Literature, 2000.

De Quincey, Thomas. *Selected Essays on Rhetoric.* Ed. Frederick Burwick. Carbondale: Southern Illinois UP, 1967.

Derrida, Jacques. "White Mythology." *Margins of Philosophy.* Trans. Alan Bass. Chicago: U of Chicago P, 1982. 207–271.

Dewey, John. *Experience and Nature.* La Salle, IL: Open Court, 1989.

Dictionary.com. Lexico Publishing Group, LLC. 3 July 2004. Translation engine at dictionary.reference.com/translate/text.html.

Di Leo, Jeffrey R., ed. *Affiliations: Identity in Academic Culture.* Lincoln: U of Nebraska P, 2003.

Doubiago, Sharon. *Hard Country.* 2nd ed. Albuquerque, NM: West End, 1999.

Dunne, Michael. *Metapop: Self-Referentiality in American Pop Culture.* Jackson: UP of Mississippi, 1992.

DuPlessis, Rachel Blau. *The Pink Guitar: Writing as Feminist Practice.* New York: Routledge, 1990.

Eagleton, Terry. *After Theory.* New York: Basic, 2004.

———. *Against the Grain: Essays 1975–1985.* London: Verso, 1986.

Eakin, Emily. "The Latest Theory Is That Theory Doesn't Matter." *New York Times*, online ed., 19 April 2003. 9 July 2004. www.nytimes.com/2003/04/19/arts/19CRIT.html.

Eco, Umberto. *Travels in Hyperreality.* Trans. William Weaver. San Diego: HBJ, 1986.

Ehrenreich, Barbara. *Nickel and Dimed: On (Not) Getting By in America.* New York: Metropolitan/Owl, 2002.

Ehrlich, Eugene. *The Highly Selective Thesaurus for the Extraordinarily Literate.* New York: HarperCollins, 1994.

8 1/2 (Otto e Mezzo). Dir. Federico Fellini. Screenplay by Federico Fellini, Ennio Flaiano, Tullio Pinelli, and Brunello Rondi. Story by Federico Fellini and Ennio Flaiano. Perf. Marcello Mastroianni, Anouk Aimée, Sandra Milo, Claudia Cardinale, Rosella Falk, Barbara Steele, and Guido Alberti. Embassy, 1963.

Elbow, Peter. "Being a Writer vs. Being an Academic: A Conflict in Goals." *College Composition and Communication* 46.1 (Feb. 1995): 72–83.

Eliot, T. S. *Four Quartets.* San Diego, CA: HBJ, 1971.

Ellingham, Lewis, and Kevin Killian. *Poet Be Like God: Jack Spicer and the San Francisco Renaissance.* Hanover, NH: Wesleyan UP/UP of New England, 1998.

Ellul, Jacques. *The Technological Society.* Trans. John Wilkinson. New York: Vintage, 1964.

Emerson, Ralph Waldo. "The American Scholar." *American Literature: Tradition and Innovation.* Ed. Harrison T. Meserole, Walter Sutton, and Brom Weber. Vol. 2: *Ralph Waldo Emerson to Sidny Lanier.* Lexington, MA: Heath, 1974. 961–975.

Epstein, Jason. *Book Business.* New York: Norton, 2001.

Everett, Anna, and John T. Caldwell, eds. *New Media: Theories and Practices of Digitextuality.* New York: Routledge, 2003.

Fahrenheit 9/11. Written and dir. Michael Moore. Miramax/Dog Eat Dog/Fellowship Adventure Group/Lions Gate, 2004.

Fanon, Frantz. *The Wretched of the Earth.* Trans. Constance Farrington. New York: Grove, 1966.

Fausto-Sterling, Anne. *Sexing the Body: Gender Politics and the Construction of Sexuality.* New York: Basic, 2000.

Federman, Raymond. *Critifiction: Postmodern Essays.* Albany: State U of New York P, 1993.

Felshin, Nina, ed. *But Is It Art?: The Spirit of Art as Activism.* Seattle, WA: Bay, 1995.

Ferraro, Thomas J. *Ethnic Passages: Literary Immigrants in Twentieth-Century America.* Chicago: U of Chicago P, 1993.

Feyerabend, Paul. *Against Method. Outline of an Anarchistic Theory of Knowledge.* London: Verso, 1986.

F for Fake (Vérités et mensonges). Dir. Orson Welles. Screenplay by Orson Welles and Oja Kodar. Janus/Les Films de l'Astrophore/SACI, 1976.

Fisher, Philip. *Wonder, the Rainbow, and the Aesthetics of Rare Experiences.* Cambridge, MA: Harvard UP, 1998.

The Flight of the Phoenix. Dir. Robert Aldrich. Screenplay by Lukas Heller. Based on the novel by Elleston Trevor. Perf. James Stewart, Richard Attenborough, Peter Finch, Hardy Krüger, Ernest Borgnine, Ian Bannen, Ronald Fraser, Christian Marquand, Dan Duryea, and George Kennedy. 20th Century Fox/The Associates and Aldrich Co., 1965.

Florman, Samuel C. *The Existential Pleasures of Engineering*. New York: St. Martin's, 1976.

Foucault, Michel. *Discipline and Punish: The Birth of the Prison*. Trans. Alan Sheridan. 2nd ed. New York: Vintage, 1995.

———. "The Functions of Literature." *Politics, Philosophy, Culture: Interviews and Other Writings 1977–1984*. Ed. Lawrence D. Kritzman. Trans. Alan Sheridan et al. New York: Routledge, 1990. 307–313.

———. *The Order of Things: An Archaeology of the Human Sciences*. New York: Vintage, 1973.

———. "What Is an Author?" *Critical Theory since 1965*. Ed. Hazard Adams and Leroy Searle. Trans. Donald F. Bouchard and Sherry Simon. Tallahassee: Florida State UP, 1986. 137–148.

Fredman, Stephen. *Poet's Prose: The Crisis in American Verse*. 2nd ed. Cambridge, UK: Cambridge UP, 1990.

Freese, Barbara. *Coal: A Human History*. New York: Penguin, 2004.

Freire, Paulo. *Pedagogy of the Oppressed*. Trans. Myra Bergman Ramos. New York: Continuum, 1994.

Friedman, Thomas L. *The World Is Flat: A Brief History of the Twenty-First Century*. New York: FSG, 2005.

Fuller, R. Buckminster, in collaboration with E. J. Applewhite. *Synergetics: Explorations in the Geometry of Thinking*. New York: Macmillan, 1975.

Galvin, Robert W. *The Idea of Ideas*. Schaumburg, IL: Motorola UP, 1991.

Garreau, Joel. *Edge City: Life on the New Frontier*. New York: Doubleday, 1991.

Gee, James Paul. *What Video Games Have to Teach Us about Learning and Literacy*. New York: Palgrave Macmillan, 2003.

Gelpi, Albert. "The Genealogy of Postmodernism: Contemporary American Poetry." *Southern Review* 26 (1990): 517–541.

Gianturco, Elio. "Translator's Introduction." *On the Study Methods of Our Time*. By Giambattista Vico. Indianapolis, IN: Bobbs-Merrill, 1965. xxix–xxx.

Gizzi, Peter, and Juliana Spahr, eds. *Writing from the New Coast*. Spec. (double) issue of *o•blek* 12 (Spring/Fall 1993). 2 vols.: *Technique, Presentation*.

Glaser, Mark. *Glaser Online*—E-Mail Edition. "Collaborative Book Helps Tech Journo Walk the Walk, 'Making the News,' interactively." 16 April 2003. www.ojr.org/ojr/glaser.

Glazier, Loss Pequeño. *Digital Poetics: The Making of E-Poetries*. Tuscaloosa: U of Alabama P, 2002.

Golding, Alan. *From Outlaw to Classic: Canons in American Poetry*. Madison: U of Wisconsin P, 1995.

Goldsmith, John A., John Komlos, and Penny Schine Gold. *The Chicago Guide to Your Academic Career: A Portable Mentor for Scholars from Graduate School Through Tenure*. Chicago: U of Chicago P, 2001.

Gonzenbach, Laura. *Beautiful Angiola: The Great Treasury of Sicilian Folk and Fairy Tales*. Trans. Jack Zipes. Illus. Joellyn Rock. New York: Routledge, 2004.

Goodman, Paul. *Growing Up Absurd: Problems of Youth in the Organized Society*. New York: Vintage, 1960.

———. *New Reformation: Notes of a Neolithic Conservative*. New York: Vintage, 1971.

Grabo, Carl H. *The Creative Critic*. Chicago: U of Chicago P, 1948.

Gramsci, Antonio. *The Southern Question*. Trans. Pasquale Verdicchio. West Lafayette, IN: Bordighera, 1995.

Greenblatt, Stephen. Letter on behalf of MLA Executive Council. 28 May 2002.

———. "Racial Memory and Literary History." *PMLA* 116.1 (Jan. 2001): 48–63.

Gunnell, John G. *Between Philosophy and Politics: The Alienation of Political Theory*. Amherst: U of Massachusetts P, 1986.

Habermas, Jürgen. *Moral Consciousness and Communicative Action*. Trans. Christian Lenhardt and Shierry Weber Nicholson. Cambridge, MA: MIT P, 1990.

Hacker, Sally L. *"Doing It the Hard Way": Investigations of Gender and Technology*. Ed. Dorothy E. Smith and Susan M. Turner. Boston: Unwin Hyman, 1990.

Hamper, Ben. *Rivethead: Tales from the Assembly Line*. New York: Warner, 1991.

Haraway, Donna J. "A Cyborg Manifesto: Science, Technology, and Socialist-Feminism in the Late Twentieth Century." *Simians, Cyborgs, and Women: The Reinvention of Nature*. New York: Routledge, 1991. 149–181.

Harding, Sandra. *The Science Question in Feminism*. Ithaca, NY: Cornell UP, 1986.

Hassan, Ihab. "Parabiography: The Varieties of Critical Experience." *Georgia Review* 34.3 (Fall 1980): 593–612.

———. *The Postmodern Turn: Essays in Postmodern Theory and Culture*. Columbus: Ohio State UP, 1987.

Hawisher, Gail E., and Cynthia L. Selfe, eds. *Passions, Pedagogies, and 21st Century Technologies*. Logan: Utah State UP, 1999.

Hayles, N. Katherine. *How We Became Posthuman: Virtual Bodies in Cybernetics, Literature, and Informatics*. Chicago: U of Chicago P, 1999.

Hegel, G. W. F. *The Phenomenology of Spirit*. Trans. A. V. Miller. New York: Oxford UP, 1979.

Hejinian, Lyn. *The Language of Inquiry.* Berkeley: U of California P, 2000.
Heller, Michael. "Aspects of Poetics." *Samizdat* 8 (Autumn 2001): 3–5. See www.samizdateditions.com.
Henwood, Doug. *Wall Street: How It Works and for Whom.* London, UK: Verso, 1998.
Highland, August. "70,000 books!" E-mail to SUNY/Buffalo Poetics discussion group. 5 Feb. 2003. Used by permission of author. Archived at epc.buffalo.edu.
Hix, H. L. *Wild and Whirling Words: A Poetic Conversation.* Silver Spring, MD: Etruscan, 2004.
Hofstadter, Richard. *Anti-Intellectualism in American Life.* New York: Vintage, 1966.
Hollo, Anselm. "Canto Arastra." *Notes on the Possibilities and Attractions of Existence: Selected Poems 1965–2000.* Minneapolis, MN: Coffee House, 2001. 222.
———. *Caws & Causeries: Around Poetry and Poets.* Albuquerque, NM: La Alameda, 1999.
hooks, bell. *Teaching to Transgress: Education as the Practice of Freedom.* New York: Routledge, 1994.
Howe, Fanny. *Economics.* Chicago: Flood Editions, 2002.
Howe, Susan. *My Emily Dickinson.* Berkeley, CA: North Atlantic, 1985.
IIT Undergraduate Bulletin 1998–1999. Issued April 1998.
"Imagine." Perf. Neil Young. Words and music by John Lennon. "America: A Tribute to Heroes." Live benefit telethon and syndicated broadcast. Dir. Joel Gallen and Beth McCarthy-Miller. 21 Sept. 2001.
Italie, Hillel. "Report Shows Big Drop in Reading in U.S." *Guardian* 8 July 2004. Guardian Unlimited Network. 8 July 2004. www.guardian.co.uk.
Jameson, Fredric. *Postmodernism, or, the Cultural Logic of Late Capitalism.* Durham, NC: Duke UP, 1997.
Jarrett, Michael. *Drifting on a Read: Jazz as a Model for Writing.* Albany: State U of New York P, 1999.
Jay & The Americans. "This Magic Moment." Words and music by Doc Pomus and Mort Shuman. *Jay & The Americans—Greatest Hits.* Curb, 1994.
Johnson, Kent. Interview with Bill Freind. *Vert* 5 (2001). 9 July 2004. www.litvert.com/KJ_Interview.html.
Johnston, Devin. *Precipitations: Contemporary American Poetry as Occult Practice.* Middletown, CT: Wesleyan UP, 2002.
Jones, Malcolm. "Waiting for the Movie." *Newsweek* 19 July 2004: 58.
Joni Mitchell: Woman of Heart and Mind. PBS American Masters. Premiere 2 April 2003. Dir. Susan Lacy.
Joris, Pierre. *A Nomad Poetics: Essays.* Middletown, CT: Wesleyan UP, 2003.

———. "one moment earlier." *Poasis: Selected Poems 1986–1999*. Middletown, CT : Wesleyan UP, 2001. 54.

Joyce, James. *Ulysses: The Corrected Text*. Ed. Hans Walter Gabler, with Wolfhard Steppe and Claus Melchior. New York: Vintage, 1986.

Joyce, Michael. *Of Two Minds: Hypertext Pedagogy and Poetics*. Ann Arbor: U of Michigan P, 1995.

———. "The Persistence of the Ordinary." *Moral Tales and Meditations: Technological Parables and Refractions*. Albany: State U of New York P, 2001. 127–138.

Kael, Pauline. *For Keeps: 30 Years at the Movies*. New York: Plume, 1996.

Kahn, Gus, and Raymond B. Egan. "Ain't We Got Fun." Music by Richard Whiting. Jerome H. Remick, 1921.

Kant, Immanuel. *Foundations of the Metaphysics of Morals*. Trans. Lewis White Beck. Indianapolis, IN: Bobbs-Merrill, 1978.

Katz, Peter. *The New Urbanism: Toward an Architecture of Community*. New York: McGraw-Hill, 1994.

Kennedy, George A. *Comparative Rhetoric: An Historical and Cross-Cultural Introduction*. New York: Oxford UP, 1998.

———. "A Hoot in the Dark: The Evolution of General Rhetoric." *Philosophy and Rhetoric* 25.1 (1992): 1–21.

King Kong. Dir. Merian C. Cooper and Ernest B. Schoedsack. Screenplay by James Ashmore Creelman and Ruth Rose. Story by Merian C. Cooper and Edgar Wallace. Perf. Fay Wray, Robert Armstrong, and Bruce Cabot. RKO Radio Pictures, 1933.

Knoblauch, C. H., and Lil Brannon. *Critical Teaching and the Idea of Literacy*. Portsmouth, NH: Boynton/Cook, 1993.

Krauss, Rosalind. *The Originality of the Avant-Garde and Other Modernist Myths*. Cambridge, MA: MIT P, 1986.

Krishnamurti, J., and David Bohm. *The Ending of Time*. San Francisco: Harper and Row, 1985.

Krugman, Paul. "For Richer: How the Permissive Capitalism of the Boom Destroyed American Equality." *New York Times Magazine* 20 Oct. 2002: 62+.

———. Letter to James K. Galbraith. *Slate* "Dialogue" 6 Nov. 1996. 27 July 2004. slate.msn.com/id/3629/entry/23738.

Kuswa, Kevin. "Machinic Rhetoric, Highways, and Interpellating Motions." *Rhizomes* 8 (Spring 2004). 17 July 2004. www.rhizomes.net/issue8/kuswa.htm.

Labor Research Association. "Low-Wage Nation: Economic Notes from Labor Research Association." E-mail dated 22 June 2004. www.laborresearch.org/story2.php/358.

Lake, Paul. "The Enchanted Loom: A New Paradigm for Literature." *Contemporary Poetry Review* (Sept. 2003). 11 Nov. 2003. www.cprw.com/Lake/loom.htm#mail.

———. "The Shape of Poetry." *AWP Chronicle* 29.2 (Oct./Nov. 1996): 1, 7–12.

Landow, George, ed. *Hyper/Text/Theory*. Baltimore: Johns Hopkins UP, 1994.

Langer, Susanne K. *Mind: An Essay on Human Feeling*. Vol. 1. Baltimore: Johns Hopkins UP, 1970.

Lasch, Christopher. *The New Radicalism in America (1899–1963): The Intellectual as a Social Type*. New York: Knopf, 1965.

Lawrence, D. H. *Studies in Classic American Literature*. New York: Viking, 1964.

Layton, Edwin T., Jr. *The Revolt of the Engineers: Social Responsibility and the American Engineering Profession*. Baltimore: Johns Hopkins UP, 1986.

Lazer, Hank. "The People's Poetry." *Boston Review* April/May 2004. 9 July 2004. bostonreview.net/BR29.2/lazer.html.

Le Sueur, Meridel. *Ripening: Selected Work*. Ed. Elaine Hedges. 2nd ed. New York: Feminist P, 1990.

Lemke, Jay L. *Textual Politics: Discourse and Social Dynamics*. London: Taylor and Francis, 1995.

Lennard, John. *But I Digress: The Exploitation of Parentheses in English Printed Verse*. Oxford: Clarendon/Oxford UP, 1991.

Lentricchia, Frank. *Criticism and Social Change*. Chicago: U of Chicago P, 1983.

———. "Last Will and Testament of an Ex-Literary Critic." *Lingua Franca* 6.6 (Sept./Oct. 1996): 59–67.

Lerner, Gerda. *Why History Matters: Life and Thought*. New York: Oxford UP, 1997.

Levi, Primo. *The Periodic Table*. Trans. Raymond Rosenthal. New York: Schocken, 1984.

Levine, Philip. *New Selected Poems*. New York: Knopf, 1992.

Loewy, Raymond. *Never Leave Well Enough Alone*. Baltimore: Johns Hopkins UP, 2002.

Lubrano, Alfred. *Limbo: Blue-Collar Roots, White-Collar Dreams*. Hoboken, NJ: Wiley, 2004.

Lutz, Tom. *Cosmopolitan Vistas: American Regionalism and Literary Value*. Ithaca, NY: Cornell UP, 2004.

Lyotard, Jean-François. Interview with *JAC*. *Critical Intellectuals on Writing*. Ed. Gary A. Olson and Lynn Worsham. Albany: State U of New York P, 2003. 144–153.

———. *The Postmodern Condition: A Report on Knowledge*. Trans. Geoff Bennington and Brian Massumi. Minneapolis: U of Minnesota P, 1986.

Magee, Michael. *Emancipating Pragmatism: Emerson, Jazz, and Experimental Writing*. Tuscaloosa: U of Alabama P, 2004.

Mahala, Daniel, and Jody Swilky. "Remapping the Geography of Service in English." *College English* 59.6 (Oct. 1997): 625–646.
Mann, Paul. *The Theory-Death of the Avant-Garde*. Bloomington: Indiana UP, 1991.
Manning, Richard. *Against the Grain: How Agriculture Has Hijacked Civilization*. New York: FSG, 2004.
Marcus, Greil. *Lipstick Traces: A Secret History of the Twentieth Century*. Cambridge, MA: Harvard UP, 1989.
Marcuse, Herbert. *Eros and Civilization: A Philosophical Inquiry into Freud*. Boston: Beacon, 1974.
———. *One Dimensional Man: Studies in the Ideology of Advanced Industrial Society*. Boston: Beacon, 1964.
Maturana, Humberto R., and Francisco J. Varela. *The Tree of Knowledge: The Biological Roots of Human Understanding*. Trans. Robert Paolucci. Boston: New Science Library/Shambhala, 1988.
Mauss, Marcel. *The Gift: Forms and Functions of Exchange in Archaic Societies*. Trans. Ian Cunnison. New York: Norton, 1967.
Mayer, Bernadette. *Midwinter Day*. Berkeley, CA: Turtle Island Foundation, 1982.
———. *Sonnets*. New York: Tender Buttons, 1989.
McCaffery, Steve. *North of Intention: Critical Writings, 1973–86*. New York: Roof, 1986.
———. "Voice in Extremis." *Close Listening: Poetry and the Performed Word*. Ed. Charles Bernstein. New York: Oxford UP, 1998. 162–177.
McCloud, Scott. *Reinventing Comics*. New York: HarperCollins, 2000.
———. *Understanding Comics: The Invisible Art*. New York: HarperCollins, 1994.
McGann, Jerome, and Lisa Samuels. "Deformance and Interpretation." 1 July 2004. http://www.iath.virginia.edu/~jjm2f/old/deform.html.
McGrath, Charles. "What Johnny Won't Read." *New York Times*, natl. ed., sec. 4: 3.
McKibben, Bill. *Enough: Staying Human in an Engineered Age*. New York: Times, 2003.
McLuhan, Marshall. *Understanding Media: The Extensions of Man*. New York: McGraw-Hill, 1965.
McLuhan, Marshall, and Quentin Fiore. *The Medium is the Massage*. Prod. Jerome Agel. New York: Touchstone, 1989.
———. *War and Peace in the Global Village*. Prod. Jerome Agel. New York: Touchstone, 1989.
Merleau-Ponty, Maurice. *The Prose of the World*. Ed. Claude Lefort. Trans. John O'Neill. Evanston, IL: Northwestern UP, 1973.
Metcalf, Paul. *Collected Works*. 3 vols. Minneapolis, MN: Coffee House, 1956–1997.
Middleton, Peter. "The Contemporary Poetry Reading." *Close Listening: Poetry and*

the Performed Word. Ed. Charles Bernstein. New York: Oxford UP, 1998. 262–299.

Moraru, Christian. *Rewriting: Postmodern Narrative and Cultural Critique in the Age of Cloning*. Albany: State U of New York P, 2001.

Morris, Adalaide, ed. *Sound States: Innovative Poetics and Acoustical Technologies*. Chapel Hill: U of North Carolina P, 1997.

Morrison, Toni. *Playing in the Dark: Whiteness and the Literary Imagination*. Cambridge, MA: Harvard UP, 1992.

Morton, Donald, and Mas'ud Zavarzadeh. *Theory/Pedagogy/Politics: Texts for Change*. Urbana: U of Illinois P, 1991.

Motokiyu, Tosa, Ojiu Noringa, and Ocura Kyojin, eds. *Doubled Flowering: From the Notebooks of Araki Yasusada*. Trans. Tosa Motokiyu, Ojiu Noringa, and Okura Kyojin. New York: Roof, 1997.

Moulthrop, Stuart, and Nancy Kaplan. "New Literacies and Old: A Dialogue." *Kairos* 9.1 (Fall 2004). 16 Sept. 2004. http://english.ttu.edu/kairos/9.1/binder.html?interviews/moulthrop-kaplan/index.htm.

Mumford, Lewis. *Art and Technics*. New York: Columbia UP, 2000.

Murghana, Fehta. "The Puncture Effect: Encrypted Space, Modernism, and the Hoarse Men of the Apocalypse." *Conspiracies, Aesthetics, Politics*. Guest ed. Chea Prince. Ed. Robert Cheatham. Spec. issue of *Perforations* 1.2 (Winter 1992): A–R.

Myers, D. G. *The Elephants Teach: Creative Writing Since 1880*. Englewood Cliffs, NJ: Prentice Hall, 1996.

Nancy, Jean-Luc. *The Inoperative Community*. Ed. Peter Connor. Trans. Peter Connor, Lisa Garbus, Michael Holland, and Simona Sawhney. Minneapolis: U of Minnesota P, 1990.

———. "Sharing Voices." *Transforming the Hermeneutic Context: From Nietzsche to Nancy*. Ed. Gayle L. Ormiston and Alan D. Schrift. Albany: State U of New York P, 1990. 234–235.

Nehring, Christina. "Books Make You a Boring Person." *New York Times Book Review* 27 June 2004: 23.

Nelson, Cary. *Manifesto of a Tenured Radical*. New York: New York UP, 1997.

———. "Murder in the Cathedral: Editing a Comprehensive Anthology of Modern American Poetry." *American Literary History* 14.2 (Summer 2002): 311–327.

———. *Repression and Recovery: Modern American Poetry and the Politics of Cultural Memory, 1910–1945*. Madison: U of Wisconsin P, 1989.

———, ed. *Anthology of Modern American Poetry*. New York: Oxford UP, 2000.

———, ed. *Will Teach for Food: Academic Labor in Crisis*. Minneapolis: U of Minnesota P, 1997.
Nemet-Nejat, Murat. "Re: about social recompense." Email to SUNY/Buffalo Poetics discussion list. 17 April 2004. Used by permission of author. Archived at epc.buffalo.edu.
———. "Is Poetry a Job, Is a Poem a Product." *Readme* 4 (Spring/Summer 2001). home.jps.net/~nada/murat1.htm.
Nielsen, Aldon Lynn. *Black Chant: Languages of African-American Postmodernism*. Cambridge, UK: Cambridge UP, 1997.
Ohmann, Richard. *English in America: A Radical View of the Profession*. New York: Oxford UP, 1976.
O'Keefe, Daniel Lawrence. *Stolen Lightning: The Social Theory of Magic*. New York: Vintage, 1983.
O'Leary, Peter. *Gnostic Contagion: Robert Duncan and the Poetry of Illness*. Middletown,CT: Wesleyan UP, 2002.
Olson, Charles. *Collected Prose*. Ed. Donald Allen and Benjamin Friedlander. Berkeley: U of California P, 1997.
———. *The Post Office: A Memoir of His Father*. San Francisco: Grey Fox, 1984.
Olson, Gary A., and Irene Gale, eds. *(Inter)views: Cross-Disciplinary Perspectives on Rhetoric and Literacy*. Carbondale: Southern Illinois UP, 1991.
Ong, Walter J. *Orality and Literacy: The Technologizing of the Word*. New York: Routledge, 1991.
On the Waterfront. Dir. Elia Kazan. Screenplay by Budd Schulberg. Perf. Marlon Brando, Karl Malden, Lee J. Cobb, Rod Steiger, Eva Marie Saint, and Pat Henning. Columbia, 1954.
Owens, Derek. *Composition and Sustainability: Teaching for a Threatened Generation*. Urbana, IL: NCTE, 2001.
Parker, Deborah. "Eco, Umberto." *The Johns Hopkins Guide to Literary Theory and Criticism*. Ed. Michael Groden and Martin Kreiswirth. Baltimore: Johns Hopkins UP, 1994. 220–222.
Peck, Dale. *Hatchet Jobs*. New York: New P, 2004.
Perelman, Bob. *The Marginalization of Poetry: Language Writing and Literary History*. Princeton, NJ: Princeton UP, 1996.
Perloff, Marjorie. *Poetic License: Essays on Modernist and Postmodernist Lyric*. Evanston, IL: Northwestern UP, 1990.
———. *Radical Artifice: Writing Poetry in the Age of Media*. Chicago: U of Chicago P, 1991.
———. *21st-Century Modernism: The "New" Poetics*. Oxford, UK: Blackwell, 2002.

———. *The Vienna Paradox: A Memoir*. New York: New Directions, 2004.

———. *Wittgenstein's Ladder: Poetic Language and the Strangeness of the Ordinary*. Chicago: U of Chicago, 1996.

Petroski, Henry. *To Engineer is Human: The Role of Failure in Successful Design*. New York: St. Martin's, 1985.

Phillips, Kevin. *Wealth and Democracy: A Political History of the American Rich*. New York: Broadway, 2003.

Pinsky, Robert. *The Sounds of Poetry: A Brief Guide*. New York: FSG, 1999.

Pirandello, Luigi. *Six Characters in Search of an Author*. Trans. Eric Bentley. New York: Signet Classics, 1998.

Pirsig, Robert M. *Zen and the Art of Motorcycle Maintenance: An Inquiry into Values*. New York: Morrow Quill, 1979.

Pollack, Norman. *The Populist Response to Industrial America: Midwestern Populist Thought*. Cambridge, MA: Harvard UP, 1962.

Pollack, Sydney. Introduction. *Sanford Meisner on Acting*. By Sanford Meisner and Dennis Longwell. New York: Vintage, 1987. xiii–xvi.

Pope, Alexander. *An Essay on Criticism: Poetry and Prose of Alexander Pope*. Ed. Aubrey Williams. Boston: Houghton Mifflin, 1969. 37–57.

Porush, David. *The Soft Machine: Cybernetic Fiction*. New York: Methuen, 1985.

Poster, Mark. "Foucault, Michel." *The Johns Hopkins Guide to Literary Theory and Criticism*. Ed. Michael Groden and Martin Kreiswirth. Baltimore: Johns Hopkins UP, 1994. 277–280.

Postman, Neil. *Technopoly: The Surrender of Culture to Technology*. New York: Knopf, 1992.

Postman, Neil, and Charles Weingartner. *Teaching as a Subversive Activity*. New York: Delta/Dell, 1969.

Pound, Ezra. *ABC of Reading*. New York: New Directions, 1987.

———. *The Pisan Cantos*. Ed. Richard Sieburth. New York: New Directions, 2003.

Pratt, Mary Louise. "Arts of the Contact Zone." *Profession 91* (1991): 33–40.

———. "Of Poets and Polyglots." President's Column. *MLA Newsletter* 35.1 (Spring 2003): 3–4.

Preminger, Alex, and T. V. F. Brogan, eds. *The New Princeton Encyclopedia of Poetry and Poetics*. New York: MJF, 1993.

Rabaté, Jean-Michel. *The Future of Theory*. Oxford: Blackwell, 2002.

Rasula, Jed. *The American Poetry Wax Museum: Reality Effects, 1940–1990*. Urbana, IL: NCTE, 1997.

———. *Syncopations: The Stress of Innovation in Contemporary American Poetry*. Tuscaloosa: U of Alabama P, 2004.

———. "Textual Indigence in the Archive." *Postmodern Culture* 9.3 (May 1999). 12 July 2004. muse.jhu.edu/journals/pmc/v009/9.3rasula.html.

———. *This Compost: Ecological Imperatives in American Poetry*. Athens: U of Georgia P, 2002.

———. "Understanding the Sound of Not Understanding." *Close Listening: Poetry and the Performed Word*. Ed. Charles Bernstein. New York: Oxford UP, 1998. 233–261.

Rasula, Jed, and Steve McCaffery, eds. *Imagining Language: An Anthology*. Cambridge, MA: MIT P, 1998.

Ratcliffe, Stephen. *Listening to Reading*. Albany: State U of New York P, 2000.

Raworth, Tom. *Tottering State: Selected and New Poems 1963–1983*. Great Barrington, MA: The Figures, 1984.

Readings, Bill. *The University in Ruins*. Cambridge, MA: Harvard UP, 1996.

Redon, Odile, Françoise Sabban, and Silvano Serventi. *The Medieval Kitchen: Recipes from France and Italy*. Trans. Edward Schneider. Chicago: U of Chicago P, 1998.

Richards, I. A. *The Philosophy of Rhetoric*. New York: Oxford UP, 1981.

Richter, Gerhard. "A Picture Is Worth 216 Newspaper Articles." Interview with Jan Thorn-Prikker. Trans. Tim Nevill. *New York Times* 4 July 2004, natl. ed., sec. 2: 26–27.

Rifkin, Jeremy. *The End of Work: The Decline of the Global Labor Force and the Dawn of the Post-Market Era*. New York: Jeremy P. Tarcher/Penguin, 2004.

Rifkin, Libbie. *Career Moves: Olson, Creeley, Zukofsky, Berrigan, and the American Avant-Garde*. Madison: U of Wisconsin P, 2000.

Robinson, Jeffrey C. *Romantic Presences: Living Images from the Age of Wordsworth & Shelley*. Barrytown, NY: Station Hill, 1995.

Roger & Me. Written and dir. Michael Moore. Dog Eat Dog/Warner Bros., 1989.

Ronell, Avital. *Crack Wars: Literature, Addiction, Mania*. Lincoln: U of Nebraska P, 1992.

Rooke, Tetz. "From Self-Made Man to Man-Made Self: A Story about Changing Identities." *Rooke Time Unlimited* 21 (January 2001). 13 July 2004. http://www.rooke.se/rooketime21e.html.

Rose, Gillian. *Mourning Becomes the Law: Philosophy and Representation*. Cambridge, UK: Cambridge UP, 1996.

Ross, Marilyn, and Tom Ross. "Book News and Publishing Industry Statistics." 11 July 2004. www.selfpublishingresources.com/Booknews.htm.

Rothenberg, Jerome. "New Models, New Visions: Some Notes toward a Poetics of Performance." *Postmodern American Poetry: A Norton Anthology*. Ed. Paul Hoover. New York: Norton, 1994. 640–644.

Rothenberg, Jerome, and Pierre Joris, eds. "Commentary." *Poems for the Millennium: The University of California Book of Modern and Postmodern Poetry.* Vol. 1: *From Fin-de-Siècle to Negritude.* Berkeley: U of California P, 1995. 24.

Rothenberg, Jerome, and Steven Clay, eds. *A Book of the Book: Some Works & Projections about the Book & Writing.* New York: Granary, 2000.

Rukeyser, Muriel. *Willard Gibbs: American Genius.* Garden City, NY: Doubleday, 1942.

Rules of the Game (La Règle du Jeu). Dir. Jean Renoir. Screenplay by Jean Renior, Karl Koch, Camille François, and the cast. Derived from "Les Caprices de Marianne" by Alfred de Musset. Perf. Marcel Dalio, Nora Grégor, Roland Toutain, Jean Renoir, and Mila Parély. Janus, 1939.

Said, Edward W. *The World, the Text, and the Critic.* Cambridge, MA: Harvard UP, 1983.

Schiffrin, André. *The Business of Books: How International Conglomerates Took Over Publishing and Changed the Way We Read.* London: Verso, 2000.

Scroggins, Mark, ed. *Upper Limit Music: The Writing of Louis Zukofsky.* Tuscaloosa: U of Alabama P, 1997.

Sedinger, Tracey. Rev. of *An Ethics of Dissensus,* by Ewa Ponowska Ziarek. *Culture Machine* (May 2003). 9 July 2004. culturemachine.tees.ac.uk/Reviews/rev25.htm.

Seltzer, Mark. *Bodies and Machines.* New York: Routledge, 1992.

Serres, Michel, with Bruno Latour. *Conversations on Science, Culture, and Time.* Trans. Roxanne Lapidus. Ann Arbor: U of Michigan P, 1998.

Shulevitz, Judith. "Sing, Muse . . . or Maybe Not." *New York Times Book Review* 1 Dec. 2002: 31.

Silk Stockings. Dir. Rouben Mamoulian. Screenplay by Leonard Gershe and Leonard Spigelgass. Play by Abe Burrows, George S. Kaufman, and Leueen MacGrath. Book (uncredited) by Melchior Lengyel. Perf. Fred Astaire, Cyd Charisse, Janis Paige, Peter Lorre, and George Tobias. MGM, 1957.

Silliman, Ron. *The New Sentence.* New York: Roof, 1989.

Silverstein, Michael. Wallstreetpoet.com. 27 June 2004. www.wallstreetpoet.com.

Simmons, Russell, Danny Simmons, and M. Raven Rowe. *Russell Simmons' Def Poetry Jam on Broadway . . . and More: The Choice Collection.* New York: Atria, 2003.

Simpson, David. *The Academic Postmodern and the Rule of Literature: A Report on Half-Knowledge.* Chicago: U of Chicago P, 1995.

Singerman, Howard. *Art Subjects: Making Artists in the American University.* Berkeley: U of California P, 1999.

Siskin, Clifford. "Epilogue: The Rise of Novelism." *Cultural Institutions of the Novel.* Ed. Deidre Lynch and William B. Warner. Duke: Duke UP, 1996. 423–440.

Sloan, Mary Margaret, ed. *Moving Borders: Three Decades of Innovative Writing by Women.* Jersey City, NJ: Talisman, 1998.

Smith, Barbara Hernstein. *Contingencies of Value: Alternative Perspectives for Critical Theory.* Cambridge, MA: Harvard UP, 1988.

Sosnoski, James J. *Token Professionals and Master Critics: A Critique of Orthodoxy in Literary Studies.* Albany: State U of New York P, 1994.

Spellmeyer, Kurt. "After Theory: From Textuality to Attunement with the World." *College English* 58.8 (Dec. 1996): 893–913.

Spicer, Jack. "Thing Language." *The Collected Books of Jack Spicer.* Ed. Robin Blaser. Los Angeles: Black Sparrow, 1975. 217–224.

Stauber, John, and Sheldon Rampton. *Toxic Sludge is Good for You: Lies, Damn Lies, and the Public Relations Industry.* Monroe, ME: Common Courage, 1995.

Steger, Manfred. *Globalization: A Very Short Introduction.* Oxford: Oxford UP, 2003.

Stein, Gertrude. *Everybody's Autobiography.* Cambridge, MA: Exact Change, 1993.

———. *How to Write.* Los Angeles: Sun and Moon, 1995.

———. *Lectures in America.* Boston: Beacon, 1957.

———. *Narration: Four Lectures.* New York: Greenwood, 1969.

Steinberg, Leo. *Other Criteria: Confrontations with Twentieth-Century Art.* New York: Oxford UP, 1975.

Steiner, George. *In Bluebeard's Castle: Some Notes towards a Redefinition of Culture.* New Haven, CT: Yale UP, 1973.

———. *On Difficulty, and Other Essays.* New York: Oxford UP, 1978.

Steingraber, Sandra. *Living Downstream: An Ecologist Looks at Cancer and the Environment.* Reading, MA: Addison-Wesley, 1997.

Steinman, Lisa M. *Made in America: Science, Technology, and American Modernist Poets.* New Haven, CT: Yale UP, 1987.

Stevens, Wallace. "The Comedian as the Letter C." *The Collected Poems of Wallace Stevens.* New York: Vintage, 1990. 27–46.

———. "World without Peculiarity." *The Collected Poems of Wallace Stevens.* New York: Vintage, 1990. 453–454.

Stewart, Susan. *Poetry and the Fate of the Senses.* Chicago: U of Chicago P, 2001.

Strickland, Stephanie. *V: Losing L'una, WaveSon.nets.* New York: Penguin, 2002.

Sukenick, Ronald. *In Form: Digressions on the Act of Fiction.* Carbondale: Southern Illinois UP, 1985.

———. *Mosaic Man.* Normal, IL: FC2, 1999.

Syverson, Margaret A. *The Wealth of Reality: An Ecology of Composition.* Carbondale: Southern Illinois UP, 1999.

Tabbi, Joseph. "Solitary Inventions: David Markson at the End of the Line." *Technofiction and Hypernarrative*. Ed. N. Katherine Hayles. Spec. issue of *Modern Fiction Studies* 43.3 (Fall 1997): 745–772.

Telefon. Dir. Don Siegel. Perf. Charles Bronson and Lee Remick. MGM, 1977.

Teresi, Dick. *Lost Discoveries: The Ancient Roots of Modern Science—from the Babylonians to the Maya*. New York: Simon and Schuster, 2002.

They Might Be Giants. "Istanbul (Not Constantinople)." *Flood*. Elektra, 1990.

Thomas, Robert C. "Whatever Intellectuals: The Politics of Thought in Post-disciplinary Societies." 1998. 24 June 2004. online.sfsu.edu/~theory/mrt/lecture.html.

Thompson, Clive. "The Poetry of Spam." 18 Nov. 2003. www.collisiondetection.net.

Tichi, Cecelia. *Shifting Gears: Technology, Literature, Culture in Modernist America*. Chapel Hill: U of North Carolina P, 1987.

Toffler, Alvin. *Future Shock*. New York: Bantam, 1971.

———. *The Third Wave*. New York: Morrow, 1980.

Tomasula, Steve. "Speaking through a Veil of Dollars: The Dialogue between Art and Literature." *New Art Examiner* 26.10 (July–Aug. 1999): 36–41.

———. *VAS: An Opera in Flatland: A Novel*. Art and design by Stephen Farrell. Barrytown, NY: Station Hill, 2002.

Trimbur, John. "Consensus and Difference in Collaborative Learning." *College English* 51 (Oct. 1989): 602–616.

Tucker, Robert C., ed. *The Marx-Engels Reader*. 2nd ed. New York: Norton, 1978.

Tufte, Edward R. *The Visual Display of Quantitative Information*. 2nd ed. Cheshire, CT: Graphics P, 2001.

Ullman, Ellen. *Close to the Machine: Technophilia and Its Discontents*. San Francisco: City Lights, 1997.

Ulmer, Gregory L. *Applied Grammatology: Post(e)-Pedagogy from Jacques Derrida to Joseph Beuys*. Baltimore: Johns Hopkins UP, 1985.

United States. National Endowment for the Arts. *Reading at Risk: A Survey of Literary Reading in America*. 8 July 2004. Available at http://www.nea.gov/pub/ReadingAtRisk.pdf.

Valery, Paul. *The Art of Poetry*. Trans. Denise Folliot. Princeton, NJ: Princeton UP, 1985.

———. "Poetry as Abstract Thought." *Critical Theory since Plato*. Ed. Hazard Adams. San Diego, CA: HBJ, 1971. 915–926.

Vaneigem, Raoul. *The Revolution of Everyday Life*. Trans. Donald Nicholson-Smith. London: Left Bank, 1983.

Varela, Francisco J., Evan Thompson, and Eleanor Rosch. *The Embodied Mind: Cognitive Science and Human Experience*. Cambridge, MA: MIT P, 1991.

Virilio, Paul. *The Aesthetics of Disappearance*. Trans. Philip Beitchman. New York: Semiotext(e), 1991.

Volosinov, V. N. *Marxism and the Philosophy of Language*. Trans. Ladislav Matejka and I. R. Titunik. Cambridge, MA: Harvard UP, 1986.

Vygotsky, L. S. *Thought and Language*. Trans. Eugenia Hanfmann and Gertrude Vakar. Ed. Alex Kozulin. Rev. ed. Cambridge, MA: MIT P, 1986.

Waldman, Anne, and Andrew Schelling, eds. *Disembodied Poetics: Annals of the Jack Kerouac School*. Albuquerque: U of New Mexico P, 1994.

Wallace, Mark. "Toward a Free Multiplicity of Form." *Telling It Slant: Avant-Garde Poetics of the 1990s*. Ed. Mark Wallace and Steven Marks. Tuscaloosa: U of Alabama P, 2002. 191–203.

Wardrip-Fruin, Noah, and Nick Montfort, eds. *The New Media Reader*. Book design by Michael Crumpton. Cambridge, MA: MIT P, 2003.

Watkins, Evan. *Work Time: English Departments and the Circulation of Cultural Value*. Stanford, CA: Stanford UP, 1989.

Watt, Ian. *The Rise of the Novel: Studies in Defoe, Richardson, and Fielding*. Berkeley: U of California P, 1957.

Watten, Barrett. "The Bride of the Assembly Line: From Material Text to Cultural Poetics." *Impercipient Lecture Series* 1.8 (Oct. 1997).

Weber, Bruce. "Fewer Noses Stuck in Books in America, Survey Finds." *New York Times*, online ed., 8 July 2004. 9 July 2004. www.nytimes.com/2004/07/08/books/08READ.html?ex=1090310833&ei=1&en=c522e111bf197fab.

Weinberger, Eliot. Interview with Kent Johnson. *Jacket* 16 (March 2002). jacketmagazine.com/16/johns-iv-weinb.html.

White, Curtis. *The Middle Mind: Why Americans Don't Think for Themselves*. San Francisco: HarperSanFrancisco, 2003.

White, Hayden. *The Content of the Form: Narrative Discourse and Historical Representation*. Baltimore: Johns Hopkins UP, 1987.

Whitehead, Alfred North. *Modes of Thought*. New York: Free P, 1968.

———. *Science and the Modern World*. New York: Free P, 1967.

Whitman, Walt. *Prose Works: Collected and Other Prose*. Ed. Floyd Stovall. 3 vols. New York: New York UP, 1964.

———. "This Compost." *Leaves of Grass*. Ed. Sculley Bradley and Harold W. Blodgett. Norton critical ed. New York: Norton, 1973. 368–370.

———. "To Those Who've Fail'd." *Leaves of Grass*. Ed. Sculley Bradley and Harold W. Blodgett. Norton critical ed. New York: Norton, 1973. 508.

The Who. "Young Man Blues." Words and music by Mose Allison. *Live at Leeds*. 1970. MCA, 1995 (remaster).

Whyte, David. *The Heart Aroused: Poetry and the Preservation of the Soul in Corporate America*. New York: Currency Doubleday, 1994.

Whyte, William H. *The Organization Man*. New York: Simon and Schuster, 1956.

Williams, Raymond. *Keywords: A Vocabulary of Culture and Society*. Rev. ed. New York: Oxford UP, 1983.

———. *Marxism and Literature*. Oxford: Oxford UP, 1977.

Williams, William Carlos. "Asphodel, That Greeny Flower." Book 1. *Anthology of Modern American Poetry*. Ed. Cary Nelson. New York: Oxford UP, 2000. 194–200.

———. *Imaginations*. Ed. Webster Schott. New York: New Directions, 1971.

———. *Paterson*. New York: New Directions, 1963.

Wilson, Rob. *Reimagining the American Pacific: From South Pacific to Bamboo Ridge and Beyond*. Durham, NC: Duke UP, 2000.

Winner, Langdon. *Autonomous Technology: Technics-Out-of-Control as a Theme in Political Thought*. Cambridge, MA: MIT P, 1985.

Wolfe, Cary. "Ezra Pound and the Politics of Patronage." *American Literature* 63.1 (March 1991): 26–42.

Wood, Robert C. *Suburbia: Its People and Their Politics*. Boston: Houghton Mifflin, 1958.

Woods, Tim. *Beginning Postmodernism*. Manchester, UK: Manchester UP, 1999.

Xerox. Commercial advertisement. CNN. 31 Jan. 2003.

Yeats, William Butler. "Among School Children." *The Norton Anthology of Modern Poetry*. 2nd ed. Ed. Richard Ellmann and Robert O'Clair. New York: Norton, 1988. 167–168.

Yurick, Sol. *Behold Metatron, the Recording Angel*. New York: Semiotext(e), 1985.

Ziarek, Ewa Ponowska. *An Ethics of Dissensus: Postmodernity, Feminism, and the Politics of Radical Democracy*. Stanford, CA: Stanford UP, 2001.

Zim, Herbert S., and Paul R. Shaffer. *Rocks and Minerals: A Guide to Familiar Minerals, Gems, Ores and Rocks*. New York: Golden, 1957.

Žižek, Slavoj. "The Interpassive Subject." The European Graduate School. 23 April 2004. www.egs.edu/faculty/zizek/zizek-the-interpassive-subject.html.

Zuboff, Shoshana. *In the Age of the Smart Machine: The Future of Work and Power*. New York: Basic, 1988.

Index

Note: Front matter, bibliography, and parts 25–29 *passim* of Track 1 are not indexed. To index the latter would have felt too much like stepping on my own lines. Indexed below are names of actual people, living or dead, including one entry for a name that was at one time thought to designate an actual person (Araki Yasusada) and one entry for a name that designates an actual persona (gazelle friedman). Also indexed are actual governmental and professional organizations, actual corporations, actual academic institutions, and actual arts collectives, operational or defunct. I've indexed a few names of (actual) authors from whom I've quoted a line without citation; a few proper adjectives (e.g., "Habermasian" yields an entry for Habermas); two fictitious collectives; and most curiously, perhaps, the actual parent companies responsible for producing those actual products mentioned in my meanderings (e.g., Chevy is made by GM, as were Rochester carburetors, hence the entry for General Motors Corporation reflects this). Finally, I've elected *not* to index publishers or presses or publications cited in my bibliography, go figure. And there's a surprise, too, for those who appreciate such things.

AAUP (American Association of University Professors), 167n1 (Track 2)
Adonis, 116
Adorno, Theodor W., 52, 98
Agamben, Giorgio, 97, 148, 166n11
Alexander, Charles, 126
Altieri, Charles, 164n9
Altria Group, 95
Amato, Joe, 9, 47, 52–55, 127
Anderson, Benedict, 50
Antin, David, 45–46, 139
Aramco, 77
Archambeau, Robert, 30
Arendt, Hannah, 36
Aristotle, 25, 167n1 (Track 2)
Armour Food, 85
Armour Institute of Technology, 85
Aronowitz, Stanley, 171n7
Artaud, Antonin, 115, 141
ASME (American Society of Mechanical Engineers), 16
Auden, W. H., 135
Auerbach, Erich, 14
Augustine, Saint, 23
AWP (Associated Writing Programs), 168n4

Axelrod, Robert, 89
Ayto, John, 19, 24, 33, 158, 164–165n9, 172n11, 176n26

Bai, Matt, 162n3
Baker, Houston A., Jr., 176n29
Bakhtin, Mikhail M., 14
Ballard, J. G., 163n7
Bangs, Lester, 141
Barfield, Owen, 172n12
Barlow, John Perry, 51
Barnard, Chester I., 89
Barthes, Roland, 130, 142
Bataille, Georges, 36, 139, 144–145, 152, 173n17
Baudrillard, Jean, 114
Bauhaus, 74, 85
Benjamin, Walter, 30, 115–116, 132, 139
Benny, Jack, 128
Berger, John, 174n21
Bernays, Edward L., 116
Bernoulli, Daniel, 12
Bernstein, Charles, 9, 35, 51–55, 117, 128, 137, 140
Berrigan, Ted, 135
Berry, Ralph, 127

Bertelsmann AG, 170n6
Bey, Hakim, 147
Bierce, Ambrose, 141
Blake, William, 135, 155
Blanchot, Maurice, 50, 139, 143–145, 147–148, 152–153, 177n31
Blaser, Robin, 114
Blind Faith, 176n26
Bloch, Ernst, 30
Bly, Robert, 135
Bohm, David, 177n31
Bourdieu, Pierre, 50, 109–110
Bousquet, Marc, 171n7, 174n21
Bramson, Leon, 44
Brando, Marlon, 175n24
Braverman, Harry, 171n7
Brecht, Bertolt, 115, 140
Brickell, Edie and the New Bohemians, 165n9
Bristol-Myers Company (Bristol-Myers Squibb), 30, 78, 80
Broderick, Harold M., 50
Bronson, Charles, 136
Bruns, Gerald L., 138–142, 144–146, 153, 155, 162–163n5, 173n18, 177n31
Burgess, Helen J., 163n7
Buttons, Red, 103
Byrd, Don, 127, 149–152, 176n27

Cage, John, 24, 139, 145
Callois, Roger, 144
Camras, Marvin, 85
Capucine, 103
Carson, Rachel, 29
Carter, Jimmy, 26
Cassirer, Ernst, 157
Certeau, Michel de, 107
Charisse, Cyd, 29
Cheek, Chris, 54, 140
Cixous, Hélène, 25
Clark, Lenard, 75
Clark, Tom, 50
Clay, Steven, 176n25, 177n30
Clements, Brian, 168n2
Coleridge, Samuel Taylor, 36

College of Sociology, 144
Collom, Jack, 176n26
Cook, Peter, 143
Corbett, John, 176n30
Corbett, Robert, 176n30
Cosby, Bill, 19
Cotter, Holland, 110
Covino, William A., 151–152
Crane, Hart, 29
Cronkite, Walter, 127
Cunningham, Merce, 139

D'Agata, John, 166n11
Daly, Mary, 151
Daly, Tyne, 136
Damon, Maria, 50
Danto, Arthur C., 44
Davis, Michael, 167n1 (Track 2)
De Niro, Robert, 116
De Quincey, Thomas, 151
Debord, Guy, 155, 163n7
Deleuze, Gilles, 155
Descartes, René, 76
Dewey, John, 43–44, 49
Dickens, Charles, 46
Disney Corporation, 170n6
Disney, Walt, 17
Dorn, Edward, 48
Doubiago, Sharon, 12, 113
Dow Chemical Company, 97
Dr. Marten's AirWair, 92
Drifters, 176n27
Duchamp, Marcel, 44, 152
Duncan, Robert, 127, 140
Dunne, Michael, 173n14
Duran, Susan, 173n14
Dykstra, Kris, 127

Eagleton, Terry, 171n8
Eakin, Emily, 171–172n8
Eco, Umberto, 178n33
Egan, Raymond B., 138
Eliot, T. S., 45, 90, 135, 154
Ellingham, Lewis, 50
Emerson, Ralph Waldo, 28, 81, 117

Epstein, Jason, 52
Euclid, 174n21

Fellini, Federico, 159
Ferraro, Thomas J., 166n12
Fisher, Philip, 174n21
Fleisher, Kass, 27, 34, 50, 127
Fonda, Jane, 12
Ford Motor Company, 85
Foreign Intelligence Advisory Board, 95
Foreman, Richard, 140
Foucault, Michel, 49, 116, 143
Fredman, Stephen, 50
Freese, Barbara, 29
Freind, Bill, 54–55
Freud, Sigmund, 112
Fried, Michael, 139
friedman, gazelle, 105–106
Friedman, Thomas L., 171n6
Frost, Robert, 38, 135–137

Galbraith, James K., 108
Galvin, Christopher, 90
Galvin, Paul V., 81
Galvin, Robert "Bob" W., 81–82, 84–92, 95–96
García Lorca, Federico, 158
General Electric Company, 77, 96
General Motors Corporation, 85, 174–175n21
Gianturco, Elio, 173n13
Gilliam, Terry, 116
Gillmor, Dan, 167n2
Gizzi, Peter, 50
Glaser, Mark, 167n2
Glazier, Loss Pequeño, 115
Goldberg, Rube, 7
Golding, Alan, 50
Greenblatt, Stephen, 39, 176n25
Guattari, Félix, 155
Gudding, Gabe, 128

Habermas, Jürgen, 148
Hacker, Sally, 40
Hammett, Dashiell, 51

Hamper, Ben, 18
Haraway, Donna J., 165n10
Haussmann, Georges Eugène, 29
Hayakawa, S. I., 85
Hazlitt, William, 117
Hejinian, Lyn, 7, 9, 13
Heller, Michael, 30, 31, 33, 153
Henry IV (king of England), 5
Herron, Patrick, 54
Hershey Foods Corporation, 69
Hesiod, 138
Highland, August, 105–106, 167n1 (Track 3)
Hix, H. L., 168n2
Hollo, Anselm, 116–117, 126, 176n25
Home Depot, Inc., 44
Hooker, John Lee, 71
Hoover, Herbert, 16, 26, 50
Hoover, Paul, 50
Hughes, Langston, 38
Humboldt, Wilhelm von, 177n31

IAMAW (International Association of Machinists and Aerospace Workers), 26
IIT (Illinois Institute of Technology), 74–75, 80–85, 87, 92–96
IMF (International Monetary Fund), 55
ISA (Instrument Society of America), 21
ISU (Illinois State University), 80
Italie, Hillel, 169n6
IUE (International Union of Electronic, Electrical, Salaried, Machine and Furniture Workers), 28

James, William, 154
Jarnot, Lisa, 126
Jay and the Americans, 152, 176n27
Johnson, Judith, 127
Johnson, Kent, 9, 53–55, 127, 166n11
Johnston, Devin, 30, 172n12
Jones, Malcolm, 170n6
Joris, Pierre, 50, 127, 149, 155

Joyce, James, 45, 161–162n2
Joyce, Michael, 117, 128–129

Kael, Pauline, 141
Kahn, Gus, 138
Kant, Immanuel, 149
Kaplan, Nancy, 170n6
Kennedy, George, 151–152
Killian, Kevin, 50
King, Carole, 103
Klossowski, Pierre, 144
Koolhaas, Rem, 74
Krauss, Rosalind, 32
Krishnamurti, J., 177n31
Krugman, Paul, 28, 108
Kuswa, Kevin, 163n7

Labor Research Association, 162n3
Lake Forest College, 30
Lake, Paul, 135, 172n9
Langer, Susanne K., 172n12
Lappé, Marc, 29
Lawrence, D. H., 11
Layton, Edwin T., Jr., 16, 20, 25
Le Sueur, Meridel, 12
Leary, Timothy, 103
Leiris, Michel, 144
Lennard, John, 11
Lentricchia, Frank, 134–135
Levi, Primo, 126
Levine, Philip, 113, 169n5
Levy, Andrew, 128
Linkletter, Art, 127
Lippman, Walter, 90
Liquid-Plumr, 28
Loewy, Raymond, 19
LoLordo, V. Nicholas, 127–128
London Philharmonic, 128
Lowther, John, 46
Ludd, Ned, 147
Lutz, Tom, 175n23
Lyotard, Jean-François, 176n28

Mac Low, Jackson, 24
Magee, Michael, 44

Mallarmé, Stéphane, 163n5
Mamoulian, Rouben, 29
The Man, 18, 41, 42
Mann, Paul, 23
Manning, Richard, 29
Marcus, Greil, 173n17
Marcuse, Herbert, 26
Marmon Group, Inc., 95
Mauss, Marcel, 173n17
Mayer, Bernadette, 11, 135
McCaffery, Steve, 155, 176n25
McCartney, Paul, 47
McDonald's Corporation, 25, 162n3
McGrath, Charles, 169n6
McKibben, Bill, 29
McLuhan, Marshall, 158
Meisner, Sanford, 174n20
Metcalf, Paul, 113
Middleton, Peter, 139, 141
Mies van der Rohe, Ludwig, 74
Miller Brewing Company, 35, 77, 80, 95, 107
Mishko, Bernice, 20
Mishko, John, 20, 21, 40
Mitchell, Joni, 143
MLA (Modern Language Association), 34, 39, 48, 55, 103, 126–127, 173n15
Moholy-Nagy, László, 19, 85
Molson Coors Brewing Company, 97, 102
Montaigne, Michel de, 81
Moore, Michael, 95, 115
Moraru, Christian, 162n2
Moreno, Rita, 128
Motorola Corporation, 81–83, 85, 90, 92
Moulthrop, Stuart, 170n6
Mullen, Laura, 126
Murghana, Fehta, 157
Murphy, Sheila, 128
Muse Apprentice Guild, 106
Myers, D. G., 113

Nancy, Jean-Luc, 139, 144, 148
NEA (National Education Association), 167n1 (Track 2)

NEA (National Endowment for the Arts), 169–170n6
Nehring, Christina, 117
Nelson, Cary, 50, 113, 168–169n5
Nelson, Lycette, 147
Nelson, Ricky, 128
Nemet-Nejat, Murat, 111–112
New Critics, 162
News Corporation, 170n6
NFL (National Football League), 149
Nielsen, Aldon Lynn, 50, 127, 176n30
Nixon, Richard, 75, 95
NLRB (National Labor Relations Board), 83
Noble, David, 171n7

O'Keefe, Daniel Lawrence, 151
O'Leary, Peter, 140
Olsen, Lance, 126
Olson, Charles, 32, 43, 139, 145, 152, 164n9
Orwell, George, 26
OULIPO, 24
Owens, Derek, 29

Paglia, Camille, 135
Parker, Deborah, 178n33
Pater, Walter, 143
Paz, Octavio, 128
Peck, Dale, 67, 162
Perednik, Jorge Santiago, 52
Perloff, Marjorie, 29, 50, 126–127
Petroski, Henry, 22, 161n2
Philip Morris Companies, 35, 77, 95
Philips, Rodney, 177n30
Phillips, Kevin, 28
Pinsky, Robert, 173n16
Pirandello, Luigi, 140
Pirsig, Robert M., 11, 14
Plato, 136, 139
Pleasance, Donald, 136
Poe, Edgar Allan, 47
Pollack, Sydney, 147, 174n20
Pope, Alexander, 51, 117, 133
Poster, Mark, 174n21

Potter, Harry, 31
Pound, Ezra, 31, 45, 52, 105, 109, 111–112
Pratt, Mary Louise, 173n15
Pritzker, Robert "Bob," 81, 84, 94–95

Rabaté, Jean-Michel, 12–13
Rasputin, 102
Rasula, Jed, 11, 50, 128, 143, 165–166n10, 168n4, 174n21, 176n25, 177n31
Raworth, Tom, 126, 142
Readings, Bill, 110, 148–149, 161n1
Remick, Lee, 136
Rich, Adrienne, 87
Richards, I. A., 23
Richter, Gerhard, 164n8
Rider, Bhanu Kapil, 127
Rifkin, Jeremy, 108
Rifkin, Libbie, 50, 109, 146
Robert Taylor Homes-Stateway Gardens, 74
Robinson, Jeffrey C., 35–37
Rolling Stones, 81
Rollins, Henry, 27
Rollison, Damian Judge, 167n1 (Track 3)
Ronell, Avital, 112
Rooke, Tetz, 165n10
Rose, Gillian, 30
Ross, Andrew, 171n7
Rothenberg, Jerome, 50, 152–153, 155
Rumsfeld, Donald, 128
Russell, Bertrand, 125–126

(SAB) South African Breweries, 95
Said, Edward, 14
Schiffrin, André, 52
Schiller, Friedrich von, 35
Schudson, Michael S., 44
Schwitters, Kurt, 4
Sealy Corporation, 3
Sedinger, Tracey, 175n22
Sexton, Anne, 135
Shelley, Percy Bysshe, 30
Shulevitz, Judith, 173n16
Siegel, Don, 136

Silliman, Ron, 128
Silverstein, Michael, 135
Simmons, Russell, 142
Simpson, David, 164n9
Siskin, Clifford, 106–107
Situationists, 163n7
Smithson, Robert, 30
Snyder, Gary, 135, 152
Spellmeyer, Kurt, 136
Spicer, Jack, 36, 47, 114, 130
Stanford University, 16
Starr, Ringo, 47
Steger, Manfred, 29
Stein, Gertrude, 47, 136, 142
Steiner, George, 14
Steingraber, Sandra, 29
Steve Katz-Ron Sukenick Dance Troupe, 127
Stevens, Wallace, 14, 75, 133, 135, 137
Sukenick, Ronald, 22
Summers, Lawrence H., 102
Swensen, Cole, 127
Swilky, Jody, 127
Syverson, Margaret A., 25

Tabbi, Joseph, 177n31
Tarantino, Quentin, 68–69
Telefon School of Embodied Poetics, 136
Terranova, Tiziana, 171n7
Tharp, Twyla, 5
Thomas, Robert C., 166n11
Thompson, Clive, 168n3
Time Warner, 170n6
Tomasula, Steve, 112, 128
Trimbur, John, 175n22
Tufte, Edward R., 164n9

UIUC (University of Illinois at Urbana-Champaign), 75
Ullman, Ellen, 18
University of Notre Dame, 118

Valéry, Paul, 11–12
Varela, Francisco J., 172n12
Viacom/CBS, 170n6
Vico, Giambattista, 141, 173n13
Volvo Cars, 70–71

Walcott, Derek, 135
Waldman, Anne, 127
Wallace, Mark, 126, 168n4
Wallach, Eli, 103
Wal-Mart, 162n3
Warhol, Andy, 44
Waters, John, 103
Watten, Barrett, 12
Weinberger, Eliot, 166n11
Weiner, Hannah, 128
White, Hayden, 91
White Sox, 75
Whitman, Walt, 49, 137, 159, 177n31, 177n32
Whole Foods Market, 70–71
Whyte, David, 134–135
Williams, Raymond, 19, 107, 154
Williams, William Carlos, 52, 135, 137
Wittgenstein, Ludwig, 45
WLMN (Worldwide Literati Mobilization Network), 105–106
Wolfe, Cary, 112
Wordsworth, William, 36, 135
Wright, Laura, 126

Xerox Corporation, 108

Yale University, 128
Yasusada, Araki, 53–55
Yeats, William Butler, 135
Young, Neil, 52

Ziarek, Ewa Ponowska, 175n22
Žižek, Slavoj, 102
Zuboff, Shoshana, 132
Zukofsky, Louis, 142

Contemporary North American Poetry Series

Industrial Poetics: Demo Tracks for a Mobile Culture
By Joe Amato

Jorie Graham: Essays on the Poetry
Edited by Thomas Gardner
University of Wisconsin Press, 2005

Gary Snyder and the Pacific Rim: Creating Countercultural Community
By Timothy Gray

Paracritical Hinge: Essays, Talks, Notes, Interviews
By Nathaniel Mackey
University of Wisconsin Press, 2004

Frank O'Hara: The Poetics of Coterie
By Lytle Shaw